WHAT COLLEGES DON'T TELL YOU
(AND OTHER PARENTS DON'T WANT YOU TO KNOW)

Trained as a professional journalist, ELIZABETH WISSNER-GROSS has been creating educational strategies for families, schools, educational programs, and school districts for the past decade, helping students, including her own children, gain admission offers into Harvard, Princeton, Yale, MIT, and other of the nation's most competitive colleges. She is a graduate of Barnard College and the Columbia University Graduate School of Journalism. Visit her websites at www.whatcollegesdonttellyou.com and www.whathighschoolsdonttellyou.com.

Praise for *What Colleges Don't Tell You*

"Insider Wissner-Gross . . . knows exactly how to help graduates gain admission to the most prestigious colleges in the country, including Harvard, Yale, and Princeton. . . . Dig in and give your kid a much-needed advantage."

—*Kirkus Reviews*

"Every outstanding performer has a coach to guide the way toward opportunities and around obstacles. In *What Colleges Don't Tell You (and Other Parents Don't Want You to Know)*, Wissner-Gross serves as a private coach, providing expert insider knowledge to families who want to get the most out of the college admissions process, and by extension, all competitive academic arenas."

—Rena P. Subotnik, PhD, Center for Gifted Education Policy, Washington, D.C.

"Wissner-Gross has found a keenly sought after niche in helping parents 'package' their children for college admissions. . . . Most helpful is [her] advice gleaned from admissions officers . . . and her reminder to stay persistent."

—*Publishers Weekly*

WHAT COLLEGES DON'T TELL YOU

(and Other Parents
Don't Want You to Know)

272 SECRETS
for Getting Your Kid into
the Top Schools

Elizabeth Wissner-Gross

A PLUME BOOK

PLUME
Published by Penguin Group
Penguin Group (USA) Inc., 375 Hudson Street, New York, New York 10014, U.S.A. •
Penguin Group (Canada), 90 Eglinton Avenue East, Suite 700, Toronto, Ontario, Canada
M4P 2Y3 (a division of Pearson Penguin Canada Inc.) • Penguin Books Ltd., 80 Strand,
London WC2R 0RL, England • Penguin Ireland, 25 St. Stephen's Green, Dublin 2, Ireland
(a division of Penguin Books Ltd.) • Penguin Group (Australia), 250 Camberwell Road,
Camberwell, Victoria 3124, Australia (a division of Pearson Australia Group Pty. Ltd.) •
Penguin Books India Pvt. Ltd., 11 Community Centre, Panchsheel Park, New Delhi – 110
017, India • Penguin Group (NZ), 67 Apollo Drive, Rosedale, North Shore 0745,
Auckland, New Zealand (a division of Pearson New Zealand Ltd.) • Penguin Books (South
Africa) (Pty.) Ltd., 24 Sturdee Avenue, Rosebank, Johannesburg 2196, South Africa

Penguin Books Ltd., Registered Offices: 80 Strand, London WC2R 0RL, England

Published by Plume, a member of Penguin Group (USA) Inc. Previously published in a
Hudson Street Press edition.

First Plume Printing, August 2007
10 9 8 7 6 5 4

Ⓟ REGISTERED TRADEMARK—MARCA REGISTRADA

The Library of Congress has catalogued the Hudson Street Press edition as follows:
Wissner-Gross, Elizabeth.
    What colleges don't tell you (and other parents don't want you to know) : 272 secrets to
getting your kid get into the top schools / Elizabeth Wissner-Gross.
        p. cm.
    Includes index.
    ISBN 1-59463-031-3 (hc.)
    ISBN 978-0-452-28854-6 (pbk.)
    1.   Universities and colleges—United States—Admission. 2.   College choice—United
States. 3.   College applications—United States. 4.   Education—Parent participation. I. Title.
    LB2351.2.W57 2006
    378.1'610973—dc22   2006011628

Printed in the United States of America
Original hardcover design by Eve L. Kirch

To Sig, Alex, Zach, and my mother, Aileen

ACKNOWLEDGMENTS

Over the years, many people have shared their information and wisdom with me, and encouraged me to write this book to share my secrets.

I was initially drawn to this topic by my Education professors at Barnard College, particularly Giselle Harrington, Susan Sachs, and Mary Mothersill; and Professor Joel R. Davitz of Columbia University Teachers' College, all of whom helped me develop a strong educational philosophy; and Professors Dennis Dalton and Peter Juviler, who were role models as exemplary educators.

In addition, I thank Dr. Jong Pil Lee of SUNY Old Westbury's Institute of Creative Problem Solving for Gifted and Talented Students, who kept urging me to write this book, and my good friend Dr. Mingder Chang for encouraging me to help students beyond my own family.

So many students have entrusted me over the years with helping them to develop their educational strategies to successfully gain admission to the most-competitive of colleges. I am truly honored to have played a role and congratulate all of them for winning some of the most coveted admission tickets. My hope is that they're all applying their education toward making the world a better place. That's what makes this whole endeavor worthwhile.

For this book, many college admissions officers were willing to generously spend time answering my questions, largely off the record. So although I am not identifying them, I want them to know that I'm enormously appreciative, and I believe that their candid responses will help readers of the book to obtain the best possible education and college admissions opportunities for their children.

I want to thank my agent, Susan Ginsburg, who helped this book find the perfect publisher, and her assistant, Emily Saladino. I thank Jill Danzig for helping me to meet Susan Ginsburg, and my good friend Linda Burghardt, for introducing me to Jill Danzig. I also want to thank my publisher, Laureen Rowland, for her insight, enthusiasm, and pace; and her assistant editor, Danielle Friedman.

I thank my parents for years of nightly dinner-table discussions on education. My mother, Aileen Wissner, has always been a pioneer of education, and I especially appreciate her willingness to discuss every nuance of educational philosophy during our numerous four-mile walks at Jones Beach.

Most of all, I want to thank my husband and children: my husband, Sig, for his encouragement of this book and his collaboration with our greatest project of all, raising two incredible sons. And I thank my two sons, Alex and Zach, both active collaborators in my experiments in education, who inspired and helped create the vision for this book. They turned out to be my greatest teachers of all.

CONTENTS

WHY YOU NEED THIS BOOK

W hen I grew up, there was a very bright local boy whom I'll call "KC," whose mother was a brilliant packager. At the time, none of us was familiar with the term "packaging," but we *did* observe that KC won every competition available. And his name made the cover of the two local papers each week. Scholarships, national awards, and recognition seemed to fall into KC's lap. KC's parents were not poor, nor were they famous. Yet when the time came to apply to college, amid the height of Baby Boomer competition, rumor had it that the nation's most prestigious colleges were actually *bidding* for KC—while the rest of us naively hoped for a single offer from at least one quality college.

We wondered how KC did it.

"He's brilliant," many folks concluded. "It comes naturally to him." Or, jokingly, "They must have put something in his water." But I wasn't satisfied, because I knew other extremely bright and talented kids who were not winning awards or being courted by colleges. So the puzzle captivated me.

Years later, when I became a parent, I realized that much of the secret to KC's success could be credited to his mother, who would scout out incredible opportunities, make sure KC had the perfect credentials to be selected, help him prepare an enviable application and résumé, and arrange the interviews and logistics. In these ways, she "packaged" him and made his application seem so appealing that he was sought after by some of the most desirable colleges and summer programs.

As a teenager, I was intrigued by KC's achievements. As an adult, I was intrigued by KC's mother and determined to uncover her secrets. I was inspired to explore new avenues of packaging beyond what she had been able to accomplish, in time to benefit my own children. In this way, I began my research for this book more than thirty years ago.

My exploration continued while working as a professional journalist when my sons were born. I gravitated toward assignments relating to extracurricular education. I wrote a column for *Newsday* called "Day Trips," in which I focused on educational family outings, another on "Kids' TV," in which I reviewed educational children's media, and wrote articles for *Newsday*'s "Travel" section on family travel, which allowed me to take my family to science museums, observatories, and geological sights around the world.

On one family trip, my older son, Alex, was eleven months old and still in a stroller when he became fascinated by a physics exhibit at a museum in Geneva, Switzerland. We had wandered into the museum about a half hour before closing time, to get out of the rain, and the curator asked us if he could show Alex an exhibit. Puzzled, we let the curator wheel the stroller to an exhibit labeled "Jakob's Ladder," in which lightning jumps from one metal rod to another. Alex was mesmerized. When the curator switched off the lights, Alex screamed and pointed to the exhibit. The curator turned the exhibit on again. Again, Alex was mesmerized. Finally at closing time, the curator had to turn off the exhibit for the night. Too young to speak, Alex screamed for at least a half hour, protesting our departure. Ever since then, we made sure to take Alex, and later, my younger son, Zach, to science museums wherever we traveled.

As both boys were growing up, I aggressively sought out other enriching opportunities for them. Because both seemed to gravitate toward math and science, we had most birthday parties at math and science museums. Family vacations were often centered on science themes. I sought out out-of-school classes and summer programs for them that taught math, science, and engineering, so they could enrich their in-school learning. As a children's media reviewer at *Newsday*, I was able to bring home new educational movies for the family to review. Most important, we *never* separated the concept of fun from the concept of learning.

To enrich the heavy doses of math and science, I had both sons audition for the New York City Opera, although neither had prior singing experience. I joked that auditioning at Lincoln Center would someday make a great college essay, even if the auditions had not been successful. But first Alex and then Zach were accepted into the Children's Chorus, which provided free voice lessons and training. Both boys played street urchins in productions of *Carmen* and *La Bohème*.

Then Zach sang a one-line solo in *La Bohème* at a NYCO gala, in which Plácido Domingo and Beverly Sills were onstage; next, he sang the part of the First Spirit in NYCO's *The Magic Flute*. He starred as Amahl in *Amahl and the Night Visitors* at Lincoln Center and did a voice-over for a Bob Dole Visa commercial that played during the Super Bowl. He ultimately starred as Miles in NYCO's *Turn of the Screw*, in which, at the age of eleven, he won raves from *The New York Times*, *Newsday*, *New York* magazine, and *USA Today*.

In 1994, I left *Newsday* and began teaching college, largely for the schedule the college life afforded. I was able to drive my kids to rehearsals and science classes. Both boys maintained their strong interest in math and science throughout this period, fully aware that their professional boy-soprano careers would end abruptly when their voices became lower. When their opera days were over, they turned their attention to winning math, science, and computer competitions.

Other parents, noticing my sons' weekly appearance in the local newspapers, began calling to ask for advice. I shared advice openly and for no charge with strangers. But gradually, my phones were so busy that giving advice had become a full-time endeavor. Rather than turn kids away because I was left with no time for any other work, I was drafted by other parents to start charging for my service. My first paying advisees were admitted into Princeton, Harvard, Yale, Stanford, University of Pennsylvania, Columbia, Harvard Business School, and Stanford Business School. Some of these students had been considered extremely unlikely admissions, so my reputation and business grew locally on Long Island. I began getting phone calls from Manhattan, upstate New York, New Jersey, Connecticut, Massachusetts, and then as far away as California.

My college admissions strategy was never to focus on making cosmetic improvements to an application, but rather to suggest ways to enhance the credentials of the applicant—to actually *improve* the applicant and tell parents about opportunities that other parents may be less willing to share and teachers might not be aware of. Instead of viewing myself primarily as a last-minute college admissions coach, I created the title "Educational Strategist," and for ten years now have specialized in finding and tailoring enriching experiences to further individual students' interests and goals. When these students apply to college, they are extremely desired by colleges, and packaging is just a matter of revealing to the colleges how accomplished they are.

By the time my own two sons applied, they were considered over-the-top with credentials and were offered admission into every college to which they applied—MIT, Harvard, Princeton, and Yale—based on their own achievements. Just to give a sampling: Both Alex and Zach were valedictorians in an extremely competitive Long Island high school. Each was named one of the top twenty high school students in America by *USA Today*. Both were among the nation's forty Intel Science Talent Search finalists (extremely rare for siblings), and Alex went on to be named a winner. In addition, Alex was chosen as one of four American high school students to represent the United States in the International Olympiad in Informatics (computer programming) in Portugal and was inducted into the U.S. Young Inventors' Hall of Fame. Zach was one of nine international winners of the First Step to the Nobel Prize in Physics while still in high school. For the same research, he won first place from the American Academy of Neurology and presented his work before hundreds of neurologists at their 2003 convention in Hawaii.

When my sons were safely beyond high school, I agreed to speak about my strategies at schools, and school districts began asking me to consult. In one district, for example, top students were consistently getting rejected from the most-competitive colleges, whereas students from neighboring districts with similar demographics were gaining admission. I was brought in (confidentially) to offer advice and helped reverse the trend.

What I Mean by "Packaging"

Ideally, packaging should be about being creative and productive and making significant contributions to the world, using the time we're given on this planet well. Sometimes the best way to motivate ourselves is by verbally sharing our experiences and achievements with others— assessing what we have achieved—putting a report of our successes into writing and accounting for our time. We "package" ourselves in conversations and on applications, and in the process, examine our achievements and goals. We ask ourselves if we are satisfied with what we see and are motivated to improve.

Packaging one's child is most constructive when used as a pretext for establishing goals, discovering aspirations, and determining ways to achieve dreams. The college application process can be viewed as an excellent opportunity for young people to self-examine and measure what they have accomplished so far and determine what they would like to achieve as they proceed. Ideally, the college application should not be the first time that students are packaged, although in most cases, it is. Life will be filled with many such opportunities.

In the meantime, **every college applicant, regardless of philosophy, engages in packaging. Merely filling out an application is packaging.** For those readers who are still clucking at the notion and ethics of packaging, note that *every* college application requires a "package" description of the applicant. Some students and families are more skillful at this, and some are less so. Some are very deliberate and organized about what they include in the package and how they present themselves, and some are very haphazard. There is nothing noble about being poorly equipped for a task. So, even if you do not like the concept of packaging, it is to the student's advantage to do it well. And it is to the parents' advantage to help their child do the best job possible.

Packaging always should be truthful. Where we see shortcomings in our own applications, we should fix them—not primarily for the purpose of enhancing the application, but for the greater goal of improving our ability to contribute to the world. If a shortcoming is spotted, the right approach is to strengthen the skill or fill the gap that appears to be a weakness—*not* to fabricate additional credentials. Parents should be very firm about this. The application process is an ideal time to demonstrate honesty and integrity. If you notice that your child lacks a sport (some colleges favor athletic students), for example, the correct approach is to find a suitable sport that your child will enjoy (hopefully early enough in high school to provide a track record). The wrong approach is to make one up, or say that the child participated in a sport or team that doesn't exist at his school.

If the mere concept of packaging your kid for college still sounds overbearing, controversial, counterproductive, wrong-headed, obnoxious, threatening, or even corrupt, note that in this competitive society, more and more colleges and academic programs are recognizing that a successful applicant is one who either can sell him- or herself, or bring in the right "board of advisers"—parents, teachers, guidance counselors, private advisers—to assist with the task. The current generation generally has come to expect heavy adult participation and no longer looks down on parental involvement as a sign of weakness. As this approach becomes the majority thinking of the applicant pool, involved parents are viewing their children's college applications in marketing terms. In fact, many savvy parents would say that lack of parental involvement or supervision in the application process is irresponsible.

Admissions officials emphasize their philosophy that **parents should not *tailor* their children to college applications.** Most college officials would encourage parents to nurture talents, rather than "force" any interests on children or design their kids to fit their perception of a particular college's needs or requirements. At the same time, colleges seem to prefer students who have specific academic **passions** (the current buzzword). And it's the parents' job to discover, nurture, and even promote or *package* those passions. Do you have trouble with that concept? Colleges once had trouble with the concept of kids preparing for standardized exams—now an assumed activity for responsible, ambitious students. Students who took prep courses were once viewed suspiciously as undeserving of their high scores or achieving beyond their supposed natural limits. Similarly, nowadays, students who have sought help in the application process are sometimes viewed by others—particularly less successful applicants—as unfairly stacking the deck, rather than as good delegators, team players, or initiative-takers. But these images are gradually changing. Teachers are volunteering proofreading and editing assistance on college application essays. College application summer camps exist to help students write better application essays. Commercial test prep centers are thriving, and many parents are hiring private college consultants or stepping in themselves to help see the student through the application process.

As with many tasks that today's parents have assumed to make life simpler for their children, more parents are assisting their teenagers in the tedious clerical processes inherent in applications, like typing in the student's name, address, and phone numbers again and again to help expedite the sometimes emotional, sometimes overwhelming process of applying to college. Of course, **each student should write his or her own essays and content,** but increasingly students are consulting with teachers and counselors for advice on what personal topic would provide the most appealing anecdotes and would most intrigue college admissions officers. Many also seek the assistance of professional editors to help clean up spelling and grammar. Today's children are more willing to bounce ideas off parents, discuss future careers, and consult adults for advice. And parents are more willing to play a larger role in the process than merely writing the checks for the admission fees, paying for standardized tests, hiring consultants, chauffeuring their kids to visit campuses, and eventually paying tens of thousands of dollars in tuition. While the parents of the Baby Boomers and Xers emphasized the importance of independence, today's parents are generally less concerned about independence and more focused on family collaboration as a way to beat the competition.

Warning: The role of "helper" is a slippery slope. Colleges emphasize that when admissions officers read applications, they seek the **"genuine voice"** (more buzzwords) of the student. This voice is vital to the application, and when it does not emerge, admissions officers will not admit the applicant—even if the essay is perfectly written and the topic is appealing. Admissions officers who read thousands of applications each year claim that they become expert at detecting essays that have been doctored up or written by others. (According to current college application lore, in this day of college-essay websites, one professor even recognized his *own* application essay in a prospective student's application.) Admissions officers look for consistency in tone, style, sophistication, and stated interests. They want parents to know that the presence of the "genuine voice" is sometimes the single most important element in deciding whether to admit.

This book contains lots of answers that you'll never see printed elsewhere, including many secrets known only to the parents of the most successful students. Succeeding in high school and applying to college are considered very competitive sports, and many winners do not share their strategies.

How to Read This Book

In this book, 272 college application secrets are highlighted in bold type. What makes these secrets secret is that few people who have this information are willing to share what they know. The least willing are usually the parents of kids who are your kids' ages. (The most willing are usually parents whose youngest kid has already gone through the system—my case.) Some of the secrets are more obvious—but may not be obvious to you. Some are controversial—with few people in authority willing to publicly confirm this.

"How does *she* know?" you ask.

In addition to working obsessively helping scores of students in recent years to gain admission into their dream colleges, I've interviewed heads of admission offices and other college representatives, many of whom were very generous with information. This book represents a compilation of my findings.

I proudly want you to know, however, that I haven't sought the endorsement of any colleges—because I know I would have to compromise or eliminate some of the less popular information if I were to seek official endorsements. And my purpose is to let you, the parents, know everything—regardless of how popular the information is among admissions officers or high school guidance counselors.

Why did I write this book for parents and not students? I figure that parents are more likely to read a book on application strategies—and have a better sense of what's at stake. Today's college-bound students expect their parents to offer full service right through high school and organize more than just soccer schedules. This is a parents' tool to successfully and intelligently oversee the application process.

WHAT COLLEGES DON'T TELL YOU

CHAPTER I

The Shoo-In Kid

The Big Question

When more than 2.94 million students graduate from more than 27,000 high schools each year in the United States—including more than 27,000 valedictorians, 27,000 salutatorians, 27,000 student government presidents, 27,000 school newspaper editors-in-chief, and about 25,000 students with verbal SAT scores that are 750 or above and 30,000 with math scores of 750 or above—totaling more than 100,000 "top kids" (assuming some kids have a combination of these credentials—otherwise more than 150,000 top kids)—why should a college that admits only 500 to 3,000 freshmen annually take *your* kid? That's a sobering question that parents must know how to answer if they want to help their kids get into the most-competitive colleges. Saying that your kid is hardworking, a great kid, top in the school, or believing that your kid is even gifted, well-rounded, head of every organization and club in school, deserving, or able to handle the workload, doesn't cut it. Getting a lovely recommendation from a guidance counselor, principal, or teacher isn't enough. To be able to state *all* of the above, isn't even enough. These are all qualities that are *assumed* of all the applicants to the most-competitive colleges.

Secret 1

In order to help your kid get into a "most-competitive" college, you must help your child craft an honest and convincing answer to the BIG QUESTION. Most people don't understand that this is the main question that "most-competitive" colleges are asking during interviews, in the college essays, and in reading recommendations. But if you know this one secret and follow up on it, you will be far more helpful to your son or daughter in succeeding at the college admissions game.

Don't relax with the notion that the college your son is aiming for accepts 1,500 or 3,000 or 10,000 students, so the odds are in his favor. Colleges take pride in admitting each student—one individual at a time. Your daughter must have her own sought-after desirable qualities. If not, *create* some while there's still time. Remember, most of the most-desirable colleges reject far more kids than they accept. So if you're counting on your child "getting in with the flow," the flow isn't getting admitted.

Granted, the 107 students out of 300,000 test-takers who received perfect scores of 2400 on the first round of the new SATs in 2005 might have deserved to feel a little more relaxed than other applicants. Placing among the country's top 107 *does* make one stand out nationally. But receiving a perfect score is still no guarantee of admission and no cause for complacency. (Top colleges love to boast about how many students with perfect scores they've turned away. And they don't like to grant admission to lax underachievers based solely on a lotterylike one-day performance on the SATs. So extremely high SAT scores alone will not guarantee admission.)

Secret 2

Behind every successful kid, there's a supportive network or individual. If you look at the enrollment of the most-competitive colleges, you'll find that most of the kids who attend have been assisted enormously by families, mentors, community members, teachers, or all of the above. The vast majority of parents of successful students can take credit for helping their kids get into the school of their choice, often investing hours to do so.

Granted, not all parents are equally capable of helping. And some parents may be too busy. Others claim to want to encourage independence (which is not achieved, I should emphasize, by ignoring a child's needs). And many, many parents claim that they would *love* to help their kids but that their kids reject any offers of assistance. That may be, but don't be fooled into thinking that some of the most successful kids just make it on their own. Very, very few do nowadays—no matter how independent their parents claim they are. Your extremely competent, deserving high school student needs your help.

Who says a parent need get involved? Why not just have the child apply to college the way our parents and their generation dealt with us—send her to her room to fill out the application form alone? When she gets good and "motivated" (translation: tired, bored, panic-stricken, sick of being badgered), the application will magically get done. After all, the rationale goes, if a student isn't motivated enough to fill out an application, how will she make it through college?

Parents who accept this line of thinking generally have children who are less successful at getting into more competitive colleges. More-involved parents tend to have more success. Involvement ranges from playing a cheerleading role to agreeing to be responsible for the dull but essential bookkeeping chores (maintaining files, monitoring deadlines, and photocopying to keep duplicates of every paper submitted) to brainstorming, reading, and discussing the student's essays.

Parental encouragement and enthusiasm have never been found to stifle kids' motivation or to slow them down. Students who have been encouraged by their parents in the application process or in other competitive endeavors never seem to be at any greater loss for motivation later in life. Among the most visible examples are televised teenage tennis stars and Olympic athletes. TV cameras increasingly show exuberant parents in the stands. In turn, the winners are increasingly thanking their parents publicly for support that ranges from building ski board apparatus in the backyard to chauffeuring an athlete to practices hundreds of miles away, from uprooting the family to be near the world's top instructor to financing expensive equipment and lessons.

To start your child thinking about colleges, show him a sample college application or take him on a college tour as far in advance as possible—eleventh grade, tenth grade, or younger—to motivate him. Make special note of the part of the application that asks for lists of activities and awards. Talk about how you expect to help your kid fill those blanks with the remaining time left before he goes off to college. Will you root for your daughter at swim meets? Will you accompany your son on Hollywood auditions? Will you pay for an archaeological dig? Will you welcome an exchange student into your home? Will you drive the family to an isolated field at three a.m. to witness an aurora borealis? Plan ahead as much as you can.

Significant achievements require lots of family legwork and lots of outside support and encouragement. Mozart could not have composed such beautiful music if his parents had not invested in a piano and arranged his performance schedule. Shirley Temple could not have reached stardom at such a young age if family members did not help prepare her for auditions. Olympic athletes require investment in sports equipment and plenty of costly training, scheduling, and chauffeuring.

The best résumés don't happen—they're carefully planned. When should you start planning? Now. As soon as you realize the value of planning. Plan *with* your child. She should be the decision maker in choosing a direction—but you, the parent, should figure out the opportunities. You're the chief scout. Find that audition, science class, rocketry camp, or architecture competition. Inspire multiple interests and expose your child to multiple fields. The younger the child is when you start, the greater the résumé and the more opportunities that will become available.

In helping to select activities, you might do so with specific colleges in mind. For example, if your son shows a strong interest in architecture and might want to be the shoo-in at architecture school, contact colleges that offer that subject to find out what experiences they value in their applicants. At a minimum, have your son pursue some of those activities in the summer leading up to senior year—preferably in prior summers as well. Sometimes some of these activities have their own prerequisites (design, drawing, or engineering courses) that must be filled summers earlier. By letting your child explore multiple interests and experiences during the summers leading up to college, he or she will develop a better understanding of how to find the best school and what colleges like to call "the perfect match."

The Best College and the Perfect Match

Which is better: Harvard or Stanford? Princeton or Yale? Virginia or Berkeley? MIT or Caltech? Bates or Bowdoin? Wash U or Hopkins? These are questions that parents often ask. Some are satisfied to base their decisions on the annual ratings in *U.S. News & World Report.* But for savvier parents, I stress that what is considered perfect for one child is not necessarily the best for another. Colleges really do differ, and smart families visit campuses to get a sense of the diverse campus cultures.

Secret 3   **Don't be fooled by a low student-to-faculty ratio, for example, on a campus where students are not supposed to speak to faculty members except during very limited office hours.** Some of the most prestigious colleges have appealingly low ratios, but all undergraduate classes may still be taught by graduate students. That famous professor that your daughter looked forward to studying government with might not be interested in discussions with a mere undergraduate. That Nobel Prize winner whom your son wanted to bounce ideas off might be on speaking tours all semester, every semester. If student-to-faculty ratio is not the best way to determine a perfect match, what is? To answer this question, parents should focus on the criteria colleges use to determine a "perfect match."

Secret 4   **Two major questions (beyond the BIG QUESTION) are the keys for determining which applicants a college should admit and which ones should be rejected. Memorize these questions.**

Question 1: Although many students could *benefit* significantly by attending a top college, how would your student *benefit most* by being at the *specific* college to which he/she is applying?

Question 2: While many students have much *to contribute* to a top college, how would your student *contribute the most* by being at the *specific* college to which he/she is applying?

These are the questions you want your child to answer on the college application form. **Regardless of whether the application actually asks these questions, these are the questions the admissions officers want answered.** Colleges view this as the *right* or "perfect match." Stated simply, the questions ask: "Why should we take you? (How would we benefit? How would you benefit?)"

On the Yale College website, the admissions staff prominently states: "In selecting a freshman class of 1,300 from nearly 20,000 applicants each year, the Yale Admissions Committee attempts to answer two questions: "Who is likely to make the most of Yale's resources?" and "Who will contribute most significantly to the Yale community?"

There's no single right answer, but there are many wrong or overdone answers. Remember: In addition to these two questions is the overall most-important question of "Why should we take you, when there are 27,000 high schools in America with 27,000 valedictorians, 27,000 salutatorians, 27,000 student government presidents, 27,000 school newspaper editors-in-chief, etc.?" If you can adequately answer these three questions—and have top SAT or ACT scores and an A-plus average—you're a *shoo-in* at the most-competitive colleges. But obviously, answering these three questions adequately is no easy task.

Lots of parents mistakenly think that the way to get their kids into college is to show pain and suffering. They believe that colleges actively seek the least fortunate. The parents bemoan the fact that they've provided stable and happy upbringings for their children, fearing that this domestic bliss will come to haunt them and that, as a result, their well-adjusted offspring will never achieve admission into a top college. This is false. Colleges are not seeking the most pitiful and depressed students to fill their classes.

| **Secret 5** | **Parents should note that the "neediest" applicant—the one who claims the most** |

problems in college applications and at interviews—is not necessarily the one that the college would see as benefiting most from the college, because the particular college may not be expert at addressing those needs. For example, a student who emphasizes a reading disability might not be viewed as able to handle the intensive reading of a competitive university. And the student who has a disability regarding pacing and speed may not be viewed as able to keep up with the rest of the students. So parents should not assume that by having their kid tell sob stories or demonstrate neediness, the applicant is more likely to gain admission.

| **Secret 6** | **When it comes to disabilities, colleges most admire students who have somehow** |

"overcome" their disabilities to look equally competitive—equal grades, equal test scores—to students with no disabilities. They don't want students whose disabilities become an excuse or crutch for lower grades or lower scores.

If your child has a learning disability and feels it necessary to divulge this obstacle in the application, he or she should be ready to also discuss how the obstacle has been overcome or compensated for. Otherwise the assumption will be that the lower grades in high school are predictors of low grades in college and possibly less success in life. Did your son come to high school from another country where English was not his primary language? Be prepared to demonstrate (through test scores, perhaps) that his English is proficient.

Different learning disabilities are treated differently. Does your daughter require extra time for exams or reading? She might not look as attractive to a fast-paced college, where nondisabled students constantly complain of time pressure and inability to keep up with the intensive load. Of course, colleges will not say that they discriminate against slower workers or slower absorbers, and most make some provision for such students once admitted. But think about it. When you're on an admissions committee of a highly competitive college, and an applicant goes out of his or her way to highlight his or her inability to keep up with the pace in high school, and you have thousands of other eager applicants, the tendency has to be to select a student who relishes the fast pace and can thrive in that dynamic. You rationalize, probably correctly, that the slower-paced student would really suffer in a speed-oriented environment—always playing catch-up, and probably requiring an extra year of college or lots of summer courses just to stay on par. You figure that a slower-paced student would enjoy a more flexible program somewhere else and would thus benefit from a less stressed environment. So you figure you're doing both the university and the applicant a favor by choosing another student instead.

Secret 7 **Gawkers and groupies are unappealing. Colleges are not impressed by families seeking "good influences" on their children.** A boy talked about his Ivy League interview where he was asked why he wanted to attend. "I want to surround myself with all those geniuses," he responded. "Maybe some of it will rub off on me." The interviewer raised an eyebrow. "Are you a genius?" The boy, uncomfortable, opted for the humble approach: "No." The interview went downhill from there. Tell your kid *not* to go to an interview with an admiring gee-whiz attitude that clearly says, "I don't fit in here" or "I'm in over my head," even if you think it makes your kid look charming. It doesn't.

Many parents believe the notion that their kids will benefit most by being surrounded by students who are somehow "above" (smarter, more accomplished) their children, who will be "good influences." Colleges don't see it this way, unless the child has had a rough upbringing or was unduly influenced by discrimination. Their thinking is that parents have had about eighteen years to provide a good influence. If the kids are still so peer-driven and peer-dependent, they're less appealing. Colleges know all too well that students who are motivated by "the influences around them," will find plenty of bad influences on most campuses. It's safer to accept a solid, well-grounded, motivated student who isn't so easily manipulated.

In plain terms, the last thing you want your child to say when asked why he or she wants to attend a particular college is "because I feel it would be a good influence on me." She should not say, "I tend to be a follower, and I need to be surrounded by stronger students." He should not say, "I tend to work up to the expectations of those around me. If there are few expectations and few achieving students around me, my tendency is to sink."

| Secret 8 | **Applicants whose primary interests coincide with the university's facilities and of-** |

ferings are generally preferred. In determining which student would benefit most by being at a particular college, the college compares the applicant's needs and interests to the services offered (and the ability of the university to accommodate that student's interests). If the student, for example, is hoping to eventually become a harpist, would an Ivy League college offer the right opportunity? Or would that student be better off at a conservatory or a liberal arts college affiliated with a conservatory or near a celebrated harp teacher's studio? Likewise, if the student aspires to become a major film director, would the student be better off at a college where film production is offered as a major—or at least as a minor?

Some people argue that with all career intentions, a liberal arts education is universally the best route. But a student who loses years of harp lessons, or goes for four years without getting to produce a film, may not benefit most from a rigid curriculum that doesn't allow enough time for the student's primary interest.

Obviously, not all applicants have passions or outstanding talents. For those students, isn't the best route automatically the most prestigious route? Again, the most-competitive colleges look for students who will *benefit most*. Students with talents and skills that are *addressed* on a particular campus are most likely to be able to develop those talents and skills at college, and are therefore most likely to *benefit most* from attending the college and be offered admission. If, for example, a student is somewhat interested in horticulture and the college offers no horticulture and has no interest in funding a horticultural club or research, the university, no matter how prestigious, may not make a good match, and they're aware of that. If the same student is willing to major in biology, knowing that his or her peers at another institution are having the opportunity to focus intensively for four years on horticulture, and still feels that he or she is getting the best education for his or her own goals, an Ivy-style university may, indeed, be suitable. The student should make this case clearly both on the application and in an interview.

Students with well-matched talents and skills are also likely (in response to the second question posed by college admissions officers) to be able to *contribute* the most to the college while they are there and, presumably, after they graduate, and enhance the quality of the match. If the college, for example, has a ballet company and no equestrian team, the talented dancer may be perceived as more valuable to campus life than the local rodeo star with a higher average and higher SATs or ACTs. If the university has a prizewinning math team, a gifted math student might be more sought after than a literary scholar with higher verbal SATs. And if the college has an undersubscribed Food Science Department and needs to fill the department to receive government funds, a student with a strong interest in solving world hunger might be viewed as a better potential contributor to the campus than a talented mathematician, a professional ballet dancer, or an accomplished rodeo star. One way to find out what departments need students is to visit the campus and ask a random student or two which majors seem to attract the fewest students. Many students will eagerly share this information with you.

On a visit to Cornell University, for example, the most commonly suggested "uncrowded" majors were Entomology (insects) and Biometry and Statistics. At the University of Pennsylvania, when an information-session leader asked the audience of two hundred visitors how many were applying to the School of Nursing, no hands went up. A follow-up call to the school revealed that of those students who choose Nursing, only 15 percent are male. Of course, these numbers could change dramatically from year to year. So parents should do their own investigating.

In selecting the right college, your child needs a solid understanding of what makes him or her a perfect match. A sample statement could be something like, "Michigan is the perfect college for me because it is one of the few places where I could major in Business as an undergraduate, while seriously pursuing my passion for Modern Dance, perfecting my ancestral language of Swedish, and playing trombone in a nationally ranked marching band." Or "Penn is the perfect college for me because it's the only undergraduate Ivy League program where I can combine my interest in Nursing with my proven track record in Entrepreneurship." Or "University of Connecticut is the perfect college for me because it's the only major university where a student can double-major in my two favorite fields: Puppetry and Ornamental Horticulture." Or "Macalester is a perfect match for me because it is one of the only colleges where, as an undergraduate, I could major in Neuroscience and minor in Legal Studies."

Do not manufacture interests last-minute or try to alter your child's interests based on what courses a prestigious college offers. (In order for your child's purported interests to be taken seriously, he or she must show a track record. If your son says, for example, that he wants to major in Puppetry, he should have some related experience listed among his "Activities" on the application.) Instead of encouraging phoniness, look at your child's real interests and see which college would academically satisfy your kid the most.

The College with the Best Opportunities

Secret 9 **The right college is the college that offers *your* kid the most opportunities for *your* kid to develop in the subjects that interest him or her most.** Try to keep this in mind throughout the application process, as other people will try to convince you that "best" equals "most prestigious."

Don't let your child choose a college based on status, the most coveted decals, the most eyebrow-raising name recognition, the most attractive campus, the best-dressed students, the largest dorm rooms, a rah-rah spirit, gorgeous weather, most gourmet food, friendliest greeters, smallest class size, lowest student-to-faculty ratio, largest endowment, largest alumni donation rate, best yield, trendiest eateries, convenient location, "winning-est" teams, "smartest students," most famous professors, or even varied majors. All of these qualities are nice *enhancements.*

The right college is the place with the best opportunities for your child and the place where your child is most likely to succeed. "Best opportunities" include the right courses, internships, jobs, academic clubs, and other exciting experiences. If you are able to find the college with the right match of opportunities, your kid will be much more able to convince the college in the application that he or she would *benefit* from being at the college and constructively *contribute* to the college—the two qualities that the colleges care most about.

Different colleges are best for different applicants. Generally, successful kids who go to the most-prestigious schools sometimes find the competition so cutthroat that they *become* unsuccessful. Many students at the most-competitive colleges, accustomed to getting top grades in high school, ultimately drop out of rigorous programs that initially interested them (Pre-Med or Physics, for example), in favor of courses of study that are popularly perceived to be easier (Media Studies or Family Studies), in order to maintain high grades. Instead of basing applications on prestige, seek a college that offers the right educational undergraduate opportunities while promoting confidence.

Remember: The big fish in the little sea (the A student in the slightly less prestigious college) often has an easier time getting into better medical, law, business schools, and graduate schools than the little fish in the big sea (the B student at the top prestige colleges). But, of course, the A student in the most-competitive college will have the most opportunities offered. Top graduate programs tend to take more students from the most competitive undergraduate programs than from significantly less rigorous undergraduate programs.

| Secret 10 | In order to help your child to create a track record in a supposed passion, be |

proactive. Seek out potential awards and prizes, and use these honors as motivation for young people to accomplish interesting and worthwhile goals. If you wait for your kid to plan his or her own strategies or find opportunities or pursue applications, your kid is less likely to be successful. Disregard other parents who tell you that their son won an Intel award or was offered an invitation to join the U.S. Biology Team or landed a starring role in a movie or signed a book contract while insisting he achieved this independently, without any assistance from adults. Any such achievement, at a minimum, requires lots of chauffeuring, extra lessons, and planning. Kids don't become winners in a vacuum. Truly hardworking, ambitious students rarely have time to search out their own opportunities. They're too busy studying, doing their homework, and taking advantage of other opportunities. The most successful students have a parent or mentor constantly on the lookout for new contests, internships, paid jobs, and the like.

The Secret to Avoiding the "Cinderella Syndrome"

Some parents will ask, "Is it possible to *plan* achievements?" Certainly. Students who wait for awards and prizes to be bestowed upon them (à la Cinderella) tend to graduate with few awards and prizes. Waiting to be discovered by the handsome prince (in this case, an award giver, prize judge, faculty adviser, or competition administrator) may work for Cinderella or other fairy tale characters. In this competitive society, parents need to be more proactive in helping the prize find the kid.

This does not mean that you should write your son's essay on a competition application or create your daughter's project in a science competition. Instead, parents should aggressively scout out suitable competitions, meaningful jobs, enrichment courses, and research opportunities, and act supportive in helping students to acquire the credentials necessary to qualify. Being willing to chauffeur your child to practices or find transportation, to tutor him or her or provide a tutor, to pay for an evening course at a local university or school to gain knowledge or skills required for an opportunity, and helping your child work out scheduling conflicts, photocopy, etc., are essential to kids' success. Too busy? Hire a private adviser or counselor to seek out appropriate opportunities for your child.

The Value of Competitions

Secret 11

Some college admissions offices have secret internal ranking systems for prizes, awards, and honors—charting which ones are more valued by the particular college, or even referring to an internal checklist. Competitive colleges *do* pay attention to *significant* competitions.

At some colleges, winners of certain competitions may even be specially recruited. University of Oklahoma, for example, is known to recruit National Merit Scholarship winners. MIT particularly values national science Olympiad winners—or better yet, international winners. (National and International Olympiads are offered in Physics, Mathematics, Biology, Chemistry, and Computer Science.) In addition, MIT seeks out participants of the Research Science Institute (RSI), an extremely selective science-research program based on the MIT and Caltech campuses, the MIT-based MITES research program, and Intel Science Talent Search winners and finalists. MIT specifically asks students for their AMC 12 (American Mathematics Contest 12) and AIME (American Invitational Math Exam) scores on the application, as does Yale, which has an "optional" section where students are asked to list "other" test results including AMC 12, AIME, Fermat (Canadian), AP (Advanced Placement) scores, and IB (International Baccalaureate) scores, among others. Caltech also looks at these numbers and favors students who have participated in Research Science Institute (RSI), NASA-Sharp Program (at the Jet Propulsion Lab, http://www.nasasharp.com), the Summer Science Institutes (in Ojai, California, and in Socorro, New Mexico), the Governors' Schools for the Sciences in every state, and most of the competitive free Science Training Programs listed at the Sciserv.org website. Caltech is also drawn to students who have conducted independent research, who have published in peer-reviewed journals, and who hold patents.

If specific competition scores are not requested on the application, wins should be communicated through the application essays. Describe any meaningful awards in detail—the criteria, competitors, significance of the honor, and winning strategy. You should not want your kid to be *solely* motivated by prizes and awards, but such rewards do provide incentive for students to work hard and achieve, and gradually discover the intrinsic value of worthwhile pursuits. That's why the awards and prizes exist—to motivate youngsters to want to do meaningful things.

Many competing parents, guidance counselors, teachers, and other supposedly knowledgeable people may try to convince parents that such incentives are artificial or even harmful. While many academic experts support sports competitions—possibly ignoring the feelings such athletic contests engender in teenagers about their physical selves—many academic "experts" oppose academic contests that challenge the students' minds, worrying that the students are being falsely motivated or that the non-winners will feel academically or intellectually inferior.

Academic contests can provide constructive risks for young people seeking adventure—and they're far more constructive than other challenges teenagers are known to be drawn to. But students who enter contests without preparation may indeed get discouraged by the challenge. Parents can help their kids prepare.

Parents should note that competition does not work for all high school students, however. Some kids get turned off or find the notion of competing for prizes and awards stifling. Without prizes, awards, and recognition, some are self-motivated to create wonderful art, or conduct valuable science experiments, or write publishable stories. Such students do their work for the love of their work and its own intrinsic value. That can be perceived as a very mature attitude, a terrific lifelong approach, and an attractive value to college admissions officers. But in order to take this approach, students have to be able to demonstrate their proficiency and expertise in the chosen art or science to the college—a difficult task, when no competitions will "vouch" for the student or "validate" the talents. Such a student must be able to produce a work of art that will genuinely impress the admissions officers— who may not be experts in the art form and may, themselves, have questionable taste. Or such a student may be required to produce a science paper or other work that makes him or her stand out from the other admissions candidates.

| Secret 12 | **A noncompeting student needs to find his or her own forum to show off or document** |

his or her talents and abilities—sometimes a much more elaborate, time-consuming, and *competitive* task than just simply entering a contest. So no, it's not necessary for *every* applicant to compete for prizes and awards in order to get into the most-competitive colleges. But since competitive colleges are competitive by definition, students who are successful in competitions tend to be looked at most positively.

A student who was applying to liberal arts colleges was eager to show me his portfolio. He had won multiple competitions, and based on his art résumé achievements—along with his high average and SAT scores—had an outstanding chance at some prestigious colleges. When I saw his artwork—which his mother (who was not an artist) raved about—I was not impressed. Although admittedly I am no art expert, I had seen many high school artists whose work seemed far more sophisticated. His portfolio contained rainbows, tulips, and sunshine—elementary-school themes. I don't know how he managed to win contests.

Should he include his portfolio in his application? "No" I responded.

The boy's track record in art contests spoke far better than the artwork itself. Contests would help him get into the colleges he most wanted. (A portfolio would have been necessary had he been applying to art schools.) Had he not won some local contests, he would have been stuck showing the colleges his art and likely would not have been offered admission.

Similarly, a boy who wrote poetry sought admission to an extremely competitive college. Eagerly, he brought me his work to read, as his doting father looked on. The poems described his sexual fantasies, and I could easily envision an admissions officer finding his writing tasteless or offensive. I advised against submitting any actual poems but recommended that he instead include a list of his literary awards and publications, which spoke better for him.

Finding an Award for Your Child

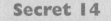 **Don't wait for a teacher to nominate your kid for an award that you think your kid could win. With many honors, the big secret is that you can often contact the contest or award givers yourself to get an application or nomination form.** Parents who wait for their kid to be noticed by teachers who are sometimes overburdened or going out of their way to be "fair to everyone," are often disappointed when their kid isn't nominated for some great opportunity. What's worse is when *another* classmate, not necessarily a better student or more deserving kid, is nominated instead—sometimes because the other kid's parents are more vocal, sometimes because the other kid (or the kid's parents) is the one to bring the contest to the teacher's attention. If you read about an older kid winning a contest that you think your kid might be eligible for the following year, don't be afraid to ask a teacher if he or she would nominate your kid. If the teacher says no, contact the contest, get your own application, and nominate your own kid. Most contests don't require teacher nominations.

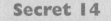 **Several high school academic contests are so prestigious that they will make your kid a shoo-in to *any* college.** These include the national

academic Olympiads in Physics, Mathematics, Chemistry, Biology, and "Informatics" (computer science); Intel Science Talent Search (top 10 winners), Siemens Westinghouse (winners only). In addition, a few summer programs have top track records in getting kids into their first-choice colleges: Telluride Association Summer Program (TASP), Telluride Association Sophomore Summer (TASS), Research Science Institute (RSI), and the Ross Program in Mathematics at Ohio State. Don't expect to hear about these from your kid's school. Often you are the one who must inform the teachers of your kid's interest, or even badger a teacher until he or she gets the appropriate application for your kid. For some of these opportunities, your kid can apply directly, without depending upon school. But for all of these opportunities, your kid must have a significant track record *before* junior year. These opportunities require lots of advance planning and preparation.

Elusive "Back Doors" in High-Prestige Colleges

Secret 15   **What if your kid is stuck on going to a particular name-brand college, although** he or she is just below the cutoff of grades, scores, or competition credentials? At many extremely competitive colleges, academic back doors *do* exist. But few universities admit to them. There's no universal major or passion that will win your kid admission to all extremely competitive colleges. And whether or not a back door stays open from year to year varies by college and department. If an undersubscribed department turns trendy the next year, the department's back door closes.

Colleges don't want you to know about current back doors, because they're afraid you'll convince your kid to switch to back-door majors or programs just to get accepted, and then switch back to the major that truly interests him or her after deceiving the admissions staff. Or worse, they're afraid that your kid will apply to a back-door major and feel obligated to stick with a subject that he or she really has no interest in— just because he or she does not want to look deceptive. Don't have your kid apply to any back doors that you know would make your kid unhappy. But if you find some that do make him or her happy, go ahead.

How, then, do you find out where the current back doors are? The procedure is tricky, unless you happen to know someone with a connection to the admissions office who is in the know. In general, the best route is to attend an on-campus information session and ask politely: "Are there any undersubscribed majors or majors that tend to be difficult to fill?" Do not even mention the words "back door." In most cases, the admissions officer running the information session will remain elusive or claim ignorance as to the existence of undersubscribed majors, and you won't get an answer. But on occasion, you might get an honest, candid, helpful response. At public colleges or colleges with publicly funded programs, you're more likely to get a response, since the university may be dependent on filling each class in each subject to continue to gain public funding for that subject— in other words, if they don't fill the classes, then the department eventually gets closed down and professors lose their jobs. (Note that willingness to pursue a course of study that is undersubscribed does not *guarantee* you admission to an extremely competitive university, especially if the kid's grades or scores are significantly lower than the college's usual range.)

| Secret 16 | If your kid's grades and test scores are within the right range, opting for a less |

popular major—and expressing this interest at an interview or on the application—could significantly enhance the chances of admission if a department is hurting for students.

If the admissions officer at the information session is unwilling to name some undersubscribed majors, one approach is to inquire about the most popular majors—to be able to safely eliminate these. Typically, the most popular majors include English, Biology, Economics, Government/Political Science, History, and Psychology. At non–liberal arts colleges, popular majors include Media Studies, Computer Studies (or Computer Science or Computer Engineering), Management/ Finance/Business, Electrical Engineering, and Mechanical Engineering.

If you are seeking a back door, avoid asking about these majors. Select something else, and phone that particular department to ask how many student majors there are in the department this year. An individual department administrator might be more willing to share information.

Secret 17 Sometimes a chatty department assistant will confide in you that the department is traditionally undersubscribed and is hurting for students. Or you might ask during a campus-information session about three majors that your kid is considering that you suspect might be undersubscribed. Pose the question the following way: "My daughter is considering three possible majors—Public Policy, Urban Planning, and Civil Engineering—and knows that she would be happiest in a smaller department where there might be a closer faculty-student relationship. Which would you recommend?" Make sure the three majors you choose are somewhat related—so that the question sounds realistic. More important, be honest—only ask about majors that might potentially interest your kid. An admissions officer who happens to know that, let's say, Urban Planning is hurting for students, might share that information at that time. Don't ask an obvious question like, "Which department is least popular?" or "Which department offers the best chance of admission?" You won't get an answer. Have your kid (not seated with you) ask about other majors: Classics, Ancient History, and Archaeology; or Sociology, Anthropology, and Linguistics.

If a student lists a department as a potential major on the application, the applicant should be able to show a track record to demonstrate that that major really is of interest. The applicant can't claim to be interested in Geology, for example, if he or she never took Earth Science or some other Geology-related course in high school when it was offered—or if he or she took the course in high school but didn't do well.

Secret 18 For the sake of comparison, a savvy parent might pick up a copy of Harvard's "Handbook for Students," in which the number of majors

("concentrators") in each department at Harvard over a five-year period is specified. Such a listing could give parents a sense of what subjects are popular at most-competitive universities in general. In a recent copy of the handbook, for example, the total number of concentrators over a five-year period were reported in the following subjects: Sanskrit, 4; Astronomy, 83; Folklore and Mythology, 67; German, 39; Linguistics, 99; Near Eastern Languages, 75; Slavic Languages, 81; Statistics, 19; Women's Studies, 98. In comparison, more popular departments like English and American Literature and Language showed a total of 1,822 majors over five years; Government, 2,290; Psychology, 1,445; Biology, 2,178; and Economics, 2,827. (These numbers include students who concentrated exclusively and those who also pursued a secondary field.)

Another way to find out about the number of majors in a specific department is to tour the university. Some colleges post photos in the hallways showing each department's current majors. Aside from building individual students' esteem, the photos help department members and other majors recognize one another—to create a friendlier atmosphere. The displays also let the visitors know exactly how many students the major has attracted.

Do you switch your kid's focus when you find out about low enrollment in a major? In general, no. But there are many circumstances where changing the kid's focus might be appropriate. Let's say your son wants to be a medical doctor—and had intended to pursue a Biology major, but you hear that the Ornithology (birds) Department lacks students. Your son says he could enjoy Ornithology, which would let him still pursue Pre-Med courses, without the cutthroat competition of the Biology Department.

A focus change, however, requires that he do more than just state an interest in Ornithology to be credible. He needs to develop Ornithology credentials—participate in a local birding club, take part in an Earthwatch Ornithology expedition [http://www.earthwatch.org/]; take a local college course; volunteer for an ornithology-research or preservation program; and join the Audubon Society. Make the interest full-blown with a legitimate paper trail. Merely saying that your son is interested in birds when he has no track record is not convincing. When he is offered an interview by the department, he should be able to speak knowledgeably about birds.

Other back doors: Nursing, Dance, and Education are still relative back doors for men. Engineering and Physics are still relative back doors for women at universities and institutes that care about trying to equalize the number of men and women (despite the uneven applicant pool). If your kid must attend a prestigious university, and his or her grades or scores fall slightly short, applying as the odd-man- or odd-woman-out, could be a solution **if these majors interest your kid**. Don't encourage your kid to enter a college this way if the courses genuinely don't interest him or her; often these programs are difficult to transfer out of.

Note that some colleges seem content to leave the ratios uneven and may not provide a good back door. At Columbia's Fu School of Engineering, women make up 40 percent. At Cooper Union in New York (which claims to be "the only private, full-scholarship college in the United States dedicated exclusively to preparing students for the professions of art, architecture and engineering"), two-thirds of the spaces were occupied by men in 2005 (and two-thirds of the applicants were men, not giving women any advantage).

The Athletic Back Door for the Nonteam Member

Everyone knows that colleges recruit for sports and that certain sports will make your son or daughter a shoo-in if he or she is athletically talented enough and has varsity experience. But what if your kid has never been on a high school team? Does that mean that she is ineligible to be recruited for athletic talent by the most competitive colleges?

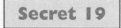 **Secret 19**   **Crew team coaches are known to *occasionally* recruit kids who've never even**

been in a boat before, including students whose academic records are not particularly outstanding. A student qualifies by first getting a good "erg score" on an erg machine (at a school or local gym). A 2,000-meter erg score of 730 for girls and 630 for boys (the lower the score, the faster you go) would pique a college's interest, according to one Ivy League coach. Students who have actually rowed on a team look more attractive to coaches, since they have a track record and are more likely to stick with rowing through college—but other students may be eligible as well. Then the coaches look for good grades and SATs, which may vary by college and student.

A doctor from Chicago talked about how her daughter's 720 erg score, solid 3.0 GPA, and 2120 SAT I score, won her offers from Harvard, Yale, Princeton, Stanford, Brown, and Penn. (One recruiter told her the "magic SAT number" was 2000.) To be recruited, the student should put together a sports résumé, including SAT scores, GPA, and what courses the student is taking in senior year. Send the résumé to crew coaches toward the end of junior year. According to NCAA guidelines, coaches may not contact the athlete before July 1, following junior year. If your kid doesn't hear after that, the Chicago mother suggests contacting the coach directly. (The most successful rowers tend to be tall, broad-shouldered, and narrow-waisted, with equal upper-and lower-body strength.) Students selected this way are obligated to attend the college that they name as their first choice. They are also obligated to participate in varsity crew once they get to college—so it is important that they actually be willing to *do* the sport, hopefully enjoying it as well.

When No College Stands Out

Parents often find themselves awaiting the great lightning bolt that will show their child which college is the perfect match. They are disappointed when no such lightning strikes. For those parents I want to offer the encouragement that the more you are able to help your child to define his or her longer-term goals, the easier the process of finding the perfect college will become, and the more likely your kid will be considered a shoo-in at a top college. Discuss goals with your child, rather than school names and reputations. Once you have an understanding of your child's dreams, you can do the research to find out which colleges offer your child the road to realizing those dreams. But first, you'll want to firm up your skills in becoming your child's advocate and opportunity scout.

CHAPTER 2

Your Role as Advocate and Opportunity Scout

It's not uncommon to hear teachers complain that their number one obstacle to teaching is loud or proactive parents who meddle too much in education. Try to always be a polite and open-minded advocate for your child, but don't let this whining intimidate you. Years from now, long after the teachers forget who your kid is, you will still feel responsible for having overseen your child's education. You should do the best job you can for your child for the limited time that you have with him.

| Secret 20 | **Always think of yourself as a home-schooling parent. The most successful** |

parents are those who treat their kids' high school as a supplement to the home-school curriculum—even if their kid attends an outside high school full time. Like it or not, parents are primarily responsible for their children's education. Many parents of "home-schooled" students (in the conventional sense) act as "facilitators" and provide a significant proportion of their children's education *outside* the home. They transport their children to a language specialist for language lessons, and to a laboratory for science lessons. The home curriculum includes values, religion, and philosophy. It sometimes includes writing, literature, and mathematics.

Parents who send their children off to school each day or even those who send their children away for boarding school have the same responsibility for their children's education. They, too, should make sure their children learn values, religion, and philosophy. They, too, should assist with communication skills. And they, too, are responsible for overseeing that their children are learning mathematics, science, and writing/literature, even if they delegate the teaching of these subjects to the high school.

Many parents ignore their own responsibility in the education process. They relegate too many tasks to the schools. They blame the schools for their kids' problems—ranging from academic weaknesses to behavioral issues. They charge the schools with lack of supervision, lack of stimulation, lack of organization, lack of values, and lack of morality. Just because a school assists in education should not mean that parents have the right to forfeit their own responsibility.

The involved parents' first job is to become informed. If you want to help manage your kids' education, you need to have an understanding of what your children are up against in the greater world. Who are the students competing against your son and daughter for a spot in their dream colleges? Don't depend on your local high school to supply the answer, even if you feel that the local high school is prestigious or competitive by national standards.

Secret 21

Admissions officers at competitive colleges secretly complain among themselves that most parents have a very poor sense of "what's out there." Parents see that their own kids are high achievers within the context of the local high school, for example. Maybe their son is a leader of many clubs. He has extremely high SATs or ACTs. He deserves to get in, right? Not necessarily.

Secret 22

The most-competitive schools look at students on a national level. To make your child a shoo-in, you must look at the national competition, and help your child find suitable forums in which to make a mark or

stand out. Very few parents understand this. Colleges tell you outright that they judge students on an individual level, based on a national pool. Let's go back then to the notion that there are 27,000 high schools in America; each has a valedictorian and a salutatorian, creating 54,000 potential competitors. Each also has a student government president and vice president, creating another possible 54,000 competitors. Each also has a school newspaper editor-in-chief, creating another 27,000 competitors, and a principal violinist, football team captain, yearbook editor, and annual star of the school's musical. There are hundreds of thousands of kids whose parents view them as the "most deserving."

Secret 23	**National competitions and honors take on greater importance in distinguishing**

top-performing kids and comparing students from one high school to another. As a general rule for national competitions, the fewer the winners and the greater the prize, the more prestige. Most parents assume that the high schools will find their kids appropriate opportunities. Very few schools—even the fanciest private schools—view this as part of their mission.

Some parents become obsessed with school politics to the point that they attempt to *get* their kid the editorship of the school newspaper or have their kid *made* captain of the high school team. This generally backfires, creating animosity among the child's classmates and sending the wrong message to the child. For the most-competitive colleges, local success is small time.

Secret 24	**If you are one of the parents obsessing about local school politics, your focus is in**

the wrong place. Is it helpful to show success in school-related activities on the application? Yes. Because some colleges view this as an indicator of how active the student would be and how much the student would contribute to the college if accepted. Also, active participation in school-affiliated activities often helps enhance a student's résumé for extracurriculars.

But a student cannot rely entirely on in-school activities to qualify for the most-competitive colleges. The most-competitive schools want students whom they perceive to be "superstars." While the student is expected to stand out in his or her local high school, the sought-after student is one who goes on to earn national stardom as well. And national recognition is far more important than local recognition. At a Stanford University info session, a prospective applicant, presumably a star of a high school team, inquired about the significance of high school sports in the college application. The information officer apparently responded with a jolting reality check: "If you're not doing your sport on a national Olympic level, don't expect to be recruited."

Think bigger. Think outside the box—or outside the school. Think nationally or even globally. And realize that if your child is not the most popular student in the school—which the highest achievers often are not—and therefore doesn't win election as student government president, editor of the newspaper, or captain of the team, your child can still get into the most-competitive schools by "skipping" or bypassing the system and going beyond the sometimes deliberately limited opportunities offered by even the most competitive high schools.

| Secret 25 | **Create out-of-school opportunities for your children, and don't teach your chil-** |

dren to accept positions that are not challenging or interesting. If your writer daughter seeks an editorship of the school newspaper, for example, and doesn't get it, and instead is asked to sell ads to help fund the publication, don't compromise. The cowering approach is to say to her, "Be a good soldier. Work hard at the lowly position that you were assigned this year. Your hard work will be appreciated, and you'll get a foot in the door. Maybe next year you'll be awarded an editorship." While that may sound like you're teaching her good sportsmanship, patience, or values, this is a case where "nice guys finish last." Instead of teaching a child patience, teach your child the importance of not wasting time, a most precious commodity.

| Secret 26 | **Colleges value creativity and energy more than patience, conformity, and "do-** |

ing time." **Colleges prefer students who *create* opportunities (or see to it that someone creates opportunities for them).**

Tell your daughter, "Quit the newspaper. Start your own underground publication and become editor-in-chief." Or "Start a different kind of publication—focused on one of your interests (a sport, an intellectual hobby, a community service in which you are active, or one of your passions)." You as the parent could then help with the setup as well as giving the publication a much wider circulation than the high school newspaper gets. Be creative. Let the faculty adviser find a student for whom selling would represent a great opportunity—a student who aspires to become a salesperson or business executive. (That's a better lesson in teamwork than dumping sales responsibilities on a student who wants to be a writer.)

Does this sound like a sore-loser or sour-grapes approach to you or some of your daughter's peers? If she is providing a positive creative solution that gives her the opportunity to edit a publication—and perhaps gives more kids the opportunity to write for a second publication—it doesn't matter that you come up with the idea to take this part of your daughter's education *outside* of the school's jurisdiction. If the school is unable to provide the opportunity that your child wants, *you* should provide the opportunity.

Many parents of juniors express panic when their son, who was supposed to get the lead part in the school musical is instead given a "nothing part." Or their daughter who was supposed to be named debate team captain is instead elected secretary whose job it is to take attendance. Parents worry that the colleges don't want to hear about internal high school politics. These parents may be partly correct. Colleges don't want to hear whining about a lack of success. The answer is *not* to attempt to play up the importance of the meager role the child was assigned—even though many high schools and teachers would tell you otherwise. When juniors and seniors do not achieve the roles they expect, their parents should find out-of-school avenues of opportunity. Don't expect to win support by complaining to a higher administrator, since most administrators won't want friction with the teacher who did not make your child star or editor.

Forget traditional channels. Take your "star" for professional auditions—or at least community theater. Take your "editor" to a local newspaper and ask what types of articles they might need—at no charge. Arrange for your debater to speak at a local political rally or at a religious organization. Schools don't have monopolies on opportunities.

Summer: The Out-of-School Enrichment Season

Secret 27

Summer is your child's chance to win the edge, to beat the competition. The most important time for out-of-school enrichment is summer—when many opportunities exist to explore and develop interests. By fall, your son or daughter should possess an entirely new repertoire of abilities. Anything else is a waste.

Downtime should provide constructive fun. Don't let your children waste their summers "hanging out." Colleges ask on the applications what the applicant did every summer starting with the summer before ninth grade. This section should be filled with many exciting adventures, challenges, experiences, and extra learning that the high schools don't offer. Summer activities often provide defining moments and grist for essays, as they promote excitement for learning.

Summers need not be expensive. Teenagers who need to work for the summer can find many enriching employment opportunities that are more inspiring than babysitting or working at a local store. Summers should be packed with activities that provide changes of pace and challenge. Here are 15 good summer suggestions:

1. Organize a community-service project, campaign, or fund-raising party.
2. Conduct science research or social science research in a laboratory or at a university (many internships are paid).
3. Practice and perform with a local theater company.
4. Volunteer at a hospital, day care center, public day camp, geri-

atric center, park, beach, zoo, or environmental center. Utilize a skill that you want to develop (EMT, teaching, caregiving, being a lifeguard, animal handling, and so on).

5. Take a paid job in a field of interest.

6. Take art classes and assemble a portfolio.

7. Practice an instrument and perform.

8. Study an advanced-level course to be able to place out of it through an exam.

9. Take college-level classes at a local community college or another college.

10. Arrange a camping trip.

11. Organize day trips by bicycle, public transportation, or by hiking.

12. Invent something.

13. Create a personal reading list and challenge yourself to complete it during the summer.

14. Write a novel or play or book of poems.

15. Develop excellence in a sport that you don't get to pursue during the school year.

Before the summer, you and your children should set goals. What would your son like to gain by the end of summer? What will he get to add to the résumé? Design your daughter's summer so that her days are crammed with activities and creativity. Variety is fine—three weeks of this, and three weeks of that, and two weeks of this. What looks most impressive to colleges, mentors, and future employers are activities that demonstrate leadership, creativity, energy, and compassion. These activities, in turn, will help your children develop into the kind of adults they dream of becoming.

What are some activities that don't particularly impress colleges?

- Ungraded high school enrichment programs on college campuses
- Fancy sleepaway camps "where the people with the best connections send their kids"

- Teen tours in which the kids sit on a bus and are led to landmarks and "sights"
- Hanging out and sleeping to recuperate from a hard-working school year
- Getting a driver's license, babysitting, and catching up on missed TV
- Sunning oneself at a beach house
- A family resort vacation
- A cruise

As a general rule, colleges don't like activities that entail lots of spoon-feeding or passive, aimless hanging out. Be wary of summer teen sleepaway "enrichment programs" (translation: expensive, uncredited high school–level courses offered on college campuses). If a course is purported to be college-level, make sure college credit is offered. Even if your daughter gets to stay on the college campus to which she is applying, such programs won't get her in. Much more impressive are summers where she carves a different path, creates an original itinerary, tries a new experience, faces a new challenge, and aggressively pursues her interests. Even those "independent" summers require parental planning.

Parents' Role Delineated

| Secret 28 | **Even parents who say they're not sure that parents should be involved in the ap-** |

plication process are involved. If your son or daughter is applying to college, you have no choice. The secret is, you're involved to some degree already. Your role might be simply paying the application fee. Or your role might be running to the post office to mail everything, ordering new printer cartridges, or buying your kid a new shirt for the interview. Or maybe you're relegated to official family badgerer, scolding your son to finish his essay. Whatever role you've taken, you're involved. Of course, you can choose how helpful you want to be.

According to observant college administrators, one of the major characteristics of today's applicants and students is much more parental involvement than previous generations. The current generation is not a "leave me alone" hands-off group that's "doing its own thing." These are children who were brought up by doting soccer parents, schedules packed with lessons and constructive activities to which parents provided chauffeuring, family vacations geared for kids' stimulation, parents who watched educational TV with kids and read to them, and parents who actively pursued quality family time.

Unlike students who were Baby Boomers or Generation Xers, today's students call home daily, sometimes a few times a day. In the age of one-minute cell-phone calls, they phone with just-left-the-classroom feedback about how they did on exams. They phone from the dorm laundry room for urgent advice on how to work a new washing machine, or in the middle of cooking dinner to find out how much spice to add. They phone when they're walking alone on a dark path late at night and don't want to trouble campus security but need to know that someone is aware of their whereabouts. They phone their parents at the office requesting a wake-up call when they're about to take a much-needed twenty-minute midday nap. They phone spur-of-the-moment when they realize they suddenly ran out of money, or they really could use some item from home that they forgot, or to get a phone number of some old high school buddy, or to hear a friendly voice wish them luck before they go for an interview. Unlike previous generations, today's students are accustomed to constant affirmation, feedback, and encouragement from parents—a strong support network from home. Few colleges, even the most supportive, claim to provide these services.

Not all colleges support increased parental involvement; some still promote a 1970s mentality. Thinking they're very liberal, for example, one prominent college has boasted in the media on more than one occasion, that it advises parents to "remain outside the college gates"— that college is a time of independence that necessitates separation. They advise parents not to contact their children too often and claim to be advocating for their students.

Administrators at other colleges have noted that the new way of thinking dictates that independence does not mandate separation, that truly independent students are not afraid to maintain strong bonds with their parents, and that strong family support is much healthier for college students. Many colleges have introduced family or parent weekends with seminars for parents and sometimes younger siblings, encouraging family involvement and support. Many have active equivalents of PTAs that are instrumental in contributing to the financial health of the university or college. In an increasingly pressured and competitive time when suicide rates among students are relatively high, many parents prefer to maintain involvement with their kids as their kids go off to college. Parents who are immediately accessible by cell phone at any hour take on a new role of off-campus adviser and cheerleader, offering encouragement and affirmation where college officials or classmates do not. Of course, there is a point where involvement can become controlling, and this is to be avoided.

Understanding the limits of this increased involvement is particularly important when it comes to delineating parents' role in college applications. Many of the colleges stuck in the 1970s would be horrified to think that parents take part in the application process beyond paying the fee and telling the high school student to go to his or her room and fill in the blanks. As a general rule, the more competitive the college, the more savvy the college is about parental involvement. Colleges in tune with the new generation of students understand that many parents hire consultants to help determine what the child's best essay might be (to brainstorm on possible topics based on the students' individual experiences), or tutors to help teach applicants how to write a more strategic personal essay, or even editors to help them fine-tune or polish their essays. Of course, there is a fine line. Most professional advisers understand that ultimately, **the essay must be written by the student**, and parents—even the most educated parents who are able to help with the consulting, tutoring, and polishing processes to help prod their children through the essay-writing process—**should not** write their kids' essays for them. Remember: The college is looking for the student's "genuine voice," and this will get buried in the prose if the student's "board of advisers" micro-manages the process.

Parents may, however, want to fill in name, address, and other rote, fill-in-the-blank information to save their child from this tedious task. Since most of this information is typed anyway, it doesn't matter who does it. And because this task is so repetitive, it might be helpful to the motivation process to free the student to devote more time to the more important task of essay writing.

Lots of parents have issues with becoming secretary, file clerk, and photocopy technician during college-application season. (Some parents actually pay their own office assistants to fill in their child's general information and make photocopies.) Some insist that this boring task is the kid's responsibility, which it is, of course. If this is your viewpoint, stick to it. Just know that applications tend to get done a lot faster and with a lot less aggravation when parents volunteer to help with the busywork. Pitching in with the application demonstrates that you value the project and are willing to sacrifice time to help your child.

 **Remember that even famous professional writers—writers of the biggest best-sellers as well as top journalists—get edited by professional editors.** While it may not be appropriate for a college essay to be heavily edited by a professional, it is not inappropriate to formulate a topic with a knowledgeable teacher or college adviser and to ask a teacher to offer feedback on an essay once it is written. Again, I'll stress that **the student always should write his or her own essay**. But that does not mean that the student should sit in a cave and not show the essay to anyone before it is submitted. Regardless of how well your child writes, he or she *should* get feedback. Using resources (teachers, college counselors, guidance counselors, college advisers, etc.) is considered a sign of maturity, responsibility, and determination.

Secret 30 **Colleges believe that students who do not use the resources available to them in high school are not likely to suddenly start using available**

resources in college. This can be perceived by colleges as a weakness or laziness—an inability to accept help, and an inability to delegate.

If your children attend a well-funded high school generously equipped with quality supplies, facilities, and faculty attention, colleges will expect your child's application to show more polish. In such a setting, more students will be competing for the most-coveted college-admissions opportunities. In order to be a contender, applicants need applications that are clean of errors in spelling, grammar, and punctuation. Savvy parents can help their children to determine who the best resources would be for proofreading, suggesting edits, and determining which qualities and credentials might be most appealing for the student to emphasize.

Organizing the Application

Secret 31 **Organizing the application process is the parents' responsibility.** Savvy parents know this. Granted, this notion horrifies some parents at first, but parents who don't play an active role in the application organization often find that there *is no* organization. This applies to the highest achievers, and most conscientious students, who are often too busy studying, rehearsing, practicing, and doing homework to focus on organization.

Unlike when you applied to college, today's applications probably require much more choreography: more pages, more fill-ins, more competition, more of an elaborate procedure. Before your student obtains any applications, you and your child can determine which colleges he or she is considering, and then make up a calendar and a series of folders or files for each school's paperwork. For each college considered, create a separate file, in which all correspondence (and printouts of computer correspondence) should be kept. Once the applications are started, note all due dates and deadlines for applications and supporting materials on a single calendar, specially devoted to the application process. Parents should know, for example, when faculty recommendations are due. Parents should plan when the kid will request a recommendation (allowing a minimum of two weeks—or, better, three—for the teacher to write the recommendation). Parents should keep track of when the teacher recommendations are actually submitted (and mark that on the calendar).

Do you worry that your son won't stay organized in college if you play such a major role in the organization process at home? Think of yourself as setting a good example. You are demonstrating organization. Despite the myths of educators, for most students—including the very brightest—if parents don't organize the applications, nobody will, resulting in missed opportunities for admission.

Typical examples of students getting rejected or deferred for lack of organization are students who forget to ask teachers for a required recommendation until specific teachers are already *booked up*; students who don't bother to obtain additional transcripts from colleges or for-credit programs that they have attended (in addition to the high school from which they are graduating); students who are too late to register for timely standardized tests, and students who are unable to get their applications organized in time to apply for Early Decision.

An otherwise meticulous senior whose parents insisted that she organize her own applications for a series of Ivy League colleges and Smith College rushed through the process without reading the fine print. The whole family was surprised when Smith sent her a congratulations letter informing her that since she had checked off the box requesting "Early Decision," she was indeed in, but also now obligated to tell the other colleges that she was withdrawing her application in order to attend Smith. She had expected to have a selection of colleges from which to choose and unwittingly narrowed her options by making a hasty mistake.

Giving Your Kid Some Charisma

Many of the most-competitive colleges prefer individuals with excellence in single passions ("lopsidedness") rather than an eclectic assortment of activities ("well-roundedness"). A secret to helping your daughter or son become most sought after by colleges is for you to become actively involved in helping him or her to develop a college-appealing passion. The current thinking is that if the college has one student with a passion for chemistry, another with a passion for the violin, and still another with a love of French literature, eventually the college will build a well-rounded class. Each student should have at least *one* different passion or sought-after talent in which he or she is an expert. The 1990s concept of a well-rounded college has evolved, and the generalist is no longer as desirable.

Secret 33

Expertise is different from mere interest. It's the parents' job to scout out a progression of opportunities, to design their kid's curriculum so that he or she becomes an expert. Kids with a passion soak up every opportunity that exists to accommodate that passion, whether it be college courses (while they're still in high school), meeting with national experts, entering national competitions to prove their expertise, or publishing writings on the topic. In the most-competitive colleges, the nation's physics champion might be seated next to the nation's top chemistry student, a winner of a national science-research contest, a published poet, and the organizer of a national campaign to end world hunger. At the very top colleges, the class roster becomes a national who's who among students. If you want your kid to play in this league, you need a game plan while the kid is still in high school. That's what other parents have done to get their kids there.

While the student with expertise is preferred, before you start revamping your kid's life, note that the passion kid is not *always* preferred over the well-rounded kid. Some colleges are still seeking a combination of generalists, and "lopsided kids." And also note that at the most-competitive colleges, even the supposedly well-rounded kids are expected to be experts in the multiple fields in which they dabble—in other words, they're expected to have multiple passions. They are preferred to the students who just dabble in multiple fields, never demonstrating excellence in any area.

What If Your Kid Arrives at Senior Year with No Passions?

| Secret 34 | **Even senior year isn't too late to create an appealing passion. But the older your** |

child is, the more likely you'll have to select a more obscure and targeted passion.

While a younger child may build on a more general interest in art or music, an older high school student needs to be able to start with a fine-tuned passion in order to jump into the competition. Sample senior-year passions could include industrial photography, art appraisal, bioengineering, American Indian music, religious architecture, Russian classic fiction, economics of Africa, opera costume design, number theory, neuropsychology, medical history, international food management, etc. Find college-level courses, programs, and after-school internships that will give your son or daughter expertise in the area in which he or she chooses to develop a passion. Have your child join related organizations that focus on that passion—even in senior year—and make sure your son or daughter participates in some of that organization's activities in the early fall.

The "Snowball Effect"

| Secret 35 | **If your daughter develops a talent, and enters a competition and wins, she is much** |

more likely to win the next competition she enters, as well. Society rewards winners. Contests and achievements help build track records and even academic pedigrees. I have observed that students who perform well in small contests often go on to win larger competitions—

and not necessarily because both sets of judges used similar criteria. Often the larger competitions ask the applicant blatantly which other competitions he or she has won. Judges find previous winners very appealing. And rewarding a previous winner is a safe way to know that your judgment will not be contested. Thus, kids who win small contests often go on to win larger contests, and this in turn leads them to accumulate opportunities that other kids of equal talent may never even hear about.

By high school junior year, many of the top competitions are impossible to break into. The game is already over. Many academic programs and contests require such a daunting accumulation of credentials to enter that the newcomer is already out of the running.

Is There a "Best Passion"?

From the college admissions perspective, kids should pursue whatever constructive endeavors captivate their imaginations and dreams, but the best passion is probably one that can be nourished on the particular college campus. So if your kid is applying to a music conservatory, a primary passion for American history might not be the "best passion," or the one to wow the admissions officers. Likewise, if your kid is applying to a Pre-Dental program, your kid's intense passion for dance might not be the "best passion." And for the kid who is applying for an undergraduate business degree, a passion for Russian literature might not be helpful. That said, embracing a variety of passions can be very helpful, as long as at least one of the kid's primary passions coincides with the curriculum of the school to which he or she is applying, and as long as the kid is able to show that he or she is outstanding in that particular field.

In fact, many admissions officers are concerned about students who seem entirely "one dimensional," worrying that the student may not be open to the broader range of opportunities offered by the college, or worrying that if the student tires of that passion, the student will burn out. In addition to the one main passion, one should also show some proficiency in other areas.

A student who applied to Princeton was asked at an interview, "Are you one of those one-dimensional science kids?" The student, whose primary passion was clearly science research, was able to cite a proven interest in classics, expertise in two sports, a deep background in classical music performance, and a passion for tracking Hollywood statistics. The kid was ultimately admitted.

| Secret 36 | **Every parent asks if there is a musical instrument preferred by colleges. If you** |

have a real choice in introducing your child to bassoon, oboe, or clarinet, you're probably wiser to go for bassoon or oboe. Colleges tend to need those instruments more. But if your kid doesn't absolutely love bassoon or oboe and *does* absolutely love clarinet (and is therefore much more likely to practice and become an expert), go with clarinet.

The retired head of a college music department argued against choosing instruments for your kid, saying that the kid should go with his or her own passion. Citing the example of harpists, he said that while harpists were once in dire demand, many college orchestras have decided not to use harp music, so that they don't need harpists. A kid who takes harp just to be sought after could be very disappointed, he said. But he added that colleges need bassoonists, oboists, French horn players, and "any college could always use a *really* top violinist."

Lots of parents misguidedly believe that the passions that really count with admissions officers are limited to science, music, and the most popular sports. But think of a university as an entire community requiring many different skills and talents.

In nurturing a passion, parents should consider the usefulness of the skill or subject to the college. Not all passions that require skill help in the college admissions process. For a passion to be useful, the college needs to have a related course, club, or program that focuses on that particular skill.

The following are some of the less useful hobbies (Disclaimer: While these activities may be useful at the appropriate university or college for an offbeat major like Circus Arts, for example, they won't be skills that the majority of most-competitive colleges are specifically seeking): tightrope, trapeze, skydiving, basket weaving, knitting, whittling, snorkeling (except Marine Biology majors), baseball card collecting, computer game mastery (except Computer Graphics majors), cooking, baking (except Food Science majors), bowling, shuffleboard, bocce, juggling, magic (except Recreation or Education majors), camping (except Environmental majors), guitar, harmonica, calligraphy, origami, scrapbooks, quilting (except Decorative Arts majors), crossword puzzles, penpals (except Foreign Culture majors), hunting, fishing, go-carting, driving, clubbing, gambling.

If your kid likes one of these activities, don't feel that you need to squelch this passion. Instead, rechannel it. Consider some new potential hobbies and activities perhaps related to your child's current passion that would translate well to the competitive colleges he's considering. If your son is into sports odds, for example, rechannel him to the stock market. Or if your daughter is into stamp or baseball card collecting, introduce her to statistics.

Last-Minute Credential Enhancement

How do you enhance the credentials of the high school junior or senior who contends to have no talent, no skills, no outstanding grades, and no outstanding selling points for college?

| Secret 37 | **The secret is that parents still can do something to help create last-minute** |

credentials that could have lifelong impact. Here are some possibilities to spark your thinking.

- A boy we'll call Matt made it through high school without participating in any extracurricular activities. His grade point average was somewhere between C-plus and B-minus. His standardized test scores were average. He didn't play sports. He didn't view himself as artistic. He never participated in community service. He never even held a part-time job and spent his summers at a golf course—playing golf, which he was not particularly skilled at—or at friends' houses. He took the courses that he thought to be the easiest in his school—no APs or IBs. Photography was his favorite. He was rejected at his top-choice colleges, but, miraculously, was wait-listed at two top state universities.

Shocked by the possibility of attending these schools, Matt and his parents began brainstorming ways to get him off the waiting list.

Matt and his parents decided to reinvent him as a photographer. He first chose a focus of nature photography. He asked the school if he could borrow a camera from his photography course for the weekend. He took a series of photographs, enlarged the pictures he liked most, and gave each a title. His parents approached the bank where they had an account, since the bank's bulletin board frequently displayed local students' work. The bank was delighted to display Matt's work. Matt arranged the photos artistically, made a banner to give the exhibit an official name, and gave himself credit for the display with a label under each photo naming the image and the photographer.

Matt could honestly report that he had become an exhibited local photographer and that his works titled "The Thorn Bush," "Reflection in a Pond," and "Ant Hill" were featured in a public exhibit. The local newspaper (contacted by Matt's mother) sent a reviewer and gave his exhibit a positive mention. In addition, the positive feedback he got from people who saw his exhibit in the bank inspired him to become much more active at school. In late April, he joined the school newspaper and class yearbook as a photographer. He faxed his added credentials to both colleges and was admitted to both.

This formative experience gave Matt a skill he eventually contributed to college.

• Jessica, an A student, played the violin and liked TV, going to parties, and shopping. She practiced violin and studied to please her parents, but showed little interest in the instrument or her classes. Her test scores were outstanding, but her application essays made her sound dull and bored.

In fact, she was coming from a family that had endured some medical hardship, and as a result, was often distracted. Despite getting all A's, she had difficulty focusing, and her application included many careless errors, which kept her from gaining acceptance to her first-choice school. She was lucky to get wait-listed at her second. The form letter from the university said that she had just missed the cutoff. The thought of being excluded suddenly motivated her.

Jessica and her parents reinvented Jessica as a caring, energetic social activist. Her mother arranged for the girl to play violin at local charity events. Jessica performed at fund-raisers for cancer research, hospitals, and disaster relief. Most of the charities were health related, for that is where her family had connections and that's what interested Jessica most. In the process, Jessica improved her violin skills, gained performance experience, helped good causes, and became more aware of public health. A few weeks later, she updated her second-choice college about her "musical tour" and documented her newfound interest in medicine. She was admitted, genuinely eager to pursue a Pre-Med major.

• Jake, a senior with below-average reading and math skills who was rejected from his first-choice Early Decision college in December, was the youngest in a high-achieving family. As he explained it, he "fell through the cracks" while his sisters went to high-profile colleges. His parents, who had a very profitable international business, wanted him to attend college, knowing that he would probably work in the family business eventually, but Jake didn't show interest in college. He hated science, math, social studies, and sports. He was not involved in social causes or community service. He did not play a musical instrument and didn't view himself as particularly artistic, but he enjoyed doodling. He never participated in extracurricular activities at school but would race home instead to watch TV or check his e-mail. Instead of studying, he spent his time playing computer games, experimenting with computer graphics, hanging out with friends, and reading comic books.

Jake's parents weren't about to let him "fall through the cracks" again. They encouraged him to reinvent himself as a comic strip artist. His parents enrolled him in a local college evening course on comic strip art, where he found it easy to concentrate, since he was encouraged to doodle in class. With his interest in comics, he quickly mastered the art form. He turned his doodles into imaginative stories, after which his parents encouraged him to contribute cartoons and illustrations to the school newspaper, literary magazine, and concert programs. Suddenly, through his art, he became a vital contributor to many school activities. Teachers noticed his work and newfound passion and gained new respect for Jake, who before had been viewed as lazy and unfocused. Jake the cartoonist assembled a portfolio by the end of senior year. He updated his college applications and submitted copies of published cartoons, and earned himself admission into a college that offered one of the top animation programs in the country.

- A junior we'll call Laura whose dream it was to become a model, actress, or rock star was never chosen for a significant acting role in school plays or musicals. Her grades were straight B's, with test scores that matched. She was attractive enough to play a heroine, musical enough to sing decently, and physically fit but a very mediocre athlete. She enjoyed art, but was a B-student there, too. Laura had a good imagination and liked to write stories, but her English grades were nothing notable. She was very caring and seemed to work well with young children, although she had no interest in teaching. At the end of her junior year, she had no outstanding credentials.

Laura's parents heard about a summer residential puppetry program that sounded interesting, and, as a cooperative family effort, decided to reinvent Laura as a puppeteer. She attended the program the summer before her senior year. There she learned how to make puppets, write scripts, and design scenery. She also designed a portable puppet theater. After the summer, her parents helped her arrange a community service "tour" of day care centers, nursery schools, and hospitals. Needing extra bodies to work the puppets, she recruited other high school students and eventually set up a traveling company (performing at elementary schools in her district). Laura, who previously couldn't get even a small part in a school show, was now the director and manager of an entire theater company. She starred in all her own shows, speaking through her puppets, and sang solos. When she applied to college, she was well received as an initiator, pioneer, talented artist, and a student who could contribute a new art form to the campus (possibly performing at local schools for good college-community relations).

• An American student named Kate who was born in China had above-average grades, low verbal SAT scores, and was bilingual. A high school senior who had been deferred in December, her strongest subjects were Latin and French. She played piano but not well. She played JV soccer in season. She didn't view herself as artistic. Although she enjoyed writing and editing, she hadn't gotten an editorship on one of the school's publications because she wasn't popular. She was one of many students to help organize her school's annual International Culture Night, but she wasn't a leader or a star. Other classmates were more musically proficient, had higher grades and scores, and were more active in school. Although she had no record of leadership, Kate was most interested in a college known for its ability to attract and train future leaders.

Kate reinvented herself as a foreign-language and culture expert. She started a foreign-language magazine, translator's club, and cultural-exchange program. She spoke to the foreign-language teachers at her school and established a series of writing contests in each language—encouraging students to submit writing for her magazine. Some teachers made the contest part of their students' homework, requiring that each student submit a story, poem, or haiku. Kate asked each teacher to pick the best pieces for publication and to recommend a student to edit in each foreign language. She immediately acquired a willing staff and plenty of works from which to choose. She asked art students to submit illustrations. Eventually, she assembled an impressive self-published magazine (a booklet stapled together and distributed to the student body) and submitted a copy with her college application.

At the same time, Kate created a translator's club. Seeing the need for interpreters to assist new foreign students and their parents at her school, which had a large international population, she coordinated student volunteers to attend parent meetings. She recruited bilingual students in fifteen languages, who were happy to assist to add credentials to their own résumés. She planned to expand the program, if successful, to other schools in her district, and then offer the school-based program as a model for public schools nationwide.

Finally, Kate set up a local cultural-exchange program. Because the students in her community came from many different backgrounds, she arranged for local students to experience celebrations in the homes of families of different cultures. For example, a Lutheran had dinner with a Jewish family for

Passover. An Italian celebrated Chinese New Year's with a Chinese family. A Korean spent Easter Sunday with an Irish family. A Hindu attended a Quaker meeting. Each student in the club hosted a student at his or her own family's cultural or religious event. Each participant then got to be the guest at another family's event.

Setting up such an organization demonstrated leadership, energy, and community service. The cultural mix also provided excellent preparation for college living, particularly for the top colleges, which value diversity. The cultural programs organized by Kate enhanced community understanding. Kate earned a reputation as a pioneer, leader, and vital contributor to her school and community. In April, she was offered Regular Decision admission to her first-choice college.

While parents can play a major role in scouting out opportunities and directions and encouraging new academic passions for their sons and daughters, this advocacy need not be limited to extracurricular support. Parents can also contribute significantly to the daily in-school experience and the way that their children are assessed, graded, and perceived in the classroom and on written records.

CHAPTER 3

Your Role in Producing High-Achievers

It is no secret that the most important single factor that colleges consider is the student's grade point average. Every college guidebook and counselor will tell you that grades bear much more weight than the application form, the interview, recommendations, essays, marketable academic passions, and test scores. But what nobody wants to talk about are the subjectivity of grades and what parents can do to help their children become high-achievers.

| Secret 38 | **Parents can have a major impact on their high school kid's averages.** This is not advice you'll get from the guidance counselor, who wants to discourage parental meddling. Nor will you hear it from the principal, your kid's teachers, or college admissions officers. And this is not advice that competing parents will share. So let's just say that this is top secret information that you can verify only by letting go of your old role of badgerer and taking on a new role of team player.

People commonly believe that parents should keep away from issues of grading. Many savvy parents of top-achievers secretly have learned otherwise. They know that students with the highest grades tend to be the most sought after. But parents are at a point in time where they're not sure or comfortable with what their roles ought to be in monitoring their kid's grades. They don't want to be overbearing. They don't want to be accused of micromanaging. Yet they know that grades have enormous influence and control over where their kid goes to college. Mention your kid's grades to someone else—bad or good—and the person is likely to think you're *obsessed* with report cards. Revealing specific grades is as taboo as discussing a person's weight or salary. The top-grade-getter sounds boastful and the bottom-grade-getter sounds like a loser; the middle is nothing to be proud of—nobody wants to be "average." Challenge a teacher's grade, and the teacher is likely to tell you that you as a parent are out of line or inappropriate, and that grades should not be your focus—or even your business. (Recent studies have shown that many teachers feel that parents are their number one obstacle to teaching.) The same holds true if your kid challenges a grade. (The kid is accused of harboring the wrong values—caring too much about a numerical designation, rather than the learning process.) So, is the answer to downplay the importance of grades at home? Not if you want your kid to be offered admission into top colleges.

Grade Grubbing 101

Secret 39   **In contrast to the public party line that encourages parents to teach their kids that it is wrong to question grades that seem incorrect, the secret that savvy parents know is that monitoring grades is responsible consumerism.** Regardless of what some "experts" might tell your kid about how kids should not be overly conscious of grades, students should be very clear on why they are being given the grades they are getting. Seeking to improve one's skills and a teacher's grading of those skills shows responsibility. Teachers have been known to call such concern for grades materialistic or greedy. Assigning what can sometimes seem like arbitrary grades is far more judgmental than receiving and questioning the numbers that can have a major impact on one's life.

| Secret 40 |

Contrary to what many people like to believe, the secret is that high school grades starting with freshman year play a very powerful role in helping to determine your child's future. You may hate the grading system, abhor the pressure, and feel that children should learn to learn for learning's sake. You might be right. Nevertheless, in today's society, no matter what your philosophy on grading, testing, and learning, grades play a powerful role in the number of opportunities that become available to your child—not just which college your kid gets into. All of the most prestigious summer internships, jobs, academic programs, science-research opportunities, national competitions, and awards require that the student submit a high school transcript. So while learning for the sake of learning is a wonderful value, learning opportunities can become limited if your kid isn't getting the grades.

Teachers, guidance counselors, and administrators tend to discourage or intimidate students from questioning their grades, by attacking their values, work habits, potential, or abilities at an age when students tend to feel insecure and vulnerable. Savvy parents reassure their kids or question the grades for them. Some students become so intimidated that even when they know that their grades are incorrect, they opt to let inaccuracies go uncontested and hope that an equal number of inaccuracies will work in their favor (a teacher gives them a high grade they don't feel that they've earned). They make a general policy of passively not questioning grades, and their parents are oblivious or leave it to the kids to make the decision on whether to question the grades.

Many parents are also terrified of questioning grades or letting their child challenge grades. Parents worry most that questioning a grade will lead to repercussions—that even if they get the grade changed successfully, the teacher will take revenge at some later date, by low-balling the grade on the next subjective essay or on class participation. Parents want the teachers to like them and their kid, and that's generally a good instinct, but parents should be willing to be the "bad guys" or "pushy parents." Teachers won't hold it against the kid if the parent is annoying. If anything, they'll sympathize.

Monitoring Grades

| **Secret 41** | **Grades are often fraught with inaccuracies, even by the most well-meaning** |

teachers. Always check the numbers. My father used to double-check the waiter's addition visibly when he went to a restaurant. People who would eat out with him would ask why he did this. He insisted that at least half the time, he found errors in the addition, usually favoring the restaurant.

His lesson can be applied to grading. Having followed grades over the years, and having taught college myself, I noticed many colleagues—particularly faculty members in non-math-related fields—who did not know how to perform simple percentage-related equations. On one occasion, in a restaurant where I was being treated by seven colleagues, I was the only one at the table who could figure out the 15 percent tip (and, yes, a calculator was available, although the calculation was simple enough to do in my head). With this understanding, I emphasize that it is important for parents to double-check kids' grades. If some teachers can't figure out a simple tip, how can they give your kids accurate grades using a rubric of say: 15 percent for the final exam, 15 percent midterm, 15 percent class work, 10 percent quizzes, 20 percent homework, 15 percent for class participation, and 10 percent for attendance? If I were to generalize, I would say that most teachers I have met are extremely honest—even if they're not mathematicians. But even honest people make mistakes. Always double-check.

| **Secret 42** | **Although this may sound extremely annoying to teachers, parents should keep** |

track of all rubrics. The clever parent is aware of (1) the high school's grading policies and has them in writing; (2) the grading rubrics of each high school teacher (and has them in writing); and (3) the score at the top of every graded test paper, quiz, lab, and essay that comes home in the backpack. Parents have a right to know how their kid is being assessed. Not only will you keep teachers accurate, you will also be alerted sooner if your child is facing any sudden academic difficulties or emotional swings.

(Think of grade monitoring like bookkeeping or balancing your checkbook. It's always responsible to check the numbers for occasional errors.) The clever parent doesn't wait until the report card arrives to be surprised.

Avoiding the Role of the Ogre

Monitoring grades should not mean pressuring your children. In contrast to the pushy-parent image, think of your family as a collaborating team, working together to help family members maintain high grades. To succeed in nurturing top-grade-getters, you'll need some guidelines.

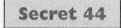 **Be a reliable advocate for your children. This deceptively simple-sounding secret is probably one of the hardest tasks for parents to master.** Being an advocate means never criticizing your child publicly or to teachers or other parents. You want your child to know that you are a reliable advocate. Parents often slip into complaining about their children, worrying that it's immodest to act as if their children are above reproach, especially in the company of teachers. It's not uncommon, for example, to hear a teacher complain about a child's study habits. Many parents, trying to sound reasonable, listen to what the teacher is saying and even agree. Parents *should* listen to what teachers have to say, but then they should not join the bandwagon and berate their child. Instead, they should discuss the teacher feedback with their child and determine a game plan for how the family will work together to improve the child's study habits.

Secret 44 **Don't pressure your child if she is genuinely trying her hardest but is unable to do better work and achieve higher grades.** Not every child

understands every lesson at the same pace. If you scold her for not achieving more when she feels unable to achieve more, she will rebel, and you will lose all credibility as a collaborator. At the same time, don't give up on her if she is not achieving to your family expectations. Instead, make it your business to work with her to see that her grades go up.

Secret 45	**Don't get stuck in the role of badgering your child to study or do homework. In-**

stead, successful parents volunteer to do it with the child, and make it fun—really fun. Studying with your daughter sends her a message that you value her work—or you at least empathize with the late-night struggle to master difficult material. Studying together also minimizes the distractions, because your child is less likely to linger on the phone with friends when he knows that his father, who has put in a busy day at the office, is waiting to study with him. It also eliminates the conflict that kids feel about whether to spend time with the other people in the household or whether to tune out the family in order to do homework or study. Studying together clearly sends the message "We're all in this together"—a most valuable message in nurturing top-grade-getters.

Secret 46	**Stay up late with your child (without complaining) when he or she has to stay**

up to complete an assignment. Suffer together, and real bonds will emerge. While you want your child to understand that you have to be awake the next morning in the office, staying up late with your child helps you to stay in tune with the curriculum and helps you stay in touch with your child's study habits. Even if your child is doing work that doesn't require your assistance, it's nice to have a companion when doing late-night homework. Stay up with your child for at least a token amount of time, if you're genuinely exhausted and are unable to stay up throughout the duration of the homework. Your good intentions will make a statement about how important you view your child's homework to be.

Secret 47

Keep track of all upcoming homework assignments, tests, quizzes, and projects— know the deadlines and how far along your child is in preparing. This prevents your child from experiencing too many "surprise assignments"—homework that even the brightest of students suddenly remember at one a.m. and that is due the next day. For the top students, high school is much more complicated than it once was, with many more AP courses offered now, for example, than ever before. It's much easier for students to overlook assignments or to misappropriate time for assignments. Parental help in overseeing the homework schedule can go a long way.

Secret 48

Compliment, affirm, and occasionally reward your child for good studying and hard work—*not for grades*, because grades are given out by teachers, and hard work is performed by kids. If you want to encourage your child to work hard, offer rewards that appeal to the child at the end of hours of hard work. Tell your daughter, for example, that she will be getting an award if she devotes three hours to studying for her Latin exam. The rewards do not have to be big, but they should be thoughtful. They can be items you planned to get for your child, anyway: a new box of felt-tipped pens, a college T-shirt, for example; or they can be little fun surprises from a dollar store. In comparison, there is relatively little benefit for rewarding high grades once the grades have been given by the teacher.

Secret 49

Supply healthful, low-fat, long-lasting foods for late nights of study (popcorn, nuts and raisins, cut-up fruit, or other things that take long to eat). Food will keep both you and the student awake and gives a reward to those who stay up late to study when they would rather be sleeping. While sleep may be important for good health, you need to support your child if he must study into the wee hours. Don't make him conflicted about whether to do school work or get enough sleep. If his course load is depriving him of sleep regularly, you may want him to drop a course to lighten the load. Or if you feel that the homework is unreasonably time-consuming on a regular basis, you might want to speak with the particular teacher to let him or her know that a disproportionate amount of time is required to fulfill class homework assignments. Assuming that your kid isn't particularly pokey, most teachers would want to know.

Secret 50 **Never tell your child you wish she were like so-and-so who gets top grades. Instead, show her appreciation for *her* hard work, whenever you see evidence of it.** If your daughter longingly mentions so-and-so who gets top grades, create a strategy to help her improve her grades. Remember: *You're a team. If your kid gets a C, then you get a C as a parent. Invest yourself in this process.*

Secret 51 **If you are unable to study with your kid (you don't know the material), keep your kid company.** Don't make studying a lonely, isolating experience. While you are keeping her company, you can tell your daughter how impressed you are with the physics that she is studying and do not understand it yourself. Let her know that she is learning something more advanced than you have learned. You can also offer to learn the material, do Google searches, and explore the subject with her.

Secret 52 **Don't switch on the TV in the background if your child is trying to work, and don't set up other distractions.** When a child has to study, the whole house has to respect that silence—even in a mansion, and even in a family with ten children. Individuals' homework is that important, and you want that message to be clear.

Secret 53 **Set a break schedule. For some students, a ten-minute break is required every hour. For others, five minutes per half hour is better.** Do not encourage TV as a break-time activity, because it gets frustrating when you have to pull your daughter away in the middle of her TV show. Instead, encourage something physically active, like playing a round or two of the popular college arcade game Dance Dance Revolution, or even playing a short piece on a musical instrument. Or break time can be snack time, or enough time for a quick shower. Break time can also provide a good discussion time. (Most kids will willingly discuss what happened in school that day at break time—because they know that if the discussion goes into overtime, few parents will interrupt to make kids go back to work. Such discussions provide a good chance for procrastination and lots of bonding.)

| Secret 54 | **Find out what tutoring options the school offers and know the schedule.** Does the |

school offer free intense tutoring, for example, for Advanced Placement exams or for the SATs or ACTs? Even if you prefer to have a private tutor for your child, the savvy parent should be aware of what opportunities the school offers. Before you resort to high-cost tutoring programs or courses, your child should sample at least one in-school prep program to see if it meets his or her needs.

| Secret 55 | **If your child is stuck on a concept that you cannot help with, hire a tutor.** A tutor can |

be an older student seeking community-service credit—and doing it voluntarily—or a certified teacher or a local college student. Don't let too much time lapse if your son's grades suddenly drop or if he complains that he is not keeping up with the class. Have tutors in mind who can rescue him before the problem snowballs. Don't make him feel bad about needing tutors—most top students hire tutors from time to time. Some parents employ steady tutors for the hardest subjects. In other cases, a tutor is needed for a one-time boost, when the student comes upon an obstacle; and once the obstacle is passed, the tutor is no longer needed. Using a tutor is *not* cheating or wimping out. Ultimately, the student must take the test and write his own papers.

Monitoring Your Kid's GPA

Secret 56	**In addition to monitoring your child's grades, also monitor your child's grade**

point average. "But isn't it the kid's responsibility to keep track of his or her own average?" you ask, since you grew up in a time when you were required to monitor your own grades—which most likely meant that nobody monitored your grades.

Yes and no. If the kid is organized and keeps track of his or her own grades, fine. But if the kid is not keeping track of grades—and relatively few of the top students do—a wise parent will step in and assist. This keeps the parent tuned in to the child's school experience. It will not harm the child's sense of independence. It will only secure the child's feelings of family affirmation and teamwork and bolster the notion that schoolwork is valued.

The approach should not be one of anger or annoyance, as in, "If you can't organize your own grades, I'm going to have to step in!" Instead, managing should be a team venture. Think of yourself as your kid's agent. "Together we'll make you succeed beyond your own expectations—where you fail, we fail."

Secret 57	**Few families know to review all rubrics with their children, preferably at the be-**

ginning of the year. If you discover that you or your child have a problem with the grading rubric, challenge it before a crisis arises. While you generally want to be supportive of the teacher (in addition to being supportive of your kid), point out to your kid any grading policy that you feel is bound to be controversial in your home. For example, "It says here that Mr. Johnson, your health teacher, plans to grade you on how clean you keep your fingernails. Will you be able to keep your nails clean all year?" While questioning the rubric may appear to be inciting controversy, it's best to clear up any conflicts in advance. Most kids don't read the syllabus independently.

Is it so important for the *parent* to understand the individual teacher's grading system? Yes, particularly if you ever want to be empowered to help your kid challenge a grade or policy or maintain an average. You don't want to be the parent who requires the kid to do farm chores—getting dirt trapped in his or her nails—before showing up at Mr. Johnson's health class. You don't want to be the poky chauffeur if your kid's first-period teacher is taking off 50 points for lateness. You don't want to refuse to make the trip home again for the nth time to bring a book to school that your kid forgot, if the teacher deducts 30 points each time the kid shows up without a book. You don't want to be the parent who insists that the kid get to bed by midnight if the deadline is tomorrow, the kid is progressing nicely, and the teacher will subtract 50 points if the work is late. In other words, a teacher's requirements could have major impact on a family's lifestyle. If you find this invasive, challenge the policy *before* your kid shows up at school with dirty nails, late for class, without a book, or rested without the assignment. Know in advance if a teacher is permitted to take off points or add points for behavior, attendance, attire, class participation, or attitude. Know the ground rules when analyzing grades.

Grade Ceilings

Secret 58 **Grade ceilings may be secretly keeping your kid's grades down. Savvy parents should find out if glass ceilings are permitted in your child's school.** If, for example, the school's grading system includes grades from 0 to 100, is a teacher permitted to say, "The top grade I give in this course is 95. Only Einstein can get a 100"? Or, "In my art class only Rembrandt gets a 4.0"? If such ceilings are not permitted—and they should not be—and you see evidence of a ceiling in your child's grades or in the class grades, you may have grounds to contest a grade. After the second week of school, speak with your child about grade ceilings and ethics, and find out if any teachers have implied such grade limits or ceilings. If perfect grades are so unattainable, ceilings may exist.

Major Disparities in Grading

| Secret 59 | Grades should be equivalent in different sections of the same course. If one teacher |

consistently gives harder exams, or a different teacher gives extra credit while your child's teacher doesn't, you have the right to complain. It's unfair to have your child penalized for "getting the wrong teacher." Have your son or daughter complain to the classroom teacher first. If that doesn't work, the parent should complain. If that doesn't work, take it to the administration with some kind of comparative evidence.

Sharing Information and Family Accountability

| Secret 60 | Your child has a glass backpack. That's the secret to staying in touch with your |

teenager. Backpacks are "family property," and parents can see inside. Can you handle that concept? Your son's closet may be private. Your daughter's bedroom may be private (always knock before entering). But the backpack and its contents are family property—nothing personal. Once you're familiar with the grading structure (which may differ from course to course), read each assignment, paper, and exam as it comes home. Go through your kid's backpack nightly if necessary. Make folders for each course. Keep score on course averages, so there are no surprises at the end of the marking period.

| Secret 61 | Grades are not secrets or personal. The secret is that they appear on the report |

card during every marking period whether or not parents choose to detach themselves during the months in between. In many households, parents let their kids decide whether or not to share grades with them. This turns into a case-by-case or grade-by-grade decision, and encourages students to show their parents only their higher grades, giving parents a skewed image of the child's performance. When report cards arrive, no one is more shocked than the parents (and the self-deceiving kid) when the grades don't measure up to the perceived average. Parents sometimes are fast to blame the teacher, when the child's grade history clearly indicated that such a low grade was warranted.

To avoid this situation, go over every grade—good and bad. Make it clear to your kid that that's the only way you can advocate for your kid effectively. Emphasize that you love your kid regardless of the grades, and you also believe that your kid is smart regardless of the grades.

At the same time, sharing of grades should not be a cause of tension or conflict. Good parenting means convincing your child (and staying true to the notion) that you are on his or her side. You are on the same "team." You are your child's advocate—always, for life. (And no, advocating for your son does not mean berating him "for his own good" for not getting better grades or working hard enough. Low grades certainly should never be perceived as a cause for punishment or "grounding"—getting a low grade is punishment enough in life, even if you and your child don't realize it yet. Witnessing low grades should not be a cause for putting your daughter on a guilt trip—as in, "We expected so much more from you. How could you have done this to us?" And low grades should not be a cause for you to belittle her—as in, "I guess you're just not as smart as we had thought," or "I guess you'll just have to settle for Stupid College or Toilet U instead of Prestige College.") You have to promise not to be angry or upset with your children if they don't get the grades you want for them—even if you're frustrated *for* them, because you know they could have done better.

When a bad grade is reported, your job is to do the following:

- Console your child who also did not want to see a bad grade (even if the kid claims not to care—most kids will claim not to care at this point).

- Inspect the paper or exam to understand why your child got a low grade. Some kids assume that low grades are a matter of luck or a matter of "the teacher hates me." Find out what caused the specific problem.

- Discuss (in a positive way) the paper or exam with your child to help your child understand why a low grade was given so he or she can improve the next time. Deal with specific teacher comments one at a time. Do not scold your daughter and say that a low grade was given because "you obviously did not put enough effort into the assignment." That's lazy parenting and not at all constructive. Instead, look for specific errors in spelling, grammar, style, and factual information. Then correct those errors, so she sees exactly the way the paper or exam should be. This is very helpful and shows that you care enough to take time out to work this through with your child—even if the teacher didn't.

- If the teacher's comments are not specific, have your child go to the teacher and request (politely) more specific comments. Vague comments like "Awkward wording," "I don't understand this," and "Where are you going with this?" are useless and not constructive, and teachers should be asked to be more specific.

- Conduct a ministrategy session with your child. Teach your child what specific steps he or she can take to improve the score next time. If you the parent are puzzled about what the kid can do to improve, request a conference with the teacher to discuss how you should guide your child so that your kid could improve the next time. Is your kid having a grammar problem? Is your kid misunderstanding some method that the teacher uses? Approach the teacher in a positive way—as if you are working as a team to help the student. At the same time, *never* be willing to agree with any insults or defeatist comments that an unsophisticated teacher might hurl at your child. (Examples: "There's nothing your kid can do to improve his writing. He's just not Shakespeare." "Well maybe if she behaved in class, her writing would be better." "I just don't like his style.")

- Figure out whether the current low grade is alterable. (Does your child have the opportunity to rewrite the paper for a raised grade? Could your child take the test again at some later date?)

- See if you agree with the teacher's grading of your child's work. If you disagree with your child's answer, try to understand how he or she arrived at it. Be supportive of the thinking process as your child explains it. If done correctly, this should be a good bonding experience for you and your child. If your daughter disagrees with the teacher on the answer, never *assume* that the teacher is right. Ask your daughter to explain to you why the teacher is wrong. If she cannot explain the difference, *then* you may assume that the teacher is right.

Failing to use an open backpack policy as a parent doesn't free your child from making the same mistakes the next time around. Discussing each grade with your child implicitly demonstrates to your child how important each grade is in the scheme of overall averages and how we learn from our errors. When you devote time and concentration to your child's studies, your child will tend to do the same. At the same time, it's important not to *dwell* on single grades, since it's the big picture that counts ultimately. Dwelling on a single grade only will depress and discourage your child from working harder.

Conscientious parents are fully on top of testing schedules. Know when each test is scheduled and when each long-term assignment is due (check out your kid's assignment book—part of the glass backpack policy). You might want to offer to study for exams with the kid. On a test day, you should know to ask, "How did the test go?" Debriefings are very important to keep you in touch with your child. Know when the grades are to be announced. (Does your child's school have a return-of-assessment deadline policy stating within how many days the

teacher must return graded work? If not, you as an active parent may
want to promote such a policy.)

Some parents keep charts of grades on the refrigerator, so family
members can easily tabulate averages. This may remind you to ask your
child about progress in courses in which there are fewer grades on the
chart. Charting also helps catch problems early on. Instead of waiting
to see the report card, parents can spot a downward trend and remedy it
by providing immediate help before it becomes a major learning problem (or track record).

| **Secret 62** | **Remember throughout this process to tell your child constantly that it is not the** |

child's ability that you are questioning. While first instinct might
be to worry that this constant affirmation gives children false hope and
failed expectations, parents need not worry about a lack of societal
dampers. Even the most gifted children with no physical or mental disabilities will likely face plenty of obstacles during the course of their
education, so parents need not fill this negative role. (For example, if
your child were blind and was determined to read *War and Peace*, would
you tell your child that he or she is not capable of reading it, or would
you find the book in braille or on audiotape instead?) Where a weakness is spotted, the parents' job is to strengthen that area or find an alternative method of passage, rather than to console the child by
doubting or negating the child's ability to ever strengthen that area.
("You just aren't mathematically inclined." "Not everyone has to be a
great speller.")

Telling your child that you are not questioning his or her *abilities* is
very different than telling the child that he or she is perfect. In the
first case, you are acknowledging that your child didn't reach his goals
but are offering encouragement to work harder to achieve them. In
the second, you are saying that your child's actions and behavior are
never subject to question and will never be able to improve—a major
difference.

In monitoring grades, explain to your child that you want to stay on
top of how he or she is being *perceived*. Grades are one indicator. And

grades also send a message to others who have access to your kid's records—teachers, administrators, and staff—about how *they* should treat your kid.

Supervising Your Kid's Organization

Secret 63

Secretly organize your child. Foolish parents complain to teachers or other parents that their kid is so disorganized or keeps a messy backpack or even a messy room. Invade. Clean up the kid's act. Never blame your child (or let a teacher blame your child) for lack of organization. "How do you teach a kid organization?" well-intending parents ask. My not-so-orthodox but serious answer is, "Don't." Take responsibility for your kids' organization. You'd be surprised how quickly your kid will learn organization, once *you* become involved in organizing your kid's backpack or room.

If you don't monitor your kid's backpack (either because it takes too much time or, more commonly, that it's too *invasive*), you'll probably find that you devote far more time to contesting grades, "invading" your kid's life, sobbing or scolding your child, and helplessly questioning your kid's time management. ("Should you really be going out tonight?" "Don't you have work that you should be doing?")

Negotiating with the School

Secret 64

The trick to successful school negotiations is that when approaching a teacher or administrator, parents should always embrace a positive attitude—a team approach. The team consists of the student, the teacher, the parent, and the administrator. The student is the most important member of the team. Memorize this concept: "We are all a team working together to do what's best for the student and the school."

When addressing a problem, students should always be the frontline. If the problem concerns overall average, the student should inquire with his or her guidance counselor or academic adviser. If it's a matter of a grade for a particular course or subject, the student should approach the teacher. The student should politely question the teacher responsible for a disputed mark, to try to gain an understanding of how the mark was determined or if the mark is, in fact, an error. If the student feels dissatisfied about the resolution or results of the discussion, then the parents should step in. Phone the school to speak with the student's teacher (in the case of a single subject grade) or the student's counselor or adviser. But do not set yourself up as an accuser. In the case of schools, accusers tend to be losers. Remember: The common interest for the student, parent, and school is to achieve fairness and accuracy. A parent should not go to the school accusingly if the parent wants to get fair results—even if the parent is annoyed by a discrepancy in grades or a scheduling inconvenience.

When going to school for your child, you use the following procedure:

- Before you take any action, arm yourself with knowledge. You should have a folder with all your child's papers assembled that were supposed to comprise that average. Make sure you have *every* paper. Use a calculator and refigure the grade according to your understanding of the rubric. If you're not sure about the weight of a particular grade, check the course syllabus. If you're unable to locate such a document or no such document exists, send your child on a fact-finding mission (to phone a classmate for a faxed or e-mailed copy of the syllabus) to get a printed copy of the teacher's rubric or grading system. If nobody else seems to have it, phone the teacher at school—leave a message if you have to. Any responsible teacher should be willing to provide this in print—even midway through the year. (If a teacher argues, "but I gave your kid one at the beginning of the term and I don't have any more left," the parent could respond politely that the teacher must have at least one photocopy-able copy—or how else is the teacher grading the students? Offer to pay for the photocopy.)

- Before taking any action, speak to your child. Make sure there are no hidden papers—papers that your son didn't want to tell you about previously, or work that your daughter forgot to hand in, or points deducted for bad behavior. If there are no skeletons in the closet, proceed.

- If your tabulations are different than the teacher's, schedule an appointment. Do this politely. Do not leave any impression with any office secretary that you are hostile, angry, or confrontational. Do not *be* hostile, angry, or confrontational. Keep remembering that you and the teacher are "a team," or "partners," cooperating to provide the best possible educational opportunities for your child. You want to maintain this positive spirit. If you're asked what the meeting entails, be upbeat, positive, and vague. *Do not* badmouth your child or the teacher. You are an advocate. Remember that.

- To help assure that there are no further repercussions against a student from a teacher, a parent might want to enlist the support of a third "objective" party—the student's guidance counselor, adviser, or other administrator. Let the guidance counselor or other administrator know that you are sure that the teacher meant no harm, but just the same, you want to make sure that in speaking to the teacher about the inaccurate grade there won't be any repercussions. Let the administrator assure you that speaking out will not be punished and that the school official will see to it that there are no repercussions.

- When you meet the teacher, be supportive of the teacher— never at the expense of your child, though. (If the teacher says something nasty about your kid, don't join in.) Initiate the conversation with a positive start. Most teachers will wait till the parent talks first, so they know what they're up against.

Talk about your child's positive experiences in that teacher's classroom. You want to establish right from the start that you intend to work together. After the initial goodwill discussion, explain that you believe that there might have been some error in the tabulation of your child's grades. Bring the folder of papers with you to document your claim. Be understanding. Be respectful. Teachers are busy people, and you want to make it clear that while you appreciate their hard work, you understand that they occasionally make mistakes.

• You may find out that there was some missing grade that your kid was somehow unaware of. If so, locate the missing document and make sure that the average is correct. The grade that the teacher assigns should be consistent with the grading rubric. Otherwise, in all likelihood, the grade will be changed. If you get the grade changed successfully, don't make a big fuss. Thank the teacher. Act like "anyone can make mistakes, and this is just a simple oversight." For that's probably true. If you fuss, the teacher will be less likely to comply in the future.

Sometimes a teacher will say, "I intentionally lowered the grade to give your daughter the motivation to work harder, because I don't feel that she is working to potential." This answer is unacceptable. Be polite anyway. Many students are *not* motivated by lower grades and, in fact, are discouraged by them. Explain that your daughter is the hardworking literal kind of kid and should get the grade that she actually deserves, based on the teacher's own rubric—not some lowered grade based on the teacher's subjective opinion.

Sometimes a teacher will concoct a new element not specified in the rubric as a rationale for a low grade, like "attitude," "energy," "class participation," "attendance," etc. If it's not in the teacher's own written rubric, it's not an acceptable excuse for lowering the grade. You the parent must insist that the child receive the correct grade according to the teacher's own "contract."

When advocating for your child, once again, there is no need to be confrontational. If you have explained your child's case clearly and you still believe that the teacher has assigned your child an unfair grade, you may take the case to a higher level—a school administrator. In general, most teachers will stick with their own grading policy (and change the grade) once the policy is in writing—as long as you have the papers to document your case.

Throughout the meeting, remember the team-spirit approach: You're all on the same side—the side of the kid. You all want what's best for the kid. Mention this philosophy often during your meeting with the teacher. That's why the teacher went into the teaching profession. That's why you became a parent. Instead of stewing about an undocumentable and undeserved low grade, you're giving the well-intending teacher the opportunity to clear up an error that was unintentional. After the meeting, it's wise to continue monitoring your child's grades—and maintaining positive rapport with the teacher. You might even send a thank-you note in appreciation of the teacher's time, but if you choose to do this, be very careful that the note does not come across as patronizing or too eager to remind the teacher that you were right and the teacher was wrong. If you find a continued bias in the grading system, you may schedule another appointment, or you may want to take the grievance to the next level.

Team Problem Solving

Secret 65 — **When there is an academic problem, it's important to create a deliberate strategy of improvement that involves the kid, the parent, and possibly**

the teacher. All three should take responsibility to see that the obstacle is overcome. If you learn from a bad grade that your child is not performing to his or her ability, determine a specific plan of improvement. To do so, ask yourself the following questions to figure out the problem:

- Is a tutor needed—either short term (to get past a difficult concept that's posing an obstacle) or long term (for a student who is constantly struggling with a difficult subject)?

- Does your child require more encouragement?

- Is your child able to focus in class? Is there some distraction in the room, or some obstacle to learning?

- Is your child organized, or is lack of organization hindering him or her? Could you be organizing your child?

- Is your child distracted at home?

- Is your child engaged in the schoolwork taught? Is the work too hard or too easy? Does your child understand how the work relates to his or her future or interests—how mastery of the subject is potentially beneficial?

- Is the teacher grading fairly?

- Does your child need you to spend more time to help him or her through a difficult unit in a course or a difficult time in school in general?

- Is your child suffering from physical problems? Hearing or vision loss?

- Is your child being overworked without enough leisure time? Should your child drop a course or sport? (Some of the problems of overscheduling have more to do with too many activities.)

- Is your child suffering from a psychological or learning disorder?

- Is your child misbehaving in some way in class? Or is it perceived that your child is misbehaving or has a negative attitude?

- Have you established good rapport with the teacher, so that the teacher is helping you monitor the child's progress or weakness on an ongoing basis (so you don't wait until report card time to get the news or confront the problem)?

- Does your child's teacher have any recommendations to help your child improve his or her scores?

- Is your child getting enough sleep?

Once the problem has been defined, the parents should orchestrate a plan of attack to help the child overcome the difficulty and to guarantee improved grades on the next report card. It's not enough to identify the setback. If your child is not earning the desired grades, you *should* take it personally. You should ask: "What more can I be doing to help my child improve those grades?" Scolding doesn't count. Badgering isn't helpful. You need to figure out a concrete strategy to help the student improve.

Too Much Homework

As American students are gradually increasing the number of AP, IB, and Honors courses that they are taking, it's not uncommon for oversubscribed students to find that they have too much homework. Parental help can certainly cut down homework time. But in addition, students and their parents need to be aware of the rules of student commitments in advance. Is a student allowed to drop a course if the course turns out to be overwhelmingly time consuming? May a student quit a team during the sport's season? How is the student penalized for dropping courses or switching to more abridged sections of courses, if such opportunities exist?

Some weeks are bound to have more academic conflicts than others. Dropping courses or activities is not always necessary. Parents can be helpful in writing notes to an academic adviser (guidance counselor) or individual teachers when the child is particularly overburdened with homework. In doing so, ask for specific remedies, so the teacher clearly understands what you are seeking. Ask your daughter's science teacher, for example, if she can have a week's extension on her Earth Science project. Or ask your son's English teacher if he can hand in his vocabulary definitions a day late. Explain the circumstances, and teachers will generally respond reasonably. In this note, make sure you don't blame your child for lack of organization or time appropriation.

Homework Supervision

| Secret 66 | **Successful parents participate in homework—even in high school and even** |

for (especially for) the most successful students. Probably the most popular homework setting in America is at a centrally located computer or the kitchen table, close to where the family action usually is at around dinnertime.

Some teachers will tell you that by the time kids are in fourth or fifth grade, children should be able to do their own homework independently; they shouldn't need parental help; they should find a quiet place to work until their homework is done. That concept doesn't necessarily work for today's kids who are accustomed to lots of adult supervision, feedback, and support. Today's teenagers often concentrate better with background noise, and many can't work best in a secluded, cloistered, quiet, antiseptic environment.

If you insist on cloistering a kid who feels more productive in the middle of the household action, no homework may get done at all. Or kids may race through their homework in record time—ignoring quality—so that they can rejoin the family sooner. The best way to tell where your child is most productive is by asking and observing.

The Valedictorian and Salutatorian

Secret 67	The **valedictorian and salutatorian are typically expected to be highly sought af-**

ter by colleges, but, in fact, such students are not always the most valued by the most-competitive colleges. Parents should not obsess over the top class ranks. Traditionally, valedictorian and salutatorian mean the one who gives the valedictory and the one who gives the salutatory speech at graduation. Most schools select the valedictorian on an objective numerical basis. The student with the highest grade point average after four years of high school is named valedictorian. The student with the second highest is salutatorian. These are not necessarily the school's two brightest kids—although one generally must be extremely bright to achieve either ranking. Students who are first and second in their graduating class are not necessarily the most popular, most academically well-rounded, nor the hardest workers. At schools that do not "weight" grades, these are often not the kids who take the most rigorous courses. These are just the two with the highest averages.

Some schools add subjective factors, like having teachers nominate students for the "role" of valedictorian or salutatorian. At these schools, the rankings run the risk of becoming political and even less significant to colleges.

Aside from gaining the honor of speaking at graduation, valedictorian and salutatorian generally get local press coverage, a moment of fame, and that's it. Financial rewards are rarely bestowed. And one must remember that there are 27,000 high schools in America, and practically every one of them designates a valedictorian and salutatorian. That means there are approximately 54,000 valedictorians and salutatorians combined in the United States. Competitive colleges want to see challenging courses on the student's transcript—more than they want to see "valedictorian." Some colleges even love to boast about how many valedictorians they turn away. At many high schools, college acceptances are announced long before valedictorian and salutatorian are announced.

Manipulating Ranking by Taking Outside Courses

 **Be aware (and possibly take advantage) of your kids' high school's policy on crediting outside courses and averaging them in to your kids' averages.** A student who had expected to become valedictorian—due to the significant gap that was seemingly impossible to overcome in the next highest average—was suddenly told that he was going to be named salutatorian instead. Apparently, over the summer, a girl who was a few ranks lower, suddenly enrolled in a bunch of college courses—not all of them challenging—and was able to earn A's. The high school had a policy of counting college A's as 99s and 100s. The lower-ranking student was able to suddenly move up during September of senior year, because these grades were averaged in with her high school GPA.

Was she wrong to do this? No. If a school's policy is to average in courses taken at colleges, she was clever to do this in order to move up to valedictorian. The kid who presumed he would be valedictorian also should have been aware of this possibility—and could have protected his place by taking summer courses.

If your kid's high school has such a policy of averaging in college courses and your kid has a high ranking, you might want to encourage your kid to take outside courses to advance or protect his or her ranking. You might prefer to change the policy of having outside courses averaged in to high school grades. According to the leading argument, letting the high school average in outside grades could allow a student to take basket weaving at some local college, and, if the student scores A's, transfer those credits to high school. If the student scores B's, the grades would go unreported. As a general rule, don't wait until policy hurts your kid's average to oppose bad policies. Overturn the policy with the help of other parents before the crisis arises.

In high schools where outside courses are credited, parents should make a point of understanding how outside grades are interpreted by the high school. Is a college A the equivalent to a 4.0 or 100 (or 5.0 or 105 weighted) from the high school? Or is the college A the equivalent of a high school 90 or 3.8? Do all outside college courses automatically qualify for credit on the high school transcript? Or do only some courses qualify—in, let's say, the sciences or humanities? Parents have the responsibility to be informed of grading policies.

Schools That Don't Rank

High schools have increasingly stopped providing student rankings, contending that such numbers hurt the majority of students. Some schools publicly name a valedictorian and salutatorian—two students who can only benefit from rankings—and then do not disclose the rest of the rankings. This does not mean that these high schools do not rank the remaining students, however.

> **Secret 69** Even if your child's high school doesn't *reveal* its rankings, most schools do have *internal* rankings and know your child's standing. Not all students benefit when rankings aren't revealed. "Nearly all schools have students listed by GPA . . . at least on a spreadsheet," according to David Hawkins, director of Public Policy for the National Association for College Admission Counseling. And for schools that do not publicly provide rankings, if a college calls to inquire about a student, most high schools will offer a "grade distribution chart" to reveal where the student fits within a graduating class.

Parents should not assume that this lack of disclosure means a win-win situation for all students. **Students in the top 5 to 10 percent of the class *lose out* in a school in which the top third of the class has A averages, and nobody is ranked beyond salutatorian.**

Let's say, for example that your son has a high enough average to be ranked number 3 in a class of 600. It's certainly to his benefit to reveal this statistic, rather than let himself be lumped in with the top 200 students, all with A or A-minus averages. Likewise, if your daughter is number 12 out of 300, or 8 out of 100, or 3 out of 45, it's more impressive to have that fact on the application.

Obtaining this statistic may be difficult if your child's school won't reveal it. But many schools that don't rank are willing to provide a percentile: Where the application asks for rank, the school writes "top 2 percent," for example. If the school is unwilling to characterize your kid's GPA, do it yourself. Try to get a sense of how many kids have higher grades than your kid. (Ask your daughter: Could you name five kids who you think have higher grades? Ten kids? Twenty? This is not an exacting science—and you probably don't want your daughter asking every classmate for his or her averages—but to the best of your ability, try to help the colleges understand approximately where she perceives herself to be within her school.) In the place on the application where the college asks for your kid's rank, have your child insert a small-font sentence (if you're doing a paper application instead of an online application): "My school doesn't rank, but I know of only two students out of 600 with higher averages."

Are Colleges Impressed with Skipping?

Secret 70

Parents who accelerate their kids and have them "skip" or take high school courses before reaching high school should not assume that any resulting low grades will be understood by colleges as immaturity. Every mark starting with ninth grade, or high school courses taken in seventh or eighth grade, counts. In most high schools, all high school–level courses will be averaged into the mix, and low marks run the risk of bringing down your kid's high school average before your kid even starts high school. (In some schools, the policy is to offer only pass-fail to "underage" kids.) Do not skip your kids if your kids are not producing top-level grades in the higher-level courses. That will only hurt them in the long run. The university probably won't be impressed if your kid has to say, "Yes, I got a C in AP Calculus C, but I took it in seventh grade." There's no shame in staying with one's grade and being the top-grade-getter.

"Shopping Around" and Dropping Courses

Secret 71

If your kids' high school has a policy of letting kids drop courses without penalty, always keep this possibility in mind. Colleges are not impressed with kids who "tough it out" in courses in which they're not doing well, and boldly struggle despite low grades. You may think this shows character. It doesn't. It shows bad judgment. If your kid is able to raise his or her marks significantly, however, toughing it out can suddenly become an impressive strategy.

When your daughter is given low grades at the beginning of a year by a teacher, you need to address the situation immediately. Is she unable to do the work? Does she need a tutor? Does the teacher seem to speak another language? Does she need to drop the course or switch sections?

Different schools have different policies regarding dropping courses. Some high schools (and many colleges, including Harvard) encourage "shopping around"; that is, they allow students to sample courses for a short specified time period before finalizing which courses they want to remain enrolled in. Students drop courses without penalty—and without their transcript showing that they dropped a course. At some colleges, students are encouraged to deliberately sign up for too many courses with the intention of dropping some, depending upon which courses seem "worst" or which courses do not meet expectations or take up an inordinate amount of time or no longer interest the student.

In other schools, the "drop" is automatically recorded on the permanent record or the college transcript. No leeway is given.

In most schools, however, the student has until a specified period of time to drop a course without penalty. (Deliberate oversubscribing, however, is strongly discouraged, particularly in large public high schools, where scheduling and budgeting changes in course enrollment can become a nightmare.) That time period varies by school, ranging from halfway through the course to a month into the course or even two weeks into the course. It is the students' *and* parents' responsibility to know when that drop date is.

The later the drop date, the more education your child is likely to get at a smaller risk—the student is free to stay in a course for a longer period of time and turn his or her grades around if they're not where they should be. If the student stays, the teacher gets a greater chance to make the lessons "gel" or "click." If the drop date is relatively immediate, the student and parent must make quick decisions, discouraging experimentation and limiting a student's exploration in order to preserve the student's average.

In a school with a very fast drop date, proactive parents might want to lobby to extend the length of the "shopping around period" for all students, if the administration is able to handle the scheduling.

When permitting your child to enroll in a course that is likely to be significantly challenging, you, the parent, should find out in advance about the withdrawal policy. You must ask yourself if it's more important that your teenager complete the course in high school or get into the "right" college and have the opportunity to take the course there.

Note that sticking with a course that lowers your kid's average can be an obstacle to college admissions. What constitutes a significant lowering of the average? If you know that your child is going to get at least a full letter grade below his or her current average—a C in the course compared to a B average, or a B in the course compared to an A average—it's probably wise to drop the course. If it's a partial grade—a B-plus compared to an A average—you might want the child to stick with the course, if it's the only B+ and if the course is genuinely worthwhile. Another option might be to find out if other grading options are offered (pass-fail or auditing credit) the earlier in the year, the better, or if another section of the course is offered, perhaps with a different teacher.

In a school in which dropping courses is frowned upon (many schools), students should avoid having to drop courses often. Parents can help by doing some preliminary investigation before registration takes place:

- Have your child ask other kids about the course in advance. (You don't have to accept every negative that other kids cite, but make a mental note if you see a disturbing pattern. Sometimes, getting the "heads-up" in advance can help you prepare your child for potential pitfalls.)

- Ask parents of older kids about the course before your kid enrolls.

- Speak to the guidance counselor or college adviser about all courses before fixing a schedule for the following year.

Adding a Course or Coming in Late

Secret 72   **If your child enters a course late, parents can play an active role in helping a kid play catch-up. Don't leave it to the school and your kid. Clarify up front what work needs to be made up. Leave nothing ambiguous.** Sometimes dropping a course means adding another course in its place and entering the new class late. Help your kid out. Take responsibility. When your son signs up for a class late in the semester—or if your son enrolls in a new school—help ease the transition. Ask to meet with the teacher separately to determine how the missed work will be made up. Perhaps some initial requirements can be skipped— since your son handed in work in the previous class during the same time period and should not have to do double work. If the teacher says that the missed work is necessary for your son to understand the context, offer to help photocopy missed handouts or to buy a review book to catch him up.

When Teachers Fudge Grades

Secret 73

Some teachers, feeling uncomfortable with percentage-based rubrics, fudge their students' grades, and sometimes the fudging works against the student. As mentioned previously, many non-math teachers and even college professors are uncomfortable with grading rubrics that rely on percentages (15 percent for the final exam, 15 percent for the midterm, etc.), since they themselves are unable to determine simple percentages and are too embarrassed to admit that they're "mathematically challenged." So these teachers sometimes purport to base their grades on percentages, when, in fact, they base their grades on educated estimates and overall impressions. This fudging can easily undermine your child's average. At a minimum, make sure that the numerical report card grades are at least equal to the grade that the child has earned.

Secret 74

Some teachers artificially lower grades based on what they think they can get away with, resorting to a game I call "Flak."*

When faculty members are pressured to widen the spectrum of grades they give (to demonstrate that they're not guilty of grade inflation), many teachers feel uncomfortable giving low grades, particularly if the entire class is performing at least B-minus work. But the teachers are told that they must give out some C's or even D's to maintain their own credibility. Cornered, they play a "game" with the class. They test the waters by low-grading a few shyer, less-competent-looking, and less-confident students on preliminary assignments. If the teachers get no flak or protest from the students for the lower grade, the teachers can relax knowing they have successfully targeted their low-grade-

*This is a secret—to which very few will ever admit, nobody will admit in public, and which I've seen many times.

getters for the year. No matter what the student does after that, the student is destined for a C or D on every essay thereafter.

Even if the student gets a tutor and makes a dramatic improvement, the teacher barely notices, having happily written the kid off as a valuable C student.

The kid that's usually targeted is the one who comes late or unprepared to class at least once, is occasionally absent, sits in the back corner, and doesn't join class discussions. He or she can be the class clown, the class pariah, or the kid with no confidence who looks self-conscious. Once that group is established, the teacher is usually able to move on to picking out the B's.

In order to minimize flak, some teachers of higher-level courses find themselves judging the students from the first day of class. The teacher realizes that the students all come to an AP, IB, or Honors class expecting to get A's. The teacher knows that he or she may give a large number of the students A's, but also that the administration expects to see a certain minimal number of B's and C's. No matter how great the group, the teacher must give C's to be credible. So the teacher starts judging the group after a few days of class, subconsciously wondering, "Who would accept a C?" and "Who would accept a B?"

The reason parents need to know about "Flak" is because you can rescue your kid from losing. If your daughter tends to be timid, self-conscious, insecure, or misses the first class, make sure that her grades aren't lowballed forever. Encourage her to politely dispute any grades that seem wrong. Remind her to smile, make eye contact, look alert, volunteer answers often, and demonstrate that she's paying attention, so her behavior doesn't reinforce a first impression that she is a pushover in the back row, but rather an outspoken advocate able to deliver flak. A student assigned to the back row might even request a seat change to become more active in class discussion. Your job as a parent is to inform your child of how he or she is being judged and to encourage active class participation.

Secret 75

Parents should be especially wary of grading in schools that boast that they have no grade inflation. These are the schools most likely to pressure teachers to artificially lower grades. In some schools, this means that the high school puts quotas on grades, and that even if a student deserves an A, a curve is imposed, and if his or her A is lower than the other A students' A's, the student risks getting a B despite the A average.

Students at Princeton have been grumbling about grading since the administration decided to take action to curb supposed grade inflation. Students contend that it has become much harder for an A student to be granted an A at Princeton than it is at Harvard, Yale, or Stanford.

Registering for an A

Secret 76

In courses where grades seem somewhat discretionary, it's smart for a student (or a parent of the student, on occasion) who wants to receive top grades to somehow notify the teacher of this expectation as early as possible in the semester. This may sound ridiculously direct, but here is how registering for an A works: The student consistently works hard and earns high grades as the semester begins and waits until a slightly lower test-the-waters grade mysteriously appears on a subjectively graded paper.

"What must I do to guarantee a high A?" the student should then politely inquire of the teacher, thus putting the teacher on notice that the student is expecting a high A in the course. (The implied message: "No, I'm not the wimp to whom you can comfortably give a B or C without a public outcry.") The teacher is then required to explain the "steps" or the rubric for earning a high A—and, if the student takes notes on the discussion responsibly (and visibly), the teacher can be held to this plan. Such a discussion puts the teacher on notice that the student is "grade conscious" and will probably complain (give flak) if the grades don't get higher. It gives the teacher the opportunity to explain what additional work (if any) and skills are needed to secure an A, and possibly gives the teacher an opportunity to adjust his or her thinking about a particular student. Assuming the student follows the teacher's prescription, the student can usually expect to see higher grades for the remainder of the course.

Don't let a teacher respond with a vague response like, "Do better work, if you want a high A," or "I only give high A's to geniuses," or "I don't give out high A's." If the teacher responds, "I bet you'll improve on the next assignment," the translation is, "Okay, you've registered your interest in a high A. I'll keep that in mind next time I'm grading papers." But the strongest teachers will show a student what can be done tangibly to improve the work for the next assignment. A reasonable teacher must be willing to provide a reasonable (and visible) rubric. A reasonable student should follow that rubric and earn the grade of choice.

Wouldn't it be terrific if teachers let your kid "register" for the grade your kid wants? Sign up for an A. Or sign up for a B or C if you don't want to do as much work. An education professor at Columbia University's Teachers' College let students sign up for grades. A specified amount of work was required to earn each grade. Students who were satisfied with lower grades and preferred to do less work were granted lower grades and were required to hand in fewer assignments. Students who wanted to go for A's were required to do significantly more work. The choice was up to each student. Surprisingly, there was a fairly even distribution. Some teachers would say that all grades are that way in reality. Students who do more work tend to earn (and receive) higher grades than students who do less work. But we all know that that's not the way it always works.

When a Student Wants to Drop a Course After Applying for College

Secret 77

Oversubscribing for courses with the intention of fooling colleges is a bad idea. As senior year approaches, students sometimes register for an unmanageable number of courses to show colleges that they are taking the "most challenging curriculum available." The students are told that colleges prefer students who take advantage of all the opportunities that their school offers. As a result, some deliberately sign up for too many courses, intending to drop one or two, once they're admitted Early Decision.

This is dishonest and looks bad to colleges. Colleges want to see midyear reports as well as end-year reports. Yes, they will notice dropped courses and will want to know why the student dropped the courses after applying. Yes, they will want to know why the student neglected to tell the college that the course was dropped after the application was submitted. Colleges have rescinded admission offers based on applicants' "bait and switch."

If the student *must* drop a course after applying, the student has the responsibility to tell the college. What are reasonable excuses to drop a course?

- The student loved the course but didn't feel he or she could devote the amount of time it demanded. So the intention is to take it again in college.

- After experiencing a full semester of the course and working hard to do well, the student realized that he or she had no interest in the subject. The preparation was time consuming and not worthwhile.

- The student won a competition and, as a result, was asked to present work elsewhere in America or abroad, and would have to miss too much class.

- The student really wanted to take another course, the schedule of which conflicted with the course that was dropped. Dropping the course allows the student to pursue an equally challenging or even more difficult course.

Attendance Grades

Secret 78

Admissions officers at the most-competitive universities say that they do not pay attention to high school lateness and absences recorded on the transcript or report card. So it's probably wise for students *not* to call attention to these statistics by writing an accompanying explanation on the application unless the absences are severe. Including attendance grades on the transcript, or indicating how many times a student was absent, tardy, or missed specific classes, is a punitive measure by some high schools. Often the absence or lateness is easily explained through medical reasons or traveling to compete in regional or even national competitions. If the student manages to achieve high grades despite these absences, the colleges don't pay much attention.

Is It Better to Get an A in a Regular Course or a B in an AP Course?

Secret 79

Contrary to what admissions officers present, there is an answer to the question of whether it's better to get an A in a regular course or a B in an AP course, one of the most common queries at college information sessions. Once the question is asked, the admissions officer laughs, and says, "It's better to get an A in an AP course." And the audience nervously laughs along, while the real question always remains unanswered.

So let me share my own observations. Average is more important. Advise your child to maintain as high an average as possible. If this means no AP or IB, so be it. With no AP or IB from a school that offers AP and IB, chances are poor that your son will get into the most-competitive colleges, but a second-tier college might grab him. Even a second-tier college will not grab an applicant with straight B's (unless B's represent the top 15 percent of your child's high school, unlikely, or your child has some sought-after skill that the college needs). If your daughter is getting A's in regular courses and can handle a few APs, have her try. Keep the course "drop date" in mind, in case she has to bail out to maintain a high average. **Ultimately, the average remains more important than the degree of challenge.** In schools where the top students typically take four or five AP classes in junior and senior year, a student who finds that program to be too overwhelming might compromise by striving for A's in one or two AP courses per year. Many "exclusive" prep schools and magnet schools do not allow students to take more than two AP courses at a time.

Senioritis

Secret 80

Competitive colleges say that they will reverse a decision if a student's grades drop significantly during senior year, if there's no reasonable explanation. And they do. At the most-competitive colleges, admissions officers say that "a few B's (may be) okay" at the end of the senior year for an otherwise straight-A student. One officer said "I'm not worried" when I see that. But a C or a D would represent a problem, and the student had better explain." And no, "Senioritis" is not a viable excuse.

Colleges *do* look at transcripts at the end of senior year. Submitting the final transcript is not just a mere formality or threat. It's important to keep working until the end. While the average can dip slightly, you'll want to help your kid avoid a severe dip. Stay on top of the kid's homework and studying.

While high school transcripts are considered the single most important factor for college admissions, standardized test scores generally act as a close second. Some colleges require SATs. Others require ACTs. Neither group of exams is considered easier. Many colleges let applicants submit whichever exams best represent their abilities. And, yes, I have worked with students who have done significantly better on one set of exams compared to the other.

CHAPTER 4

Helping Your Child Excel at Standardized Testing

"**M**y daughter is a top student, but she really isn't a good test-taker," a father commented, prefacing a question at a well-attended information session at a most-competitive college. "And I don't feel that her test scores begin to reflect her abilities or who she is."

"Well, then, tell her to raise the scores so they *do* reflect her abilities," the admissions officer snapped. "We don't expect our students to be born knowing everything, but we expect that if they're aware of a weakness, they remedy that weakness rather than make excuses for it. Tell her to learn how to take the SAT and then retake it."

| Secret 81 |

The most-competitive colleges generally don't sympathize with kids who label themselves poor test-takers when it comes to standardized tests. The colleges claim that these exams really work as indicators of who will perform well in college. Colleges much prefer kids who beat their own obstacles. After all, the logic goes, how are you going to survive college if you're not good at high-pressure exams? Are you going to restrict yourself only to courses that require papers for assessment right from the start?

Most colleges say that they find these standardized tests to be very useful in comparing students nationally. While grades and transcripts demonstrate what a student has achieved and is capable

of continuing to achieve within his or her high school or a similar setting, standardized tests are said to provide a more expansive comparison. To succeed, students need to be able to demonstrate past success in
addition to capabilities for continued success in the future. Yes, some
colleges claim that they do not find these tests helpful, but the majority
of colleges in America do use standardized exams.

Each year, about 1.4 million college-bound seniors take the SATs
before they graduate, according to the College Board, which administers the SATs. More than half of the college-bound students take the
exam for the first time before the end of their junior year. Because of
the prominent role of these exams in competitive college admissions,
parents should not wait until midway through junior year to start
thinking about test-taking strategies for your children. Investigate prep
courses, tutors, and the concept of independent-study preparation as far
in advance as possible (which does not necessarily mean having your
child *take* the actual exams years in advance).

Should My Kid Prepare for the SATs and ACTs?

Secret 82

**A responsible student is expected to pre-
pare in advance to take the SAT or ACT,
unless he or she can get a perfect score without preparation.
In contrast to years past, nowadays it's considered foolish and
irresponsible to view the test for the first time on the day of the
exam.** A student no longer looks smarter for rationalizing to an admissions officer, "Yes, but realize that I achieved *that* score without any
tutoring or test prep at all." Instead, such a student appears naive and
unprepared. Thirty years ago, conventional morality dictated that it
was *wrong* or even *unethical* to get tutored or take a prep course for the
SAT or ACT. The popular thinking was that the exam tested one's
"raw" aptitude. Students who sought tutoring or prep courses often
did so clandestinely (as if they were secretly stacking the deck in their
favor).

Scratch that concept today. Remember: The SATs and ACTs are not IQ tests. They test ability but not necessarily "raw ability." "Raw" is no longer encouraged or admired. Today's wisdom mandates independent study, private tutoring, or participation in a prep course to guarantee that one achieves good results. Test-prep courses have evolved into a major American industry, in excess of $250 million annually.

Independent Preparation

Secret 83   **The secret to test preparation is practice, practice, practice.** This does not have to entail an expensive course. If you can motivate your own son, have him practice at home. Time him. Score his practice tests. Go over the wrong answers and figure out why they're wrong. Have him take the next practice test. Some test-prep companies offer free diagnostic exams in which the student shows up at a test site in person, takes a sample test, and receives a score within a week. There is no obligation to register, but the aim is obviously to sell a test-prep course to the student. The diagnostic test benefits the student by providing a sense of how much preparation needs to be done and in which areas, before the actual exam, as well as the experience of taking the test in a real-time environment and pace.

A student can administer his or her own diagnostic test by purchasing an exam review book and taking a sample test. The books provide the answers, so students can score themselves, identify their own weaknesses, and work on strengthening them. Many highly motivated students successfully opt to do all of their own preparation—without a course or tutor. Over the years, the test-prep CD-ROMs and accompanying workbooks have become fairly entertaining—no more flashcards-style drills—with cartoon clips and other humor interspersed to make the experience more captivating. I also recommend purchasing a vocabulary memorization book, since verbal portions of the exams require a good command of traditional "SAT words."

Test-Prep Courses

Secret 84 **Groups magically make tedious studying more palatable. If you find it impossible to motivate your kid to study, sign him or her up for a course.** Test-prep courses are expensive, usually costing in excess of $1,000 when offered by major companies. The rationale, for those who can afford the price, is that the most expensive private colleges may cost more than $160,000 over four years, so an extra $1,000 or $2,000 to help guarantee that the student will have the opportunity to attend the school of choice for that six-figure amount is worth the investment. For those with the funds, this is probably the most popular and successful method of preparation. Instead of badgering your teenager to study, you either chauffeur her or give her the car keys, both easier tasks.

The course provides discipline and familiarity with the test and testing environment. Students see their peers taking tests, and practicing becomes much more socially appealing. Also, at the course, trained exam experts answer questions. At home, you answer the questions. And often, even the most educated parents are unable to get into the "mind-speak" of the test writers.

Major test-prep companies guarantee that their own instructors have scored a specified minimum score and are experts at taking and therefore teaching the exam. The minimum, for example, at Stanley Kaplan is 90th percentile. *Princeton Review* claims a minimum of 95th to 99th percentile "with exceptions for extraordinary instructors." If your child is consistently achieving higher scores on practice exams, think twice about paying for a program. While the discipline is good, it may not be worth more than $1,000 to you.

Choosing the Right Prep Course

There is no one "best prep course." A lot depends on your kid and your family's interests. Location is often a factor. Some students prefer to be near home, with friends, and within easy commuting reach. Some kids can't focus when they know other kids in the room.

Ask questions before you enroll your child. Some programs group the kids by perceived ability, determined by the initial diagnostic exam. At one location, for example, two concurrent courses (higher and lower level) were offered. A student who was strong in math but was weak in verbal, for example, was put in the low-level class, which helped his verbal, but not his math. For students with balanced abilities, however, such groupings can work well.

Class size matters if your child will only ask questions when the class is small. Some kids prefer the anonymity of large classes. Others require individualized attention.

What guarantee does the prep course make?

Some guarantee an increase of 100 points or more, or your money back. Some guarantee 100 points and promise that your kid can retake the course if the score doesn't increase that much, but they offer no money-back guarantee. If the course doesn't work for your child the first time around, note that there is no reason that the course will necessarily work the second time either. You may prefer a money-back guarantee.

What happens if your child misses a session? Let's say there's a family wedding coming up on a weekend test-prep-class day. Find out how the test-prep center makes up the missed lesson. Is your child very busy on weekends? This may be an important consideration. Some programs will let your kid sit in on a comparable class at another location, to make sure your child doesn't miss the work. Some will provide missed notes. Some will allow you to "meet" with an instructor online. What works best for your child?

Schedule is also important. If you find it impossible to wake your child on the weekends, don't sign up for an early-morning Saturday course. If your child is a serious hardworking student, you might think twice about signing up for a weekday course, when homework will usurp any free time. Most serious courses meet twice weekly. This prevents students from forgetting material.

Summer Program SAT Courses

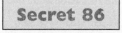 **Unless summer prep programs are run by the major test-prep companies—which specialize solely in preparing kids for standardized tests— summer classes offered as one recreational activity option at unaffiliated teen programs tend to be useless.** Many recreational teen summer programs (camps, teen tours, etc.) offer test-prep courses as a side option to make parents feel good that their child is at least accomplishing something during the summer. Be wary of these—the courses rarely measure up to the more serious test-prep-company programs, have no guarantees, and are often taught by "camp counselors," who might specialize in swimming or arts and crafts, but may not have mastered the SATs or ACTs themselves.

Students commonly complain about coming away from such teen programs more confused about standardized tests than when they entered, wasting valuable summer days and spending money on poorly planned courses that did not ultimately raise their exam scores.

Private Tutors

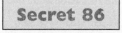 **If you hire an SAT or ACT tutor, make sure the tutor isn't just "babysitting" your teenager, while the kid takes practice tests.** Your child should take practice tests on his or her own time and prepare in advance to ask the tutor questions and have the tutor demonstrate how to solve specific problems. Tutoring ranges in price dramatically from minimum wage for a fellow student, to $800 per one- to two-hour session, with a minimum of ten sessions paid upfront to private independent tutors. *Princeton Review* charges $200 to $400 for private tutors for the SAT IIs, including physics, and the company also offers "Review-a-trois," in which a few students share the cost of a tutor.

Be skeptical of any tutor who claims to guarantee a specific score.

Private tutors can be very helpful. They can tailor a study program to suit the needs of your child. In other words, unlike in the prep courses, if your kid is getting 800s on the math SAT but 400s on the verbal or the writing, a tutor can focus solely on your child's weak points, without wasting time on the math, which needs no further attention. A good tutor can pinpoint and intensively focus on improving the kid's skills.

But, buyer beware. I've seen parents hire $650-per-hour tutors only to see the kid's three-part SAT I score increase by a total of only 10 points. And money-back guarantees are not always helpful, particularly if the student does poorly on the June SAT in junior year and now must wait for the October of senior year to retake the SAT. You may get your money back, but you could lose the opportunity to get your kid into the college that he or she most wants.

Cramming

Secret 87

Cram as much as you can! Conventional wisdom tells kids not to cram for standardized tests. Teachers and the test companies themselves tell you to prepare gradually over a long period of time. Yes, your children should prepare gradually over time to fully utilize their long-term memory, but a popularly guarded secret to success is letting your kids also utilize their short-term memory to win many extra last-minute points on standardized tests.

The most effective last-minute cramming includes vocabulary memorization for the SAT I verbal and foreign language SAT IIs, and formula memorization for math and science SAT IIs.

"Why do I have to cram?" your daughter might ask. "I'm just going to forget it all anyway." The truth is that much of what is crammed won't be forgotten—at least not for the test, and much will be remembered long after. As for that which *is* forgotten in the weeks following the exam, don't worry. The testers don't care what you recall *after* the exam. They only test what you know *during* the exam.

"Cram Day"

Secret 88   **The secret holiday called "Cram Day" is an occasion when smart kids study.** Standardized tests are usually given on Saturdays or Sundays. Let your kid take Friday off from school. If possible, take the day off from work. Friday is "Cram Day," a family holiday. Wake the kid early in the morning. Make a favorite luxury breakfast—waffles, pancakes, yogurt parfait, or exotic omelets, and let the studying begin.

Families that honor Cram Day have reported to me that their kids' scores have gone up at least 70 points and up to 150 points, directly related to the information they crammed the day before. Words that were memorized and math problems similar to those solved the day before often appeared on the test.

If Cram Day seems tedious or stressful to you or your kid, remember: "Cram Day is *ephemeral* (a common SAT word). It won't last forever." Have your kid memorize that slogan. I'd bet the word shows up on his test.

You are the emcee of Cram Day. Engaging your daughter is more likely to make studying *happen* than locking her in her room.

Avoid phrases like the following:

"It's your test. Why should I help you?"
"Preparing is your responsibility."
"I can't take the test for you, so why should I study with you now?"
"I took the SATs (or ACTs) already when I was in high school. Now it's your turn."
"Why did you save it all till the last moment? You should have been studying a word a day for the last two years."
"Go study. I'll be around if you have any questions or need help."

The Suzuki violin method attributes a lot of its success to parents working *with* their kids. Instead of isolating a three-year-old child and telling him or her to go practice, the parent pulls out a violin and practices alongside the child, thus endorsing (through actions) the task. The same success can be found by parents of teenagers. Proactive parents provide motivation, emotional support, and genuine empathy for the stressed-out teenager. Try memorizing words along with your kid.

Here are some ways to participate:

- Make a quiz-show game out of the vocabulary words, grammar rules, or math problems the night before the exam. One parent or a sibling runs the show. One parent is the opposing contestant. (If only one adult is available to help, make the family dog, cat, or goldfish the other contestant. The emcee can answer for the family pet.) Play in the style of *Jeopardy!* or even *Family Feud.* But regardless of your style of play—*and this is really important—let the kid win. No matter what.* Nobody needs to be defeated on the night before the SAT or ACT exam. If necessary, change the rules constantly so that the kid keeps winning. (Parents with deficient egos—those insecure parents who insist on beating their kids at everything to show their kids how smart they are—should refrain from this study technique completely.) If the kid keeps getting things wrong, make sure to get *more* things wrong. Look up each answer to determine who is correct (and, more important, to learn the correct answer). **If you want to get really into the game, shop for a series of prizes in advance.** In the same tradition that Americans shop for Super Bowl Sunday, shop for Cram Day Friday. This will keep the game going for hours. Go to a dollar store (if you have one near you) before Cram Day and stock up on cheap trinkets that your kid might enjoy (glow-in-the-dark pins, a rubbery bouncing ball, a mini-Frisbee, a plastic flower, marbles, a tacky-but-funny statuette or paperweight). Make sure your kid wins a prize once an hour for every hour of study.

- Provide refreshments for Cram Day—something that your kid enjoys and that represents a rare treat. (Instead of rewarding your kid on the day that the test results are reported, reward your kid for his or her hard work and dedication to create good results.) Make popcorn or bake cookies to cheer up a child who is stuck with the task of memorizing hundreds of definitions and formulas or taking lots of practice tests. Popcorn munching keeps a weary kid (and parents) awake. If the kid is on a diet, or if you're worried that snack food will send the wrong message at this desperate hour, make air-popped salt-free popcorn, or carrots and celery.

- If you're creative, help make up mnemonic devices for your child to memorize each word (language SATs), formula (for science SAT IIs and math exams), or fact (history and science SAT IIs).

- Link people you both know with hard-to-remember adjectives. For example, a word that commonly appears is "pernicious." Whom do you and your kid know that's "pernicious"? Hopefully someone whose name starts with a *P* or has some of the letters of *pernicious*. Let's say, Cousin Nic is perNICious. Likewise, whom do you know that's "parsimonious"? When you quiz the kid on each word, each word gets a laugh as the kid recalls, "Cousin Nic can seem perNICious because he drove his brand-new car into a ditch and destroyed it," and "SIMON in my English class is parSIMONious when it comes to lending lunch money." The rule is that you have to create a whole sentence that explains the definition. Warning: This game may cause occasional outbursts of laughter during the test as the kid envisions relatives and friends being used as mnemonic devices.

- Make up word-association songs and rhymes. The sillier the mnemonic songs and rhymes, the more memorable they become, and the better kid does on the exam. Creative parents seeking to relieve the boredom of cramming might make up a rhyme, a riddle, or even a series of songs defining some of the vocabulary words. Obviously, you should focus only on words that the kid doesn't know. Don't waste your time on the ones that he or she knows. Parents and kids can even use songs they both know or TV commercial jingles and substitute in vocabulary words that will help remind the test-taker of the meanings. Do you need to make up hundreds of songs and rhymes? No. Use this device only for some of the information that requires memorization—mix and match your techniques for the most entertaining and memorable studying.

- In supervising your kid's cramming for a test, make sure the kid takes the same breaks—at least ten minutes per hour—that are used in regular studying. Break time should not mean requiring the kid to do chores. Chores are not allowed, because studying itself is a chore. Breaks can mean any of the following: eating a meal or snack, jogging around the block, chatting with parents (on a non-emotional topic), browsing through a magazine, or taking a quick shower. Bathroom breaks don't count as breaks, unless the kid gets lost in procrastination in the bathroom. For a kid who appears to be suffering, a quick jog or physical exercise activity is often best because it gets the endorphins working, gives new energy, and changes a negative mood to positive. Avoid activities that are likely to engross the child and extend beyond the allotted time. (Don't let the kid get caught in a good novel, talk on the phone, watch the beginning of a half-hour TV show, or play a captivating video game. Otherwise, the parent becomes the ogre who has to stop the fun "just at the best part.") Always determine in advance how long the break will be and announce it clearly before the break starts. Make sure the child understands the length of the break with a nod or some acknowledgment. ("Would you like to take a ten-minute break?" The answer will always be yes.)

| Secret 89 | **Establish and announce the study schedule in advance.** |

The night before the exam, the student should get a good night's sleep (at least eight hours). When you begin studying together, let the child know when the end of studying will be. ("We will work for two hours, then break for dinner, then work another two hours, with ten-minute breaks in between and hourly prizes." Or, "We will attempt to do six hours of studying with ten-minute breaks each hour. At the end of the session, there will be a grand prize.")

| Secret 90 | **Provide a Grand Prize.** Provide a larger award for a full cooperative day of cramming. |

Prizes are excellent motivations. Don't worry that your kids will learn to be motivated by bribes rather than by "the intrinsic value of education." Be reasonable. We all bribe ourselves through painful situations. We buy ourselves a supermarket treat for tedious grocery shopping. The pediatrician gives our kids a lollipop or a well-decorated BandAid. Cramming is one such occasion where a reward can be very motivating. For one of my students who loved gourmet cooking, a very dramatic sandcastle-shaped baking pan was the grand prize. Other grand prizes have included just-released CDs, DVDs, books, college T-shirts (or something else from a college store), a 3-D jigsaw puzzle, a real fossil, and tiny powerful magnets.

Parental Empathy

| Secret 91 | **If your child is not motivated to study, try taking the practice tests alongside your child. Buy yourself an identical copy of the review book.** |

Sit down next to your child and take practice exams with him or her. You don't have to ace the exam. You don't have to impress your child. You just need to keep your kid company and empathize with his or her experience. Together you can laugh about some of the more boring reading passages and some of the more difficult math problems. This experience will help you build a common bond and reinforce both those areas that your kid is strong in (as she explains what you've done wrong) and weak (as you correct her mistakes).

Are There Colleges That Don't Require SATs or ACTs?

Secret 92

Some of America's very top colleges don't require SATs or ACTs. You probably won't want to broadcast the names of these colleges, unless you want your kid to face increased local competition for admission. If your son or daughter is among the kids with top grades but whose abilities are not reflected by standardized test scores, such colleges might be worth serious consideration. Although not submitting a test score might seem to imply that the student did not do well on the SAT or ACT, some highly independent colleges—many of them very highly "ranked"—claim to look beyond scores to see the total student. These are not "hippy" schools or laid-back unstructured do-your-own-thing, touchy-feely places, but rather, colleges that maintain their own standards without conforming to other colleges' criteria.

Among the colleges that do not require scores are Bates and Bowdoin (both excellent colleges consistently ranked highest among small schools) and Mount Holyoke (a top women's college). Connecticut College, Hamilton, and Union will let you submit SAT II scores instead of an SAT I or ACT. Pitzer College—part of the Claremont College group (reciprocity with prestigious Pomona, Claremont-McKenna, Scripps, and the hard-to-get-into engineering school Harvey Mudd—all within easy walking distance on the same shared campus just outside Los Angeles)—does not require SAT I scores.

Middlebury College, also one of America's top small colleges, lets students choose which standardized test scores to submit. If you don't like your SAT I, submit three AP exam scores, three IB scores, or three

SAT IIs. Browse a list of hundreds more listed alphabetically by state that don't require ACTs or SATs at www.FairTest.org.

Secret 93	**If your child wants to attend one of the colleges that does not mandate SAT or**

ACT scores and your child has excellent scores to report, go ahead and have them sent. Yes, the scores will generally help—even at colleges that claim not to care.

What's a Good Score on the SATs?

Secret 94	**No score is a guarantee of admission to any private college.** In fact, at information

sessions, Harvard's administrators seem to like to boast about how many kids with perfect 1600s on the combined math and verbal portions of the SAT I the university rejects. Almost 1,000 American students scored 1600s in 2003, according to the College Board, which administers the SATs. More than 25,000 students achieved a 750 or above on the verbal SAT I (12,888 males and 12,226 females in 2003), and more than 30,000 scored 750 or above on the math SAT I (21,033 males and 9,407 females). In the SAT I, in which the writing portion was added in 2005, a total of 107 students scored a perfect 2400 on the first round. Boys and girls score somewhat comparably on the verbal exam, but notice the discrepancy on the math SATs: More than twice as many boys got top math scores in 2003.

College admissions officers stress that top SAT scores are no guarantee of admissions—colleges look at the "whole person." They like people with lots of extracurricular involvement, lots of enthusiasm and expertise (a "passion") for what they do. Kids who just study without contributing to the community around them are considered undesirable by many of the most-competitive universities. Obviously, though, it's better to get a 2400 than a 2300. And it's better to get a 2300 than a 2200, etc. But a 2400 is no guarantee of admission.

How Your Kid Compares

Secret 95

Scoring 700 does not make one a genius. More than 66,000 students nationwide score 700 or above on the SAT I verbal, and more than 92,000 score 700 or above on the SAT I math each year. Knowing these statistics should help you understand where your child fits in with the national pool. In the 650-plus range, more than 150,000 students score 650 or better on the verbal, and more than 200,000 students score 650 or higher on the math.

Is There a Minimum SAT or ACT Score That's Considered?

Secret 96

Although very, very few admissions officers will ever admit this to you, there are minimum-score cutoffs in admissions. College officers will tell you that if a candidate who the college really wants has 100 points' lower score than the other candidates the college usually accepts, the admissions office will make an exception. Note that exceptions are just that—exceptions. For whatever reasons, many parents count on their children being the exceptions. Although colleges say that there's no ultimate cutoff, for some of the most competitive colleges, 1550 combined math and verbal is a typical "first round," "first cell," "first consideration" cutoff. Most colleges have multiple rounds of consideration. The next round might include students with 1500 to 1550, and a third round might include 1450 to 1500. Eventually, the class is filled.

Exceptions are rare and are most likely to be granted to an underrepresented population or a student whose talent a college particularly needs (a sports star). So officers feel they are justified in saying that there is no minimum. And they'll say (with a smile) that they welcome applications from a wide range of students with "good" SATs or ACTs.

But they won't define "good." Note that having the largest possible applicant pool benefits the college's final yield (lowering the percentage of acceptances and enhancing the college's prestige).

Perhaps the admissions officers imagine that the audience to which they speak is composed of some nearly extinct population with A-plus averages and athletic stardom. For a rare student with that profile, there may not be an absolute minimum score. For the rest of the world, of course there's a minimum score. But, hey, you never know who is asking the question. Moral: Have your kid apply to a college that accepts kids with scores within your kid's range. And don't rely on admissions officers to reveal that range honestly.

| Secret 97 | The best way to find out which college accepts scores within your kid's range and a |

similar academic profile is to compare your child's statistics to the statistics of previous classes from your kid's high school. Many high schools compile statistics of previous classes, independent student averages, standardized test scores, and which colleges accepted and rejected each individual student. Usually, the students' names are not provided. If your children's high school does not compile or divulge these statistics, check neighboring districts or comparable high schools. Such lists can be extremely instructive.

Unbalanced SATs and Grades

| Secret 98 | If you have a kid who gets high grades but low test scores and a kid who gets low |

grades but high test scores, the first kid is far more likely to get into a better college. The message here is that parenting is a long-haul project, and no single day of outstanding testing can rescue a brilliant student who doesn't apply him- or herself throughout the school year in his or her high school career. Most students achieve SAT scores that are comparable to their grade point averages in school. Kids with high-A averages in very competitive high schools, for example, are most likely to score 2100s and above on the SATs. But it's not that un-common for a bright student who does not apply him- or herself to get low grades, but very high SATs (above 2200 or even 2300, let's say). It's also not so unusual for a kid who gets very high grades consistently to bomb on the SATs or be labeled a bad test-taker.

Neither situation is looked upon sympathetically by the most-competitive colleges. If these colleges, however, had to choose among the two types, most would prefer the "bad test-taker." Colleges don't like students who don't apply themselves throughout high school and feel that low grades in a much less competitive setting (high school) are probably an indicator that the students won't apply themselves in college—or won't know *how* to apply themselves.

Slightly more interesting to college admissions officers are students with consistent high grades who somehow bomb on the tests. If the discrepancy is really large, the student can sometimes include a note in the "anything else you'd like to tell us about yourself" section of the application. Perhaps the student just blacks out with fear every time he or she has to absorb a reading-comprehension passage. This does not make for a great college candidate, however, because most college pro-grams include many tests and reading assignments. The student would have to explain convincingly on the application why his or her reaction to SATs or ACTs is different from his or her response to other college-style exams.

Another reason for a student bombing on SATs might be that the student, in a panic, tends to overinterpret, creatively interpret, or re-spond too literally to directions. A good explanation in an essay accom-panying an application would cite specific problems that the student got wrong, explaining the student's interpretation, and why that re-sponse seemed more reasonable than the supposedly correct answer. To take this approach, the student would have to purchase a copy of the exam with answers—most are available for purchase through the Col-lege Board. The student's explanation should demonstrate an under-standing of the test-giver's answer. This excuse would be bold and should resort to good solid logic—but that's what the most-competitive colleges are looking for anyway, isn't it?

A third reason that a student might bomb is weak time management. A novice might reasonably misappropriate time. This argument works only if the score rises significantly on the second try. In this case, no explanation is needed.

Do Colleges *Really* Only Count the Highest Score?

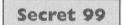 **Regardless of what you secretly suspect, most college admissions officers who say that they only count your highest standardized test scores, really do only count the highest scores.** So, if, for example, a kid gets 400 verbal and 800 math and 800 writing on the SAT the first time, and 800 verbal and 500 math and a 500 writing the second time, the resulting score counts as an 800 plus an 800 plus an 800—for a total of 2400. Although many parents are skeptical, admissions officers say they really do only count the highest standardized test scores, because they want to see what the applicant is *capable* of achieving. They really don't care as much about tabulating weak performances.

How Many Times to Take Standardized Tests

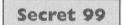 **Contrary to what everyone else will tell you, there is no maximum number of times to take the ACTs or SATs. Take them until you're satisfied.** No, most colleges don't average your scores together, after you've taken the exam for the third or fourth time, as some rumors suggest. Most colleges still only count the highest scores in each category. Does it look bad to take the exams more than two times? According to a spokeswoman from Grinnell College, studies have shown that standardized scores rarely increase significantly after two tries. But she emphasized that there is no limit, except the cost of taking the exam and the stress it puts on your child and your family. (Sometimes, knowing that

the student may retake the exam multiple times can calm the student.) Would an admissions dean raise an eyebrow if a kid took the exam five times? Perhaps it would look odd, she said, but it wouldn't stop the applicant from getting in. And if, on the fifth try, the student's scores suddenly popped up, those fifth scores would be the only ones counted.

An admissions director at Baylor University, Stephanie Willis, said applicants should "take the exams as many times as they like." She said that if the initial results are not as good as expected, it looks impressive to see students who are "willing to work and keep trying" instead of giving up after one or two tries.

Practicing for Exams

| Secret 101 | Parents have reported success with having their children take standardized tests |

annually, starting in sixth or seventh grade for practice without requiring expensive test-prep courses. By junior or senior year, the test is old hat. The students are not nearly as nervous as their peers, because test-taking has become an annual event. Of course, if you're not seeing gradual improvement from year to year, a family might be wise to abandon this as a sole strategy as junior year approaches, and SAT and ACT scores start to "count."

Is it harmful to have your child take the exam at a young age? If presented correctly, the experience should not be terrifying or in any other way detrimental. Explain to your child that he or she is taking the exam as practice—to experience the timing, setting, and exam format—and that it doesn't count for college. Emphasize how impressive it is to be one of the youngest students sitting for the exam. When the scores arrive, show your child how his or her scores compare to college-bound high school seniors (noted in the report that gets mailed to the student), and explain that your child can expect even higher scores the next year when the exam is taken again.

I urge students who aspire to win the Physics, Math (AMC), Chemistry, Biology, or Computer Olympiad exams as juniors and seniors to first take the qualifying exams in ninth and tenth grade to get a sense of the individual exam, the setting, and the timing. I tell them not to worry about their scores at all—even if they get zeros. The purpose is to get acquainted with the test-taking process. My students who have gotten negligible scores on the exams in ninth and tenth grade have gone on to become semifinalists, finalists, and even national winners of Olympiads.

Secret 102	**Many parents have their children take the SAT before their thirteenth birthday to**

qualify for the Johns Hopkins Center for Talented Youth (CTY) summer program that is considered a significant credential by top colleges. Some middle schools and junior high schools encourage parents of top-achieving children to have their kids take the exam; others do not. If you have younger children who might benefit from this program, which is offered on college campuses throughout the country, don't wait for your child's school to tell you. Investigate it yourself at http://www.jhu.edu/gifted/.

Which Math SAT II Is Better?

Secret 103	**If your kid has the math background to take the SAT II Math 2C, tell him or her**

to go for it. The 2C exam has historically been more forgiving of errors than the supposedly easier 1C. The past exams have been designed so that a student is permitted to make more mistakes with fewer points taken off per error on the 2C exam. A top math student took the SAT II 1C and achieved a score of 730 in her early years of high school. The same student took the SAT II 2C, considered a more advanced-level exam, and achieved a perfect 800. Pleased with the 800, and frustrated by the 730, the student decided to go back to the easier 1C exam, just for the fun of it, to see if she could perfect her score. Second time around, she got a 780. The third time around, she got a 780. It took four tries for her to achieve the 800 on the 1C exam, whereas, she got a perfect 800 the first time around on the 2C exam.

Though it may sound odd, and though few kids take the test four times, scores are often higher on the more challenging exam. When considering the two exams, have your child examine the 2C and see if all the problems are potentially doable. If some material has not been studied yet, your child might be stuck with the 1C. If you're not sure if the material has been covered yet, you or your child might ask your child's math teacher which test your child should take.

Alternate Test Dates

The SAT date exemption doesn't only apply to religious conflicts. It also applies to academic conflicts (a rarely divulged fact). For example, a student who was originally scheduled to take an exam on a Saturday in June won a major science competition and was invited—all expenses paid—to present his work that weekend in another part of the country. The junior needed the SAT II for his college application, however, and no more exams were scheduled until October of his senior year. The student was able to schedule a makeup SAT exam day with his own high school (the high school had to arrange a proctor), due to his "academic conflict." The student took the test on a weekday, upon returning to school. The score took longer to process, but otherwise, there were no hitches. More commonly known: Tests are also administered on Sundays for students who have religious conflicts with taking exams on Saturdays.

Why Take the PSATs?

Secret 105 **The PSATs represent the first time that high school students get a real sense of where they rank academically on a national scale. But**

otherwise, the PSATs may be useless for many or even most students who participate. Some people say that the primary purpose in taking the PSATs is to "practice" for the SATs and to qualify for a National Merit Scholarship. But a better way to practice for the SATs is probably to take an SAT practice exam. Almost 3 million students take the PSATs annually. Of those, about 10,500 receive some form of related money from National Merit (odds of about 1 in 300), which uses the exam as a qualifier for their scholarships. Students from all over the country—including from schools that usually depend primarily on the ACTs—take the PSATs in October of junior year. Besides practicing for the SAT and trying to qualify for a Merit Scholarship, one more reason that people take the PSAT is that it is required in applying to some summer-research opportunities and science competitions that specifically ask for PSAT scores. If none of these possibilities applies to your kid, you might reconsider making your kid take the PSATs.

PSAT Awards

There are five ways to win money from earning a high score on the PSATs:

1. a corporate-sponsored scholarship
2. a college-sponsored $2,000 scholarship
3. a National Achievement $2,500 Scholarship (minority students only)
4. a National Achievement corporate scholarship (minority students only)
5. the mysterious National Merit $2,500 Scholarship.

To win money from a corporation, the high-scoring student generally must be the child of an employee of a corporation that helps sponsor the PSAT. The *PSAT Guide* contains a complete list of sponsoring companies (609-771-7070). To win the $2,000 college-sponsored scholarship, you need to apply to one of the more than 200 colleges that participate, also listed in the *PSAT Guide*. (Note that none of the Ivy League schools, Stanford, MIT, Caltech, or Chicago is on the list.)

Now comes the more mysterious one—the $2,500 National Merit Scholarships. About 16,000 semifinalists are named nationally, 90 percent of whom become finalists (based on grades and follow-up SAT scores that "verify" the PSAT results). So, if you think your kid is guaranteed to get into a most-competitive college based on being a National Merit Scholarship Finalist, guess again.

From the list of more than 14,000 finalists, about half win money, mostly through corporate- or college-sponsored awards. But 2,500 win money without having their parents employed by a sponsoring corporation and without regard to college choice or race. How is this determined? To qualify for consideration, one must be a top scorer in his or her state. Minimum qualifying scores differ by state.

Secret 106

The hardest locations from which to qualify for a National Merit Scholarship are Maryland (222 points minimum to qualify in 2004); Massachusetts (222); New Jersey (222); and the District of Columbia (222). The easiest states in which to qualify in 2003 were Arkansas (202) and West Virginia (202); and in 2004, Mississippi (204), Wyoming (204), and the U.S. Territories and Commonwealth (204)* In New York in 2003 and 2004, the qualifying score was 218, and in California, the score was 216 and 217.

You qualify based on where you attend high school, and not where you sit for the exam. The perfect score is 240 points. The minimum qualifying score is determined by the proportion of graduating seniors in the state. So, if for example, State X accounted for 10 percent of the graduating seniors, then the top 250 students (or 10 percent of the 2,500 award recipients) would be chosen from State X. As a result, the exact qualifying score numbers change from year to year, depending upon the outcomes of the exam—but states tend to maintain their status in relationship to one another.

---

*Scores provided by Gloria Davis, Director of Public Information, National Merit Scholarship Corporation.

Selecting the Final 2,500 National Merit Winners

An outside committee composed of fourteen people meets annually for one week in January in Illinois to choose 2,500 students from the list of finalists to receive National Merit Scholarships of $2,500. The committee consists mostly of guidance counselors and college admissions officers, and they divide into fifty "teams" to decide which kids to pick from each state. Obviously, each committee member sits on multiple teams. Finalists within each state are pitted against one another.

Every application is read, according to Gloria Davis, Director of Public Information for the National Merit Scholarship Corporation. A very large state might have up to three teams that determine preliminary selection (pulling out kids who are clearly weak, and identifying strong candidates). A final team might evaluate the middle. Candidates are discussed in terms of course work and test scores. "Often recommendations or essays are the determining factors," says Davis. At the end of the week, all the decisions have been made.

How important is National Merit? Some colleges claim that they assume that all their candidates will be named finalists or scholars, so they are not impressed. Colleges that offer scholarships to Merit Scholars probably care the most. Among the most prestigious colleges that offer up to $2,000 to National Merit Scholars are Bowdoin, Brandeis, Carleton, Emory, Grinnell, Harvey Mudd, Johns Hopkins, Northwestern, Oberlin, Pomona, Rice, Scripps, Tufts, UCLA, University of Chicago, University of Illinois, Vanderbilt, Washington and Lee, and Washington University in St. Louis.

How Impressive is "Commended"?

 Being "commended" by the National Merit Scholarship Corporation is just as impressive as saying that your kid is among the top 50,000 kids

in America. While that statistic may indeed be impressive, it won't get your kid into a most-competitive college. Many parents of commended students—that is, 34,000 students nationally, who score *below* semi-finalist status—assume that their kids are hot candidates for the most-competitive colleges. They want to highlight the commended status on their kid's college application. Don't—even if your son is the only commended kid in his high school. If you add that 34,000 to the 16,000 students with higher scores, you realize that your commended son is one of 50,000 high scorers in America. This won't wow the most-competitive colleges.

PSAT Alternate Locations

Secret 108 **You can have your child take the PSAT at a school other than his or her own. Some high schools often don't like this information publicized because it creates extra clerical work.** Students generally take the PSATs at their own school in October of junior year. If your daughter can't be at school for the exam, or if she prefers a different environment (where friends and peers aren't present), it is possible to arrange *in advance* to have her take the PSAT at another high school. To do this, phone the desired high school directly and make arrangements. It's important to phone as far ahead as possible, since a limited number of tests are given to each high school. Also notify your daughter's high school of your plans.

Each high school has a different procedure for admitting "outsiders" to the exam. Find out what proofs (IDs) your kid needs to bring, what exact time to show up, and where to report. You'll probably want to walk in with your kid early that morning, to make sure the school has made proper accommodations. If one high school tells you in advance that it would have problems accommodating your child, reserve at another school.

Practice PSATs

If PSATs were meant to be practice for the SAT, many parents of sophomores are now requesting that their kids *practice for the practice*. Many sophomores take the PSATs to practice for the junior-year PSATs. Savvy parents who believe that practice makes perfect should request to have their kid take the PSAT during October of the *sophomore* year as a dry run for the following year, if they think that their kid's scores will come within range of earning a Merit Scholarship or winning them a good summer internship. But don't wait for your school to notify your son or daughter of this practice opportunity. Some schools notify all sophomores of this option; some only notify students who are considered "above average" or "top," and some don't tell any students. In addition, some states, some school districts, and some individual schools provide full funding for the exams—so the juniors (and, at some schools, juniors and sophomores) don't have to pay for it. Other schools charge each student. Some schools *require* the exams of all sophomores, some only require the exam of "top" students, and some announce the exam and let students decide whether to take it. (That information may never come home.) If you want your sophomore to take the exam but your school refuses to make the exam available, contact a neighboring school—a private school or school in a nearby district—in advance to arrange for your child to take the test at a different location.

Studying for PSATs

Secret 110

Regardless of what other parents or your child's guidance counselor may advise about preparation, if your child plans to take the PSAT, encourage your kid to study in a structured way. Even if others argue that your child need not study and that the PSAT is meant to reveal the child's baseline aptitude, have your child prepare. Nothing is to be gained by taking the test with minimum preparation, except low self-esteem. The information that a child learns in preparing for the PSAT can be applied toward the SAT and ACT also, so getting started early on a PSAT-SAT study plan can be a wise investment.

The best way to help your child prepare is by working with him and a review book or CD-ROM within a deliberate, prearranged, agreed-upon plan. But if such a plan interferes with your own work schedule, inquire about local PSAT prep courses. If no PSAT course is available, register your kid for an SAT prep course, or seek out a tutor. Whatever method you choose, have your child review the exam material thoroughly.

Beyond Grades and Standardized Exams

While transcripts and standardized tests are generally the most influential elements of a college application, other factors, including recommendations, interviews, and essays, can also play a significant role.

Secret 111 **A well-planned college visit can be the determining factor in whether the student is offered admission.** College visits should not be treated like casual daytrips, with a quick drive-by or walk-through. A serious, well-planned visit should ideally include having the student attend at least two sample classes, a student meeting with professors in an academic field or fields of interest, an on-campus interview with an admissions officer or department administrator, a tour of the facilities or laboratories that especially interest the student, and a possible weekend sleepover in a dorm.

If the visit allows the student to really immerse him- or herself in the college, the information gleaned can be very useful in writing the application essay and for interviews. By the end of the visit, the student should be able to cite many concrete reasons why the college represents the perfect match.

CHAPTER 5

Arranging a Winning College Visit

 **Contrary to what some parents assume, all colleges really are different.** Yes, your kid can apply to colleges without visiting them, but doing so is a big mistake. All have very different cultures—even if their prestige is the same or comparable. Brochures and view books do not communicate these differences clearly. You have to walk the campus to get a sense of the place. Some families wait until the kid has been accepted into the college before traveling to see the school, as a means of saving money and not investing emotional energy into a college that doesn't accept the child. While the strategy may sound sensible, it's far better to visit the college *before* applying—to see if it's worth applying to and to have a better sense of how to apply intelligently. If your child likes the college, she should refer to the visit in her application essays or correspondence, and this will add more weight to the application.

Arranging the Visit

Secret 113 **It's perfectly acceptable for parents to phone the college to get answers to basic travel-related questions, like "When are group tours sched-**

uled?" "When are information sessions offered?" "Could my kid meet with a professor?" "Could my child sit in on any classes?"

While some admissions officers fantasize that the prospective applicants are the ones making the travel and interview arrangements, in most applicants' homes a parent is likely to make the plans—particularly if the visit entails hotel stays. (Most parents aren't going to relegate the family hotel and travel plans to their kids!)

Before the visit, inquire about setting up an audition (for a music or theater student), or a meeting with the coach of a sport in which your kid is particularly talented. If your kid has *a particular interest*, find out in advance if tours are offered at the facility where your child is most likely to want to spend time. For example, University of Pennsylvania offers a separate tour of the Wharton School (management) and a separate tour of the Engineering School that prospective students can take in addition to a more general campus tour. Cornell offers separate information sessions for its undergraduate colleges in addition to a campus-wide tour and information session. The Claremont Colleges offer separate tours and information sessions for each college.

| Secret 114 | I've seen aggressive kids practically talk their way into a college by "chatting" with |

an admissions officer. Visit the admissions office when you visit a college with your child.** Even if no on-campus interviews are offered, the admissions office usually coordinates tours and information sessions, and you might get lucky and get to speak with an admissions officer on the spot. Make sure that your child is prepared for such an occurrence. Bring along an extra résumé just in case.

| Secret 115 | **Most colleges do not use caller-ID.** Parents of high school seniors frequently ask one an- |

other in hushed tones if it's *wrong* for parents to phone colleges for information, particularly information that they know their kids will never take the time to call about—financial aid, course requirements, etc. Ten years ago, it was *wrong* for parents to phone. Only students were supposed to call—if anyone called. Nowadays parents phone far more frequently, and their calls are treated courteously. (Colleges even report that they get many phone calls from angry parents after the kid is rejected. And admissions officers generally take these calls and talk to the parents patiently, without checking caller-ID.)

Part of the problem is that kids are in school during office hours and unable to access a reliable phone. They don't want to call from cell phones, use of which is not permitted in some high schools. During prime phoning hours, the most motivated students are busy at school or engrossed in extracurricular activities and don't get home until the admissions offices are long closed for the evening. If the kid wants the question answered, the parent has to phone.

Nevertheless, parents worry that by calling an admissions office they are inadvertently alienating admissions officers and reducing their kid's chances of being admitted. They picture an admissions officer saying something like, "It's Mrs. Smith again with another annoying question. If I get one more call from her, I'm rejecting her kid." Or they picture the admissions officer saying, "Doesn't Mrs. Johnson read? All information is available on the Internet or in the brochure."

Be courteous. Check the college website or brochures to seek your answers before phoning. But if you don't find your information, most colleges surveyed will respond to your call courteously. Admissions offices queried said they do not know or keep track of who calls unless the caller identifies him- or herself.

Secret 116

If you don't voluntarily identify yourself by name, the person answering the phone at the college rarely asks you to. Instead, you can identify yourself abstractly as "a parent," "a recommender," or "a teacher."

A woman answering the phone at one of the most competitive Ivy League colleges' undergraduate admissions office said her office phones *do* identify caller numbers, but they don't identify the names. And no, they don't mark down each time a caller from the same number phones, nor do they focus on identifying the caller. So theoretically, if you have a question to ask, you can say you're the anonymous Ms. or Mr. Smith and ask without fearing that they're going to track you down and reject your kid.

Other prominent colleges said they have no caller-ID at all, that parents are welcome to ask questions. Parents should recognize, however, that admissions offices tend to be busy, and parents should be considerate of officers' time.

Secret 117	**As a general rule, colleges that feel more secure about their image are more willing**

to entertain questions from parents. This may mean that they have greater staffing capabilities. The colleges with less secure images (and probably smaller staffs), sometimes have a tendency to scold parents and say staffers are too busy to handle individual questions. Parents may expect that the way they are treated on the phone will mirror the way that their kids would be treated at the college. If inquiries are met with respect, it can be safely assumed that campus policy and culture dictate that people should be respected and welcomed. Of course, everybody can have a bad day now and then, even the nicest receptionist. But if phone inquiries are repeatedly met with annoyance in multiple departments, take that as an indication. There are colleges where the majority of the faculty and staff members are disgruntled. And yes, this will impact your kid's education.

Tours and Info Sessions

Secret 118	**Student tour guides are more likely to give you the inside view if you can ply**

them off script. Do not despair if your campus tour is led by a current student, rather than a more public-relations-savvy admissions officer. Some college-tour canned speeches focus heavily on the "lore," traditions, architecture, and history of the college. Most give an overall sense of what's valued on campus—scholarship, social life, inventiveness, the honors system, social action, etc. Some guides are more willing to share their application strategies. Parents often nuzzle up to student guides to ask about campus politics, attentiveness of advisers, dorm and food quality, and ethnic diversity. Don't judge a college completely by the student guide, however, particularly if you feel that you're getting a skewed picture.

Follow up your tour with an information session. (Sometimes the order is reversed.) And if your child is planning to meet with any faculty members or admissions staff, try to complete the tour and info session before the meeting, so that your kid has some familiarity with the campus layout, culture, philosophy, and overall environment *before* the interview.

Siblings may attend tours and info sessions, too, as long as they're well behaved and nondisruptive. If possible, two parents should attend. Don't get overly preoccupied with family members' clothing. At a minimum, wear shoes that allow you to walk comfortably for distances. Wear comfortable but neat clothing. The applicant should wear casual interview clothes, if no interview is planned. That way, if a spur-of-the-moment opportunity arises (and yes, this does happen sometimes), the applicant is reasonably comfortable and appropriately dressed. If an interview has been arranged for the same day, the applicant should wear regular (business) interview clothes (either a suit or sport coat for males, and a skirt suit or pantsuit for females).

Arrive early. During high school holiday weeks, tours occasionally fill up at some colleges, and you may be asked to wait for the next tour (sometimes hours later). Bring along a pad of paper, if possible. You may want to jot down notes, particularly on topics you want to address later at the info session.

Sign in. Most colleges have a sign-in sheet. Sometimes this sheet determines who is on which tour—first come, first served. The sheet also helps colleges keep track of who attended and sometimes puts you on their mailing list. At some colleges, the sign-in sheet or separate cards that the applicant is asked to fill out will request SAT scores, grade point averages, and other information to see if your kid is someone they want to recruit. Leave blanks if you think your numbers may improve, or don't fill in the card at all, since these cards could show up in your application file.

Allow plenty of time for your visit. Tours usually last about an hour, depending upon the size of the campus. Info sessions usually last another hour, including a presentation by a university administrator and a question-and-answer session. Plan to spend extra time on campus after the tour and info session. Sample campus food. Visit the student center, if such a facility exists. Observe the other students on campus. Read the bulletin boards and campus newspaper to get a sense of the campus's pressing needs, issues, and upcoming events.

Tours usually take you to some of the campus landmarks. You'll probably see the stadium, if the campus has one within easy proximity to the main campus. You'll probably see the largest auditorium on campus, the main library, the athletic facilities, the student-activities center, and a sample lecture hall and classroom. You'll probably be taken past the bookshop, past some symbol of the campus, and a few on-campus eateries. Many college tours *do not* include dormitories, and the guide will cite reasons why nobody may see the dorms. A student guide might take you to his or her dorm, however. On some campuses, a pristine "sample dorm room" is set up for parents to see, so that no student is responsible for maintaining a spotless room each day for visitors to inspect. But parents commonly complain that once their kids attend the college, they never find a dorm room that really looks as good as that model.

Many parents try to schedule their kids' college visits to coincide with at least one weekend night to get a sense of campus social life. Is it a "suitcase school," where kids go home every weekend? Or does the college provide enough activities to keep students engaged on campus? What are parties like? Are they open to everyone, or is it necessary to join a fraternity, sorority, or private club to be included?

In addition, it's helpful to include a weekday, so that your child can attend a class or two on subjects of interest. Do not sit in with your child. Find out if the large classes break up into "recitations" or "tutorials" or "breakaway sessions," where students get more individualized attention and can ask questions and participate in discussions in a smaller group. If such smaller sections exist, who teaches these? Full faculty members? Grad students? And who grades papers?

Secret 119 **The campus placement office can be very revealing in terms of the kinds of opportunities that will be available to your kid.** Is it active or passive? Does the office help find and create internships and challenging opportunities? Or does it merely help the kids find babysitting and bartending jobs? Does it post any job that comes along—ranging from working in the college library to ushering at a nearby theater? Or does the placement office simply hand you a thick binder filled with résumés of illustrious graduates and tell your kid to contact some of these alums for an "information interview" (translation: some blind phone calls, we don't know if the alum even is in a position to hire or if the alum's office has any openings)?

What to Watch for on a Campus Visit

Many parents are confused about what to look for when they visit a college campus—that on the surface, all colleges appear similar despite some cosmetic differences. But real differences exist that could shape your kid's education and experience significantly. The following are guidelines for what to watch for.

Your first priority should be to get a sense of the academic environment. While other teenagers may tell your daughter that what's most important is the sorority scene, or your son may hear that the workout facilities are what should be the deciding factor, focus your campus visit on the academic environment. Among the most important questions to ask are whether students are encouraged to think and question. Do students interact with their professors outside the classroom? Are such outside interactions generally limited to office hours? Do academic departments sponsor open-to-all-students activities? Do guest lecturers come to the campus, or is there not enough of a scholarly audience to attract them? Do professors within the department offer open lectures frequently about their research and latest discoveries? Are the professors even conducting research or making discoveries? Or is there little intellectual interest (or no budget) for such activities on campus? How active are academic societies on campus? Are the honorary societies merely certificate givers and new-member-initiators, or do they coordinate any academic activities? Most parents hear about colleges in which the professors invite the class to dinner—is there more than one professor on campus who does this? Do students ask questions at the end of lectures or in smaller breakaway sessions? Or is there no opportunity to ask questions?

Secret 120 **Before your child applies, make sure the college is not a "wannabe" college where the students are constantly bemoaning the fact that they are there.** These are easy to detect if you know what questions to ask. Check out the location. Does the campus overlook another "superior" college? Do students all say that they wish that they were somewhere else? Was the college you're visiting the first choice of most of the students you meet on campus? Or was it everyone's "safety school"? The giveaway for a large wannabe university is when you ask at the info session which graduate schools the alums attend and they name many prestigious universities but not their own.

Secret 121 **Beware of colleges that make even introductory courses and other academic opportunities inaccessible till sophomore or junior year.** Your daughter won't be happy if she can't take the courses that interest her or start her on her major for a whole year. That famous Economics course that your son wants to take may require sophomore standing because there is too much demand. Or your daughter the Pre-Med isn't able to get into the overcrowded introductory Biology course until sophomore year. When visiting the campus, find out if freshmen are welcome to get involved in all activities (theater company, college newspaper, radio station). Or do students generally have to wait a year or two before they may participate in a meaningful way? Such exclusion could have significant impact on your child's college experience.

Secret 122 If course reciprocity is a major factor in selecting a college, during your visit, check the practicality of the arrangement. Sample the shuttles provided, compare the academic calendars, and ask current students if the reciprocity is really viable. (Have they taken courses on the reciprocating campus? If so, was their experience positive?) For example, try going roundtrip from Haverford to Swarthmore, Wellesley to Harvard, Smith to Amherst, Bryn Mawr to Penn, or Westminster Choir College to Princeton. Do buses arrive often or infrequently (making it difficult to take advantage of the opportunity)? When sampling the shuttle ride, get off the bus, walk around, and take another shuttle back. Don't just ride roundtrip—or you won't get a sense of the reliability.

At some colleges, the reciprocating college has a completely different vacation schedule, thus requiring any students who want to take a course there to work right through vacations. Some students who have taken courses at reciprocating colleges talk of grade discrimination— professors favor their own college's students, since they are most accountable for those students' grades. Many colleges will not count courses taken at a reciprocating college toward the core requirement or toward the major—sometimes defeating the purpose of taking the outside course. If you're drawn to a college for its course reciprocity, make sure the arrangement is what you expect.

Secret 123 On campus bulletin boards, beware of too many ads for tutoring services. If there are many such announcements, does this indicate that lots of students are "falling through the cracks," and the university isn't meeting their needs, so the tutoring business is booming? At colleges where tutoring is included in the tuition, such listings are not as prevalent. (Also check campus newspaper ads.)

Secret 124   **Pick up a copy of the campus newspaper to get the inside scoops.** Every newspaper will have some articles that deal with current issues as well as accomplishments. If the tone is completely negative and if the issues are issues that you or your child don't want to live with, that's a bad sign. Are the workers universally disgruntled? Are drugs a big issue? Is the college eliminating a department, program, or activity that your daughter is most interested in? Is the college adding a new exciting program that might interest your son?

Secret 125   **The way that the college greets visitors often mirrors the way that the college treats its own community.** If there's a welcome session in which food is served, are the refreshments appealing and reasonably generous? This may sound like a ridiculous criterion, but I have found that private colleges that welcome people "cheaply," with, let's say, a small plate of processed cheese cubes and hydrogenated oil crackers, or a few plates of supermarket packaged cookies, tend to follow through and treat their students cheaply. Will the college balk for financial reasons, for example, when your kid wants to form a new academic club? Will the college cater the event nicely if your kid invites a world-class speaker to address the students? The food does not have to be costly. It just needs to demonstrate respect. One admissions office, for example, offered freshly baked chocolate chip cookies and freshly brewed coffee and decaf—available all day to visitors. This wasn't the top criteria that impressed potential applicants or their parents, but it certainly made a memorable impression—and made the students feel comfortable and welcome. A small New England college invited an unidentified visitor to come back the next day for free buffet breakfast.

Secret 126   **Watch for subtle campus social patterns that can be very revealing.** Do students look alone and alienated? Or on the other extreme, does everyone walk around in large groups as if they're afraid to walk alone? Do women ever walk alone on campus? Is everyone coupled off? Do students seem to know each other? Do they stop to say hi? Do professors say hello to students as they pass each other on campus—or is there an invisible line separating professors from students?

One of the more interesting social settings I have seen was at Olin College, a new free-tuition engineering school in the outskirts of Boston. On an unannounced walk-in visit to the cafeteria, I saw all of the students—an eclectic and diverse-looking group—eating together family-style, crowding in at long tables nearest the food, while the rest of the cafeteria was empty. Nobody sat alone. A cafeteria supervisor proudly boasted, "We get the best kids." And she pointed out some young professors who were seated among the students. "That's the way we eat here. We're a family."

| **Secret 127** | **Make a point of observing the interaction between professors and students, as an in-** |

dicator of the campus educational process. At some colleges, students depend more on peer interaction to learn, while at others, discussions with professors play a major role in the educational process. Notice how students refer to their professors. Do they use a title and last name or are they on a more casual first-name basis? How do professors view/treat undergraduates? How are undergraduate ideas greeted by faculty members? When you seek to meet with professors, do they seem readily and eagerly available? Are professors' doors generally open, regardless of office hours? Are office hours accommodating and clearly posted? Is the university proud of its students' academic accomplishments? Do they display the students' accomplishments anywhere so that professors and visitors can see?

| **Secret 128** | **While most colleges that are not affili-** **ated with a single religion or ethnic group** |

claim to have diversity, observe the cultural mixing.

The ethnic composition and interaction will differ dramatically on different campuses. Does the college drag out its one minority ethnic administrator for the information session so everyone can see? Or are there many diverse staff members at the college? What about the student body? Is there a rich diversity? Do you see students of different backgrounds interacting? Or do they self-segregate? Are dorms "voluntarily" segregated?

Secret 129 **At some colleges, fraternities, sororities, eating clubs, and secret societies dominate—not just the social life, but also the overall setting.** One secret society, for example, is located right in the middle of the Yale campus tour route. Campus tours at University of Virginia describe some of the lore of secret societies as part of the presentation. At Princeton, an entire street of mansions is home to exclusive eating clubs. Other colleges have fraternities and sororities with varying degrees of elitism and influence. Whether these organizations intrigue or turn off your child, if you have questions regarding the influence of elitist clubs, you might want to ask an admissions officer or even a college student on the side: Do the clubs discriminate? Do they haze? Is "rush" a major focus that could distract from the learning process? Is there any kind of "social elite" on campus, and would this be a problem for your kid? Are there Honors students that your kid would either be part of at the expense of other friends, or excluded from? Are all campus programs merit-based or are some programs based on social standing and family legacy?

Secret 130 **Even if the campus tour does not take you inside a sample dorm room, you can usually find a willing student to invite you in to check out the housing facilities while you are visiting the campus.** While housing should not be among the top criteria in choosing a college, lodging can easily interfere with an education if your child isn't comfortable. To have specific questions answered pertaining to your child's needs, you would probably want to speak with a residential director or a current student. More general questions will probably be answered during the information session. Are students assigned housing based on hobbies and interests, their own input, or lottery? Is campus housing based on the residential college system? Do students race off campus at the first opportunity? Are dorms segregated ethnically? Do Honors students live in separate dorms? Do students prefer on-campus or off-campus housing? Is housing a major distraction for students? How long does the college guarantee housing?

Secret 131 **While junior years abroad can be extremely educational and supportive of independence, mass exoduses sometimes indicate campus claustrophobia, boredom, or lack of stimulation.** Don't become too starry-eyed when the campus guide tells you that every student takes his or her junior year abroad. On some campuses, it seems that all of the juniors are gone—the relatively few remaining juniors feel lonely and excluded. But leaving the campus could mean requiring five years instead of four to graduate. If your child wants to major in the sciences, ask if the study-abroad programs could accommodate her major. Would she have to spend extra time in college in order to graduate?

Secret 132 **The laundry room in a dormitory can sometimes give you an insight into the safety and sense of trust on campus.** At some colleges, students have to watch their clothes spin round and round, lest someone walk off with their laundry. On other campuses, while the machines are in operation, nobody is monitoring them. Some college dorms even have the laundry room wired up to signal the students' computers when the wash or dry cycles are finished.

Secret 133 **Student centers are often the best place to get a sense of the vibrancy of a college if you have limited time to spend on the campus.** If the college has a student center, don't just look at the exterior architecture. Go inside and see if students are excitedly working on projects and activities. Or is the student center relatively foreboding and dead—hidden behind an armed guard? If the center has a cafeteria, go past it. (Cafeterias are always bustling. But what about the other student activities?)

Secret 134 **When you visit the campus library, look to see if anyone uses it.** College tours will try to impress you with the number of volumes. But check out whether most students do most of their research there. Is it an appealing place to study? When a book is assigned reading, are plenty of copies readily available, or do you see a signup sheet at the librarian's desk where students have to reserve required reading weeks in advance? How often has your kid used the library in high school—or has most of his or her research been Internet- or textbook-based anyway?

Secret 135 **While you don't want to embarrass a student tour leader, there are some questions for which you may get helpful answers if you can ask privately.** Feel free to hang back so you can ask the guide certain questions off to the side. For example, does the campus "honor system" ever lead to students tattling inappropriately or framing each other? Is underage drinking secretly encouraged (that is, the university buys the drinks)? If several colleges share the campus (an engineering, nursing, agriculture, or women's college, for example), are students at some schools considered "higher-class citizens" than students at other schools on the same campus?

When to Visit Colleges

Secret 136 **The best time to visit colleges is junior year, preferably during February or spring break (not summer, not Christmas) when the colleges are in session but the high schools aren't.** This gives the student the opportunity to sit in on classes and meet professors. Visiting during the summer before junior year gives a somewhat skewed picture of the campus (since the campus is relatively empty), but a summer visit can tell a student if he or she thinks the campus merits a serious school-year in-session visit. If you can't travel during the school year, summer visits are worth pursuing at a minimum. But beware: When visiting a campus that has a cold winter climate (for example, Cornell, Michigan, Rochester, Bates, Dartmouth, among others), don't forget that the pretty flowers you see in summer vanish rather quickly when the fall semester starts and the days get colder and shorter.

Secret 137 **Don't send your kid on a college visit with his or her good friend.** Your son is much better off making up his own mind, rather than depending on a high school buddy's opinion. Friends tend to have other agendas. They want your kid to go to college near where they'll be. Or they want your kid to go to a college that *they* can get into. Or they want your daughter to go to a college that has great parties so that they can visit often. Friends often prejudice kids about college choices.

Accessibility of Professors and Sharing of Ideas

Secret 138 **If access to and interaction with professors are vital to your child's education (and they *should* be), check out the "openness" and accessibility in advance.** This can vary by department within a university, so check specific departments that interest your child.

A prospective student missed a day of school to travel a few hours by car to one of the nation's most competitive Ivy League universities for a prearranged noon meeting with a professor. The student arrived early, but the professor had forgotten the meeting and didn't show up. Figuring that the professor was surrounded by students after a fascinating lecture, the student waited a half hour in the hallway. Then the student went to the department secretary's office down the hall and knocked on the door. Although the secretary clearly was inside (her phone conversation could be heard from the hall, and her office lights were on), she didn't respond. After the professor still did not arrive, the student began to knock on the doors of neighboring professors whose lights were on and who also could be heard speaking on their phones. None of the professors responded.

Finally, after a full hour, the secretary opened her door. When the puzzled visitor asked if the secretary had heard his knocks, the secretary openly and unashamedly admitted that she had heard the knocks but that they'd occurred during her lunch hour, during which she's not obligated to answer her door. The visitor then asked her if that was the case with all of the professors who were clearly in their offices ignoring his knocks. She smiled and explained that the reason *they* didn't answer their doors was because they are only required to do so during official office hours. (She also scolded that the knocking was an intrusion.)

Although the student did not get to meet with the professor that day, the visit was highly informative. The student got a clear picture of this particular university's unwillingness to merely help out a stranger, much less be available for unscheduled intellectual discourse. This was not the intellectual environment that the student was seeking.

In contrast, at Princeton University, the same student had a pre-arranged meeting with a science professor and was invited to sit in on the professor's class. When he met with the professor after class, he was impressed that the professor kept his door open. A professor from across the hall, who had overheard part of their conversation, eagerly dropped in to participate.

Some top colleges encourage students to rely more on interaction with other students for intellectual stimulation and feel that professors are supposed to keep their distance. Others pride themselves on faculty-student interaction and collaboration.

One-Time Meeting with a Professor

 **For serious students, it is beneficial to arrange a meeting with professors before submitting an application; this meeting may be referred to in the application.** Many top students do this. Before arriving on campus, a parent should arrange for the student to meet with at least one

professor in a department in which the student is most interested. Parents may escort their child to the meeting but should not stay for the meeting—even if invited. Nor should they linger conspicuously near the professor's office or meeting site, or pace about impatiently, rushing the discussion.

In addition to giving the prospective student a good sense of the college, such meetings can be very helpful to the student when it comes to writing essays for the college application. If a student can cite a meeting with a specific professor as part of an essay—particularly if the meeting is productive, positive, and a convincing factor for the student—the citation could demonstrate the student's serious interest and informed perspective on the college.

To prearrange the student-professor meeting, the parent should contact the department secretary (if the admissions office doesn't handle these arrangements). Ask the secretary if the department designates a particular professor to meet with prospective students.

Secret 140 **Prepare your child to discuss relevant issues or questions in the professor's area of interest.** You as a parent can "pull articles" from the Internet written either by or about the professor, so the kid reads up on the professor's work and can discuss it intelligently. Don't expect your kid to run to the library to eagerly find sources—even if the kid really wants to attend the university and even if the kid really wants to study with the professor. Such an activity seems foreign to even top students. If the professor has published relatively little, or if the professor's works aren't readily available or understandable, try to find an interesting magazine article that relates to the professor's field that your kid can discuss. Have your kid also prepared to ask educated questions about the professor's topic.

Secret 141 **Some professors have far more power in admissions than they confess. Some don't even realize they have it. Some know they have power and don't want you to know, in case they don't want to recommend**

your kid as a result of the meeting. Most professors will tell you up front that they are not involved in admissions—beyond answering questions about their department.

Should you believe this? Not entirely, but understand that a professor is generally obligated to give you such a speech. If the meeting goes badly—if your kid seems to be on an entirely different wavelength, or if the chemistry somehow doesn't mesh—chances are the professor will not mention your kid again to an admissions officer. If the professor is very impressed, it's more likely that the professor will dash off a quick note to the admissions committee recommending your child. But there's no guarantee that if your kid is recommended by the professor, the kid will be admitted. (Some professors and some departments wield more power than others.) If your daughter meets with the professor and writes about that meeting as part of her application, it's likely that a member of the admissions committee might contact the professor by phone or e-mail, asking for the professor to comment on the meeting. So make sure she only mentions the meeting if she is sure that the meeting went well and the professor was reasonably impressed.

A positive meeting could be helpful for admission. For that reason, if a professor agrees to meet with your son, make sure he sends a thank-you note to the professor after the meeting. This will remind the professor of your son's name as well as the positive nature of the visit, which could be helpful if he refers to the meeting in his application.

Do not expect the professor to write a lengthy recommendation as a result of the meeting. Few will. Most would be annoyed at the prospect of being asked to write a recommendation for a student they only met for twenty minutes to an hour.

Getting to Know a Professor

Secret 142

Don't assume that your child will get an outstanding recommendation just because you paid for him or her to take a summer course with a professor. Some parents sign kids up for summer courses or research internships as a means of gaining an "in" with a professor or department and with the hope of seeking a weighty recommendation at the end of the program. This works sometimes, but the professor has to truly be impressed. There is no guarantee. A student took part in an intensive summer music workshop run by a noted Ivy League professor. Although they had met each other before the summer, during the program, the student and professor didn't get along. Despite the hefty fee that the parents paid for the program, no recommendation resulted.

Sitting In on Classes

Before visiting a college, arrange to have your kid sit in on at least two classes. Most colleges will welcome prospective students' visits in specified classes, often larger lectures, where the presence of one more student won't be noticed. But some colleges also allow visitors in small classes. Once again, parents should scout out the details and make the arrangements. First phone the admissions office in advance to ask if visitors may sit in on classes.

Some colleges have a daily listing of classes that are open to visitors. Some require that individuals make private arrangements with the department secretary to sit in. Don't have your kid sit in on any course that doesn't appeal to him or her. Do not sit in on the course with your child, unless the course has more than two hundred students in the lecture hall, and your kid isn't embarrassed to have you sitting next to him. Don't hang around the halls. Give your kid space, and let him imagine that he is an actual student in the class.

Select courses that are not too advanced, so that some of the material is understandable. Otherwise, the lecture will seem boring, and beyond reach, or difficult to evaluate in terms of its relevance. No matter how self-assured, your kid should probably be instructed not to ask questions at the lecture. At many colleges, it is not customary to ask questions during or after lectures—discussion of the material is saved for smaller group sessions.

At a college in which the lectures are small, questions may indeed be welcomed. But your child should introduce him- or herself to the professor before the class starts, because it's likely that the professor will know all the students by name in the small class, and he or she may be embarrassed not to recognize your kid or be able to call your kid by name when a hand is raised.

Your kid does not have to be nervous about a classroom visit. Professors will not call on a visitor as a general rule, unless the visitor volunteers an answer. The visit is not in any way viewed as an audition or tryout for admission.

Instruct your child to stay throughout the lecture, and check how long it will be. Leaving early, no matter how boring, is impolite. If she knows in advance that she cannot sit through the entire class—perhaps she is scheduled to meet with a professor an hour after the class begins—either skip that course, or notify the professor in advance that, after an hour, the student is intending to make a silent exit. This way the professor will not be offended. Usually, longer classes have breaks, anyway, and such a break would be the best time to leave. A visitor who plans to leave early should take an aisle seat, so that he doesn't have to step over other students or interrupt the lecture to exit the hall.

Beware: The Fashion Judges

As a rule, fashion is not a good way to determine which campus provides the right education for your child. But parents should observe whether students dress very differently from the faculty. Are the faculty very formal, while the students are very casual? If so, does this promote a generation gap or break in interaction between professors and students?

Students contend that observing any overwhelming appearance trends on campus gives a sense of students' values. Kids returning from campus visits often tell parents about the attire. "That was an Abercrombie campus," a prospective college student told her parents after the tour. "I prefer a Gap campus." Other students count the tie-dye shirts on campus (implying "hippy" schools) or the Burberry scarves (implying a conformist, fashion-obsessed campus) or preppy clothes. On some campuses, parent visitors commonly remark on the prevalence of blue hair, pierced belly buttons, and partially exposed tattooed rear ends.

Campuses really do differ in appearance and culture, and you want to make sure your kid will be reasonably comfortable within it. Do the students all conform to a "uniform"? If so, would this be stifling or comforting to your kid? Do the other kids focus more time on shopping than on studying? At some rural women's colleges, it's not unusual to come to class in pajamas on cold, dark, wintry mornings. Would this feel welcoming or too laid-back? At some campuses, students wear business suits to class to feel professional, and at others, religion-governed attire (sleeves for girls and no beards for boys at Brigham Young) may dominate, according to the college's religious affiliation.

Once you've visited a campus, if your child decides to apply to the college, it's time to get an understanding of who the people are that determine whether or not your child will be offered admission. Knowing your audience can better help you "package" your child most effectively, help target the application, and gain an admission offer.

CHAPTER 6

Knowing Your Audience:
Who Is Judging Your Kid?

In writing successful applications, your child needs to know his or her audience. Many kids write their essays as if they were chatting with a best friend who understands all of their personal references, appreciates their social gossip, and agrees with their perspectives on religion and politics. Such essays may seem out of context to admissions officers and can easily be misunderstood.

In this category, I would include one student's essay about his imaginary friend, another student's confession about how phony behavior made her popular, an essay apologizing for the way a boy treated his annoying younger brother, a complaint about a minister's sermons, an item-by-item critique of another girl's wardrobe, a fight with the applicant's high school principal, and a rationale for why freshmen deserve to be treated badly.

While applicants should realize that probably at least one of the admissions officers is a recent graduate, the applicant should not assume that even this peer admissions officer will appreciate essays that are angry, cruel, and/or confessions. Nor should the applicant assume that any of the admissions officers have a common heritage or common hobbies and interests.

 **Secret 143** | **Admissions committees are very different today and far more diverse than they**

were twenty and thirty years ago. Understanding who is reading your kid's application is important in guiding the application process. At non-religion-affiliated colleges, envision a group that is younger than you, multiracial, and includes at least an equal number of women and men.

Admissions officers are often as diverse as the students whom they accept, heads of admissions say. What they have in common is that they tend to be open-minded, outgoing people who care about their college and want to open doors for the most accomplished, upbeat, eager, committed, creative, and energetic group of students that they can attract.

Parents surveyed tend to picture a homogeneous admissions committee, regardless of the college, consisting of about eight to ten white men with frosty gray hair. They wrongly assume that all are above the age of sixty, some above the age of seventy. All wear conservative striped ties (or an occasional bow tie), stiffly pressed white Oxford shirts, and stuffy tweed jackets, some with suede elbow patches. Some even wear suspenders. Everyone is serious at all times, even the guy with the bow tie. Nobody smiles. Humor is not appreciated—especially not teenage humor. Nobody is easily impressed. There is no ethnic or religious diversity, except that maybe one or two members of the committee have sophisticated and intimidating British accents. One or two might have beards. For women's colleges, the image is very similar, except that women are more of a presence, and they wear sensible business suits (with skirts) instead of tweed jackets and ties. Some wear pearls. All wear eyeglasses.

That's the admissions committee of the 1970s, according to college administrators interviewed for this book. At MIT, for example, the admissions committee in recent years has consisted of thirteen full-time staffers plus ten to twenty faculty members who choose to participate. (Nobel Prize winners have been known to sit on the committee—before and after winning their world recognition.) In contrast to old stereotypes, admissions committees at coeducational colleges tend to attract more women than men, and at most of the most competitive universities, the staff consists mostly of younger people in their late twenties and thirties. Associate deans include largely people in their forties and fifties (the same age as the students' parents, for the most part). And the head deans, of which there is generally only one or two, are usually around age fifty and up. MIT's admissions staff has included whites, Asians, blacks, Hispanics, and people who would describe themselves as multiethnic. The committee in recent years has included more women than men, with members varying in age, religion, and background, including some (but not all) MIT graduates, and some (but not all) holders of advanced degrees.

Brandeis University's admissions committee also has more women than men. The ten officers range in age from recent graduates (ages twenty-one to twenty-two) to early sixties. Although the university was originally founded as a Jewish institution, the committee claims a wide ethnic mixture—with "every constituency represented." Each staffer specializes in a different geographical area of expertise. And one member specializes in international grading systems to admit foreign students.

At Washington University in St. Louis, twelve officers—more women than men—make up the staff. From this group, smaller committees along with deans determine admission to the different colleges on the campus. The committee does not include faculty or students. The oldest member of the staff is Director Nanette Tarbouni, forty-eight in 2006, and the group is very diverse. "In order to seek diversity in our student population, we have to embody that diversity in our staff."

At all three universities, women head the admissions staff, and all three admissions teams are representative of current admissions-staff composition.

Caltech has six admission directors, including three women (two African American; one Asian) and three men (one Hispanic; two Caucasian).

| Secret 144 | The applicant should note that no singular culture should be presumed to be "right culture" on the application, that the person reading the application may come from a completely different background |

and may not share your child's artistic taste, politics, religion, interests, or TV choices. At the same time, the essays should not assume that the reader of the application has no appreciation of ethnic or popular culture.

Ethnic Quotas

Secret 145	**Most colleges claim adamantly to have no quotas. But if you visit different cam-**

puses, you will see significant ethnic differences. And you can't help but notice that although quotas may not be called "quotas," certain ethnic limits still prevail.

MIT is one of the handful of private college campuses I have seen where quotas really do not seem to exist. The famous physicist Richard Feynman attended MIT as an undergraduate years ago, when he was denied admission to Columbia University due to a once-dominant ethnic quota system at Columbia.

But at some other highly reputed universities, diversity is less apparent. At the info session of an Ivy League school reputed to be less diverse, the tour leader stated that his college had no quotas. "The only limitations we have," he offered, "are the actual limits of the U.S. population. We seek to mirror the rich diversity of America." At first, that concept sounded very democratic. When pressed further by the man questioning, he said that if the population of a U.S. ethnic group made up 5 percent of the American population, then his university tried to reflect that percentage in its incoming class, by offering 5 percent of its places to members of that ethnic group. That formula suddenly seemed too ethnic-centered (translation: quota-based) for many of the visitors. So although he claimed his college had no ethnic quotas, the system he described was the opposite. On a visit to the campus, comparatively few faces of color were seen.

Most colleges will tell you that they have no geographical quotas, except some state universities tell you up front that they are required to take significant percentages of students from their own state. And some

Ivy League schools say that they could fill up an entire class with students from the New York tristate area, the Washington, D.C., area, and California if they based their admissions solely on objective numbers and scores—so they limit students from these regions. Although colleges claim to have no regional quotas, if your child is committed to getting into a specific competitive college, check the admission statistics from your kid's high school and nearby comparable schools. While colleges may not have fixed or written quotas, as such, patterns emerge when comparing statistics of accepted students from a single high school, community, county, or region from year to year.

Regional Quotas

Secret 146

Whereas colleges that claim to have no regional quotas *do* vary the actual numbers taken from each high school each year, they tend to take similar numbers from the same schools and the same region on average over a period of a few years. Being aware of this should not discourage you from supporting your kid's application for a reach (or hard-to-get-into) school, but should help you to plan a strategy in case your kid is attending a school that has no history of getting students into the college that your child wants to attend.

College representatives will emphasize that if Prestige U, for example, sees ten kids in your high school that would add considerably to Prestige's student body, Prestige U may take all ten this year, and none next year from your high school. And those claims can be proven in exceptional years, perhaps, when a group of extraordinary students coincidentally or otherwise seems to be graduating from the same high school in a single year. But look at the long-term picture or trend, and you'll see a pattern that sure looks like a geographical quota. (If your daughter attends a magnet school where fifteen kids got into Prestige last year, expect about fifteen this year. If your son attends a competitive public school where two got in last year, expect one to three to get in this year. If your child attends a "feeder" prep school that got six in last year, expect five to seven this year. If Prestige U has taken no kids from your kid's high school for ten years, don't expect your kid to get in unless you package your kid completely differently and make sure your kid's credentials are far superior to what Prestige has been shown so far from your kid's high school.

Many parents mistakenly believe that college admissions committees like to take turns with schools or entire school districts. They comfort themselves with the notion that "Prestige U hasn't accepted anyone from Smalltown, USA, in five years, whereas the neighboring Achievertown, USA, has gotten ten students into Prestige U in the past three years. It's definitely Smalltown's turn." It's just not true.

Parental Paranoia:
Where Other Parents Get Their Information

Many public and private schools produce annual reports detailing their most recent graduates' college application results. For those who can get their hands on a copy, such reports are hot bedside reading in many households. These reports can be both entertaining and one of your most enlightening tools in the college application process. If your child's school does not provide such a report, locate the nearest *comparable* school that does, and request a copy.

Report styles vary by school. In general, they consist of lists of students (names are almost always omitted) according to ranking or GPA (grade point average), SAT I and ACT scores, and SAT II scores. Now here's the fun part. The report indicates colleges to which each student was admitted, and colleges to which each student was rejected. This is obviously extremely helpful when determining to which schools your own child should apply. Armed with your child's GPA, SAT I (or ACT), and SAT II results, for example, you can find graduated seniors who had similar statistics to your child's and get a sense of which colleges are within reach.

Some of these summary reports are more elaborate, listing how many Advanced Placement and Honors courses each student took, clubs in which the student participated, or other credentials. Some indicate whether a student was admitted Early Decision, Early Action, Rolling Admission, Second Early, or Regular. Some indicate which school each senior ultimately chose to attend.

Caution: When analyzing college application reports, note that there are lots of missing variables that do not appear in the report. For example, few reports will indicate whether a particular student is a member of a "sought-after underrepresented minority," or has a rare talent like a mastery of the French horn or bassoon, or holds an Olympic sports medal, or is third-generation legacy, or has won the Intel Science Talent Search, or has published a novel, or has starred in Hollywood. So if your kid, for example, has a 1410 SAT and a 4.0 GPA, and you see in the report another kid with the identical numbers who gets into Prestige U, you can't assume that your child will automatically get in as well. The other kid might be an oboe virtuoso who composed a concerto that was played at the White House. Or the other kid might have won a bronze medal in Olympic gymnastics who published her autobiography that became a national bestseller. Or the other kid might be the school's student-government president who also teaches her native Spanish to handicapped children and starred on the county lacrosse team.

Overall Procedures

Secret 147   **Admissions committees and procedures vary dramatically from one university to the next.** Parents tend to picture a committee seated around a large conference table, picking apart one candidate at a time, determining which teenager is worthy. They imagine that the committee is sometimes charitably willing to grant admission to those who are deemed "able to handle the work" or "very deserving of a chance." They call out the names, the parents think, and everyone gives an opinion. "Jessica Jenson." "Not impressive enough," says one member. "I'm not amused by her essay," another detractor agrees. "But she's president of the student organization," says a defender, "so she deserves a chance." "But her teacher says she's only among the top fifty students in the school—we can do better." "Okay. No Jessica Jenson."

Parents imagine that admissions officers pore over each kid's essay writing style for hours—picking at each grammatical error they spot with an occasional "Aha!"—demanding only publishable-quality material. Parents and English teachers alike seem to think that what's most important about the essay, is how well the student writes, rather than what the essay says. But content is even more important.

In some committees, although all applications are read more than once, some names never come up for group discussion. Some universities reportedly hire outsiders to come in and read the applications and make the determinations. At many colleges, the entire committee never meets as a large group, but instead, subcommittees meet and write notes to one another. Some have very structured discussions, others are very informal and even arbitrary. When the coffee is bad, nobody may get accepted that morning.

How the Student Is Discussed

Secret 148   **How much discussion is devoted to a particular candidate varies. If the candidate is a so-called shoo-in or an instant reject, there may be little or no discussion.** Oh, to be a fly on the wall in the admissions office when they're discussing your kid! You could write volumes about your own kid, so you easily imagine the committee engaging in an hour-long discussion, weighing your kid's numerous merits and enjoying his or her personality or sense of humor as it emanates from his or her beautifully written essays.

But admissions committees don't have hours to devote to each applicant. Remember: Your kid's application is guaranteed a specified number of *readings* that varies from college to college (but is usually not secret)—but not necessarily *any* discussion. If the candidate is more borderline, discussion could last for twenty minutes, and admissions officers could even go home puzzling over individual situations. One admissions director claimed to remember practically every applicant in a given year at a college that attracts well over five thousand applicants. But that involvement cannot be expected at most large universities.

Some families devote so much energy to preparing their kid for college and college applications (shuttling the kids to prep courses, tutoring their kid, helping the kid fill out the rote information on the forms, proofreading essays, photocopying ad nauseum, among so many other duties) that when they imagine that the admissions committee only took three minutes to admit their kid, they feel cheated and disappointed—*even though their kid got in.* This is obviously silly. Of course, you'll never know how long the discussion lasted, anyway.

Do admissions officers pick at grammatical errors in conferences? Not really. But they may make note of errors they notice, when reading the application. If the application is sloppy (meaning errors in facts, spelling, grammar, and style), the haphazard quality or carelessness of the applicant is bound to be noted as a negative factor during any group discussion. The most-competitive colleges expect clean, error-free, computer-printed applications.

Secret 149 **Many colleges have their own rating systems for applicants typically based on a formula that combines grade point averages (weighted or unweighted according to their own system) and standardized test scores, in that order of importance.** Then they rank additional factors (extracurriculars, community service, essays, and recommendations). The highest-ranked applications within that system are generally considered first. Most universities claim to eventually read all of the applications—regardless of ranking. Some claim to read every application multiple times—even those with atypically low grades and scores. Most of the most-competitive schools give each application at least two readings (and two rankings, which may be averaged together). Caltech claims that three people read each file. At most colleges, after each series (or grouping) of applications is read and ranked, the committee meets, and decisions are made.

Parental Paranoia: Do Admissions Officers Check Applicants' Credentials?

The more grandiose the credential, the more likely it is that an admissions officer will check it out. Also, if any information in the student's application and another student's application from the same school conflict (both students claim to have founded the same organization, for example) the error is likely to be noticed.

Obviously, it's very difficult when you receive thousands of applications to check the accuracy of each one. For each school and course that the student claims to have attended, transcripts are requested, so that information is verified. For major competitions that the student claims to have won, lists of winners are readily available online. If it's a contest that would have major impact on admissions, the admissions officers are generally familiar with the list of winners. Likewise, if the kid claims to have a high national ranking in a sport, it's relatively easy for the college coaches to check the accuracy of the claim.

When it comes to lesser credentials, claiming to be head of a student club or founder of an organization, admissions officers will check the application for consistency. If an applicant, for example, is an accomplished musician who spends every spare moment pursuing the clarinet and takes the bare minimum of required science courses and then suddenly lists founding a physics club among his credentials, something is suspicious. The admissions officers might call the school for verification, especially if two kids from the same school claim to head the same club.

Once your child has a sense of who is reading the application and how the application is being evaluated, filling in the short answers and writing the essays becomes an easier and more logical task. Many colleges are using the Common Application, so it's not unusual for students to have to figure out the majority of answers once. (Of course, even colleges that use the Common App often ask supplemental questions as well.) In any case, the task of filling in the application merits some careful thought, as there are wrong answers and wrong ways to approach even the shortest fill-ins.

CHAPTER 7

How You Can Help with the Application Forms

Lots of applicants have the same questions—many of which are not answered in the application-form directions—and many of which seem silly to have to phone an admissions office about. So this chapter focuses on some awkward questions that despite their trivial nature, require an intelligent answer, and some of the vital information I have gleaned from working with college applicants over the years.

When Does the Application Process Start?

Applications generally become available around the end of August or beginning of September of each year. You can obtain applications in many ways:

- online to be filled out online
- online to be printed out and filled in on paper
- e-mail a request to the college to have a printed application sent by regular mail
- phone the college to have an application sent by regular mail
- mail a postcard to the college indicating your child's interest and providing your child's name and address
- sign an attendance sheet at the college's admissions office during

a visit or at a public-information session and request an application

- have your child sign an attendance sheet for the specific college at a college fair or when a college representative from the particular college visits your child's high school and have your child request an application

Once your kid has the application, parents should set up a file for that college immediately. (The college will also create a file on your kid as soon as the first part of the application is submitted.)

Organizing Your Accomplishments

Secret 150 **The student should start by assembling two separate listings of accomplishments and activities in advance: One should be formatted like a multi-page résumé; the other should be in the form of a chart.** The chart should feature the following columns: Activity; Position or Office Held, Year of Participation (9th, 10th, 11th, 12th), Hours Per Week; Honors or Awards Won. Parents can be most helpful in assembling both documents, or may even choose to create both documents without the child's participation to expedite the process. Every job, activity, and honor should be listed on this chart.

Once you have a comprehensive chart, format the same information into a formal résumé if your kid doesn't already have one. Although experienced job-seekers may tell you that the résumé should all fit on a single page, ignore that advice, since this isn't a job résumé. Use as many pages as you need. Most applications ask for a list of extracurricular achievements and activities. Having this material organized into both a chart and résumé (preferably stored on the computer) is extremely helpful in easing the process and saves hours of work.

Secret 151 **In addition to using the résumé for your kid's college application, make sure your**

kid brings a copy to his or her guidance counselor. Student résumés should be updated frequently, and a new copy should be filed with the counselor or college adviser each time, keeping the school in touch with what the student is doing—even if the adviser doesn't ask for one, and even if no other kid in the high school is doing this. First of all, such a résumé will inspire your kid to want to "fill it up" with meaningful awards and activities. But in addition, when an out-of-school opportunity arises, and the school is called to recommend the most qualified student, guess whose résumé will be the only one handy? Some of my students have gotten otherwise hard-to-get internships and awards by having the only résumé on file.

The résumé should be more descriptive than the chart. If your child wins the National Science Prize (fictitious award), for example, the résumé should spell out how many other people were considered for this award and how many other winners there were, so the admissions officers fully appreciate the significance. The entry might say: "**National Science Prize 2007**: Named the only First Place National Winner (for Oncology research conducted at Massbridge Hospital) of 20,000 top U.S. high school science students who applied; January 2007; sponsored by the U.S. Science Association." Note that some competitions have multiple "First Place" winners.

The basic sections of the student résumé should include Awards and Honors, Education, Academic Activities (and offices held), Organization Memberships, and Summer Employment. In addition, the student might want to include sections on Athletic Achievements, Music (or Art) Activities and Achievements, Internships or Summer Programs. A very accomplished student might want to create separate sections for International and National Awards and Honors, Regional Awards and Honors, and High School Awards and Honors.

Students with particularly strong community-action involvement might use "Community Service" as the first category on the résumé, or more specifically "Disaster Relief," or "World Hunger Prevention Activities," or "Plant Conservation."*

---

*See the appendix for sample résumé.

The Education section should include the student's grade point average, number of AP, IB, and Honors courses taken, any college courses taken while still in high school, and standardized test scores. Do not feel obligated to include all standardized test scores if you're not pleased with some results. Also show all final course averages if you're pleased with them.

Is It Better to Apply Online?

Secret 152

All official application forms are given equal treatment regardless of whether they're filed online or on paper, and regardless of what the colleges say they prefer. Even if a college specifies that it "prefers" that the applicant apply online, that does not mean that they prefer the applicant *who* applies online. Online applications are less wasteful of paper and easier to process. But a candidate who applies on paper will not be given lesser treatment. Nor will a paper application or printed application look more aesthetic to a college.

Secret 153

Paper applications give you more control if you're not completely satisfied with the format that the online application provides. When you have greater control of the margin size, spacing, and font size, for example, you can squeeze in more information. If you feel that you have no information that needs to be included beyond what you are asked to include, then file your application online. It's much easier. Examples of information that works better on paper:

- The student has more SAT II or AP scores to report than space allows.
- The student has more significant awards and honors than space allows.
- The student wants to report more *meaningful* activities (most applications limit your listing to seven).

- The student needs space to report additional offices held, additional courses currently being taken, and additional summer jobs or summer activities.

Paper applications let you write in the margins, but computer applications do not. But be careful when altering margins. The admissions committee is likely to make multiple copies of your application—so that more than one person can read it. If you write too far into the margins, the information may not be picked up on the photocopied versions. If you have more information than they provide space for within their margins, being afforded the "luxury" of writing slightly into the margins can be a major benefit and can put your kid ahead of the competition, assuming the additional information isn't just fluff and is worthwhile. I have never heard of a kid who was penalized for cramming in too much information, as long as the extra material was all readable and providing new information. (Colleges may resent cramming in repetition.)

Are the Odds Worse If My Kid Doesn't Apply Early?

| Secret 154 |

Early Decision *does* improve your child's chances—since huge percentages of the entering classes are accepted Early Decision from a much smaller pool of applicants. Many colleges will tell you the opposite. Ignore that advice. Even the most-competitive colleges that offer Early Decision "begrudgingly," claiming to dislike Early Decision, take huge percentages of their students Early Decision and have continued to increase those numbers after complaining about the system. As college admission becomes more and more competitive, my advice to applicants is to choose a realistic reach school and apply by the November deadline (exact date varies by college and year) for Early Decision or Early Action—whichever they offer.

What constitutes a realistic reach? Your child's grades and scores should be well within the college's range—not lower end. He should, in fact, be completely qualified numerically. In addition, he should have interesting talents that the university will want and quality experience and evidence to back that up. If his grades, SATs, or ACTs are not quite what the college is looking for, don't waste his Early Decision single application on that college. It's not a realistic reach—unless you have some fantastic connection, or your kid is a legacy kid (parents or grandparents attended). The most-competitive colleges have become so competitive that they are all "reach" schools for even the most qualified candidates who meet all of the criteria. Harvard admissions officers even boast at the college's information sessions that if Harvard administrators threw out the applications of the entire class that it accepted in any recent year, Harvard could completely fill another entire class at least with totally qualified students. So don't expect them to make an exception for your kid if he or she does not meet the bare-bones criteria. Instead, find a college that will be happy with your kid's scores and transcript. And reach for that school.

Parental Paranoia:
Would Colleges Find Out If My Kid Applied to Two Colleges Early?

Applying to more than one college Early Decision is considered dishonest, but the secret is that colleges generally do not know if you do it. Nevertheless, do not let your kid apply to more than one Early Decision.

The basics: Early Decision is when you apply to one school exclusively in November and promise to attend that college if you're admitted in December—the decision is binding. Early Action, on the other hand, allows you to apply to multiple colleges. And if you get accepted Early Action, you can choose which college you ultimately want to attend. You don't have to be brilliant to see that the second option is far more appealing. Why would anyone apply to a college Early Decision if they have the option of applying Early Action? The answer is simple: Most colleges offer only Early Decision. For the relatively few top colleges that offer Early Action, a third program has been introduced, Single-Choice Early Action. Under this program, the student may apply to only one college Early Action. Once the applicant is either deferred, rejected, or accepted (in December), the applicant is then free to submit additional applications. But initially, only one Early Application may be submitted (in November).

Armed with that information, you now are ready to ask how colleges will find out if your kid applies to more than one Early Decision or Single-Choice Early Action college. An admissions representative at Columbia claimed that colleges communicate with one another after decisions go out. He said colleges share lists of accepted students with colleges that are members of the same organizations. But an admissions director at Dartmouth said no such communication takes place—and she said, to her knowledge, no colleges exchange lists of accepted students.

So let's take away the fear factor. Regardless of whether colleges actually exchange lists, college admissions officers contend that applying to more than one college Early Decision is dishonest and unethical—since by applying, the student signs a document promising to only apply to one.

Handwriting or Typing?

Secret 155 **Typed and computer entries are generally preferred over handwriting, no matter how artistic your kid's handwriting is.** An art student applying for an art college insisted on handwriting her entire application using calligraphy techniques she thought she had mastered. Apparently nobody had the heart to tell her, once her application was completed days later, that some of the fancier serif letters were impossible to discern, rendering her essay almost illegible. Imagine an admissions officer reading thousands of applications, struggling to interpret individual letters in essays. While she wanted to impress admissions officers with her creativity, she was rejected from the very colleges that she thought she would impress, possibly because they couldn't read what she wrote.

Admissions officers don't like handwriting. In fact, Stanford University's application says, "We strongly prefer that you do not print or handwrite your responses." Gone are the days of sloppy papers with messy Liquid Paper or Wite-Out corrections, erasures, and careless errors. Going are the days of calligraphy on applications. Brown University, which in recent years required that students handwrite their essays to help personalize the process, now lets students type the essays and submit their applications by computer.

If your kid handwrites the essay, will the college bring in a team of handwriting analysts to reveal that he or she is nervous or ill-suited for the college? A Brown admissions officer laughed at the thought.

Would a Photo Give My Kid an Edge?

Secret 156 **Do not submit a photo unless one is specifically requested or unless your child needs to communicate something that cannot be written in words.** You have nothing to gain by submitting an unsolicited photo—no matter how adorable you think your kid is. Many colleges state up front that they prefer not to receive unsolicited photos. As a general rule, no matter how good the photo, photos do not help the application. That said, of course there are exceptions:

- If the college specifically asks the student to submit a photo (rare), submit a photo. Brown is one of the few colleges that requests a photo. Is the aim racial profiling? No, a Brown admissions officer insisted, noting that the application already asks about ethnic background openly. The aim is to show the admissions staff who the kid is—so that if an admissions officer, for example, had already met the kid, a photo would be handy. Or sometimes, she said, a photo is very revealing, depending upon the location and the circumstance in the photo. Is the kid performing a feat? Does the kid's personal photo contribute new information to the application?

Brown is not the only college that welcomes a photo. Rice's application potentially invites a photo as well. On the application, an empty box is drawn—next to it, a label says "please fill in the box with something that appeals to you"— not necessarily a photo, but an opportunity for a photo. Stanford also has a blank box, but it doesn't need to be occupied by a photo. Directions: "'A picture is worth a thousand words,' as the adage goes (but you're limited to the space provided). Attach a photograph no larger than 5×7 inches that represents something important to you, and explain its significance."

- If the student is a member of a rare, very-sought-after minority, and the application doesn't make that apparent (although it should), a photo could help.

- If the student's essay or application describes a physical handicap that the student has overcome, and the successful recovery from which is somehow evidenced in a photo that's not too scary or gory.

- If the student has achieved some feat that needs to be documented in a photo—climbed to the top of Mount Everest, for example. Most achievements can be documented by descriptive words or by citing recognition or as part of an essay.

Tip: If you send a photo, never send your only copy—and don't expect to have the college return the photo. Identify the kid (first and last name) and the high school on the back of the photo.

Newspaper Clippings

Secret 157 **Don't submit newspaper clippings.** Newspaper clippings take up extra space in the application folders, which makes the folders cumbersome and may annoy the file clerks. Parents always ask if a neat collection of local newspaper announcements in which their kid is mentioned would impress the most-competitive colleges. Answer: No. Many kids who are competing for the most-competitive colleges have scrapbooks at home that are filled with their news clippings. Instead, mention some of the local newspapers that have interviewed the student as part of the "awards and honors" listing on the application. More important, the student should list on his or her application the awards won that merited newspaper coverage—that is far more impressive to colleges.

The exception is if a student writes articles for a local newspaper. The student, particularly a student who is applying specifically to a journalism program, might want to include some. If the student has won journalism awards, however, it's probably better to list the awards and leave the particular articles to the imagination of the committee— if clippings aren't specifically requested—since high school articles are rarely impressive journalism.

Parental Paranoia: Can an Application Be Sabotaged?

Colleges say they never withdraw a candidate without speaking directly to him or her. Have any enemies who might want to prevent your kid from attending college? Don't worry about your kid being framed—or facing made-up charges—if your kid has nothing to hide. You will be contacted if anyone tries to libel you or prevent your kid's admission. Such foul play is not unheard of on Broadway or in Hollywood, and parents of college applicants can learn a lesson from stage mothers and fathers.

The mother of a boy who made the last cut and was one of the final three kids to be called back for a Broadway audition got a phone call from the casting agent, just as the two were leaving their house for the audition. The agent wanted to know why the mother had canceled the audition.

"But I didn't cancel," the mother said, a bit confused.

"We just got a call from your son's manager saying that he was no longer interested in the part," the agent said.

"But my son *is* interested in the part, and we didn't call his manager, and we didn't cancel the audition. We were just on our way to the audition now."

"We just got a call from Ms. Hanson [not her real name], the famous Broadway manager, saying that you just spoke with her and canceled the audition."

"We don't know Ms. Hanson," the mother responded. "And she is *not* my son's manager. So please do *not* cancel my son's audition."

The audition was then *un*-canceled. When the mother and son arrived at the audition place, they were asked to scan a list of about forty names to see if any of the names of the children listed were familiar. Puzzled, the two of them obliged, and sure enough, they recognized only one name.

"That's your saboteur," the casting agent said with a detectivelike "Aha," explaining that such backstabbing was not entirely uncommon on Broadway. The mother of the less successful kid apparently posed as Ms. Hanson on the telephone and attempted to cancel the successful kid's audition out of jealousy. The less successful kid had already been eliminated from contention during previous auditions. "We get these calls all the time," the casting agent said, "and we treat these trespasses very seriously."

What is your chance of having the same thing happen when your kid applies to college? Can another parent pretend to be you and sabotage your kid's application or cancel your kid's interview? No, say the admissions officers. Another parent cannot phone and have your kid withdrawn from the applicant pool. All such withdrawal requests are only recognized if they appear in writing. When university admissions officers receive such a letter, they contact both the high school and speak to the candidate directly to see if the candidate does indeed want to withdraw his or her application. That is the procedure at most of the most-competitive colleges.

What If I Don't Own a Typewriter?

| Secret 158 | **Nobody owns a typewriter anymore. But there is a way to submit a paper application that looks like it was typed without requiring a typewriter.** |

Do the following:

1. On a separate clean piece of paper, type (on the computer) and then print out just your kid's responses to the questions.
2. Cut out those answers from the clean sheet of paper and tape them (using "invisible tape") to the application in the correct spaces.
3. Bring the completed application to a photocopying place to photocopy the taped pages—so that it *looks* as though you typed the answers neatly right onto the application.
4. Submit the photocopied clean version.

For those able to locate a typewriter, the thought of trying to align the application so that the letters get typed onto the proper spaces seems overwhelming. I prefer computer typing, because it allows a change of font size and style. When you lower the font size to fit words, don't go far beyond specified word limits, or the admissions officers will be annoyed. After you've read thousands of essays, you *know* when someone is squeezing in more words in 11-point type, and it can be irritating. But changing the font is very helpful if your kid has won more awards, for example, than the application provides room for, or participated in, let's say, more than seven "most meaningful" activities over the course of four years of high school, or if you want to show off more test scores than the space allows. How small can you make your font? My general rule is to make your font size no smaller than the application questions' font size. It's not uncommon for an application to have its questions written in 10-point or even 8-point. But on online applications, the font size automatically goes to 12 point. Stick with a 10-point minimum sans serif type—with *no* fancy curls—something easily legible, like Arial. You don't want your words to be too small— but it's reasonable to assume that if they can read their questions, they can read your answers, if you use the same or larger font.

"But if the application provides a given number of lines, and I have more to say, can I ignore their lines?" you ask. Yes. Let's say they provide seven lines and you have nine lines of really worthwhile information. Lower your font size and type up your nine lines of prose on a separate clean piece of paper. Cut out the response as a block—rather than cutting out each individual line of text. Tape the whole block onto the application, covering up their underlines. Don't let any of their underlines stick out. Keep the application neat-looking and easy to read.

What About the Stationery?

Secret 159

You don't have to submit the application on the actual paper that the application arrived on. Some of the colleges use very fancy stationery for their applications. What happens if you tape the information onto the application and then photocopy it onto cheaper paper or paper that is not identical? Or what happens if you accidentally spill coffee on the application and want to have the application photocopied onto a clean sheet that won't show the coffee stain? According to Princeton, one of the colleges that uses very attractive stock for its applications, the application is regarded no differently if it arrives on less fancy paper. So relax.

Questionable Nicknames, Screen Names, and E-mail Addresses

Secret 160

Make sure your kid does not sabotage his own admissions by putting inappropriate, suggestive, self-incriminating, tasteless, or questionable e-mail addresses in his college application. Often the front page of the application asks for the applicant's name, address, and e-mail address. I have seen high school seniors who, in big, bold letters, provide e-mail addresses like (none of these are actual screen names, but you get the gist) Naked1, or Sexy1, or Druggy2, or XFelon3, or Crack4, or Jailbird, or Dumbchik. If your kid has an inappropriate e-mail address, change it to something less "cool" and less obnoxious.

The same goes for nicknames. Many applications ask your kid for his or her nickname or "name by which you prefer to be called." Make sure your kid is reasonable. "Joe" is fine for Joseph, and so is "Joey." "Snugglebottoms" is not okay. Nor is "Carrottop" or "Crackbaby." While this may sound obvious to parents, keep an eye on the front page of your kid's application, particularly if your kid has a less-than-conservative nickname or e-mail address. Many bright kids have stupid e-mail addresses—partly because many precociously set up their e-mail when they were much younger. This lack of judgment shouldn't follow them to college.

What If They Ask Where Else I'm Applying?

Secret 161

When asked where else the applicant is applying, he or she should cite comparable colleges. It's not completely uncommon for a Regular Admission application to ask the applicant to list the other colleges to which he or she is applying. The question is odd, in that students are afraid to list less competitive colleges, lest the college think that they're less competitive or less motivated applicants. At the same time, the applicant doesn't want to list more competitive colleges, lest the college conclude that the candidate is really only viewing the college as a "safe" school or alternative.

If the application is Early Decision or Early Action, the candidate is off the hook and can claim to only be applying to the one university—so far. But if the application is for Regular Admission, the applicant realistically must list some other colleges. List colleges that are comparable and to which the student actually intends to apply. Don't let your kid list safeties. If the question is asked on an application to an engineering school, let's say, don't let him or her list a music conservatory as a second choice. In other words, try to keep the application consistent—even if the kid is multitalented. College admissions officers may not understand or appreciate great variety, even if they claim to like well-roundedness or diversity. They'll be confused, or, worse, they'll assume that the applicant is confused. While it's good to have many talents, the applicant should also portray a clear sense of direction—not necessarily specifying the major, but the general direction of engineering, liberal arts, music performance, management, or nursing, etc. (Wrong answer: A combination of Juilliard, RISD, St. Olaf's, Harvey Mudd, Ohio State, Brigham Young, and Hampshire.)

Is It Okay to Mention Our Religion?

Secret 162

Mentioning religion is fine, as long as the reference is not gratuitous. If religion is a vital part of an important activity in which your kid takes part, there is nothing wrong with your kid mentioning it. If your daughter, for example, has collected $20,000 worth of clothing for the Salvation Army, the Jewish Heritage for the Blind, or a Buddhist temple destroyed by a tsunami, the religious affiliation is appropriate. If your son, however, merely "attended religious school for five years" or "mosque" or was confirmed, that is a gratuitous mention. If the kid graduated at the head of his religion class, or took part in a religious pilgrimage (not just a religious "teen tour") to another part of the world, or helped organize a religious charitable-relief program, then a mention of the activity could be very interesting on an application. In other words, colleges that are not affiliated with religions are most interested in what your kid *does* and accomplishes, rather than what religious institution your family attends or affiliates with. (For colleges that are affiliated with religion, however, affiliation could be an important factor.)

Do not let your kid try to convert admissions officers to your religion on the application. Do not let your kid show intolerance of anyone else's religion on the application. Do not let your kid talk about the values being better at your kid's religious day school than at the nearby public school—that smacks of prejudice.

Religion, like political affiliation, still potentially invokes prejudice. The vast majority of admissions officers are probably the most unprejudiced people you'll ever meet. That said, as a general rule, tell your kid to avoid gratuitously mentioning religion. Admissions officers will dispute this—but they have to.

Will My Kid Be Penalized for Controversial Politics?

Secret 163 **Despite stereotypes that self-proclaimed experts have about colleges being very liberal or very conservative, a kid who labels him- or herself as an in-the-box by-the-books party member is very unattractive to the most competitive colleges, regardless of the party.** College applications are not the time for your kid to campaign for office, promote a controversial candidate, or declare party affiliation and enthusiasm. Stay clear of conventional politics and simplistic political self-classification in the college application. Nowhere on the application does it ask which political party your kid affiliates with. Don't offer the information gratuitously or the essay will sound like party propaganda. Much more interesting and attractive to colleges is the creative and independent thinker.

If politics is genuinely an important aspect of your kid's life, she might want to write about specific activities and experiences—not about the party line.

One very politically active applicant, for example, wrote a very compelling essay about differences in the way she was treated in working for two different campaigns. She described how a third-party presidential candidate discussed issues with the volunteers, made a point of remembering each volunteer's name, invited their feedback, and inspired them to work harder. In contrast, in a traditional party senatorial campaign, the candidate never even cared to meet the volunteers, who were given no assignments, and sat idly day after day, until they finally quit, disgruntled because their support didn't seem to matter.

Should the Kid Be Up Front About Criminal Blemishes?

Secret 164 | **Although it may be tempting to keep any criminal blemishes secret, students are wiser to reveal all infractions up front on the application.** Students with a criminal record are advised by admissions officers to be up front about their wrongdoing, even if an application doesn't ask. The student should describe the problem and how it has been overcome or how the student has changed in an essay on "anything else you'd like to tell us about yourself." When writing an explanation the student should clearly explain the infraction, express remorse, describe any restitution performed, and detail changes that the applicant has made to guarantee that such an infraction will not occur again.

Is It Okay to Mention Financial Need?

Secret 165 | **Most colleges will say that they never discriminate against students with financial need, but many do.** At colleges that claim to be "need blind," seeking financial aid generally won't hurt your kid's chances—particularly if the college really wants her. Does your kid bring something extraordinary to the campus? Is he a famous performer? Does she have a skill that the college is dying for? But be careful: Most colleges no longer say that they're "need blind." Some have changed the wording slightly to say that they're "need sensitive," "need aware," or "need conscious." These colleges may indeed discriminate on the basis of finances if they so choose.

Filling in the Blanks

Secret 166 **Make sure that your child has filled in all the blanks on the college application.** A kid who has all seven (or more) "most meaningful activities" listed, is much more impressive than a student who struggles to fill in one or two spaces. Even a kid with a single strong academic passion—an astronomy aficionado, let's say—should have at a minimum lots of astronomy activities to list (for example, High School Astronomy Club, volunteer at Urbanville Observatory, volunteer docent at Urbanville Planetarium, member of the American Astronomy Association, etc.). For students with more eclectic interests, try to vary the types of activities listed, to give the college a sense of the student's versatility. (List a sport, art, and community service activity among the academic activities.) I recommend filling in the "Job Experience" section completely, and if the student has never worked, I encourage the kid to start working now—tutor somebody, babysit, design a website for someone. In addition, students who don't find enough room to fit all their activities into the limited space where they're asked to list how they spent past summers, are much more appealing than kids who have nothing substantial to list.

In overseeing the fill-in portion of the application, parents should realize that there is more than just name, address, and phone number. And some of this information could have significant influence on whether or not an applicant gets in.

Once you have an overall perspective on the application's fill-ins, it's time to focus on the more challenging part—the essays. Although many students treat these two parts as separate entities, you want to make sure that the information provided in both sections of the application is consistent. The essay should not merely restate the other information on the application, nor should it contradict.

CHAPTER 8

Overseeing the College Application Essays

Imagine yourself on the admissions committee for an extremely competitive college. You have thousands of very respectable applicants. They all have standardized test scores well above your college's minimum. They all have A or A-plus averages. An initial reading of the applications by a committee already weeded out the kids with lower scores, lower averages, or other indicators that they would not be able to keep up with the competition at your university. Now you're left with thousands of applications and only, let's say, one hundred remaining spots. Do you try to make a purely numerical-based decision so your job is easy? No. Probably not, unless your college is part of a public university. You take pride in your job, and you want the most interesting, energetic kids to gain admission—you're specifically seeking out kids who will somehow add to your wonderful university, or kids whose needs can *only* be fulfilled at your university as opposed to other colleges.

Most kids' needs can be fulfilled at multiple universities—so you're looking for that special kid who needs *your* college. All of the remaining thousands are well qualified. All can benefit from an education at your university. But you can't accept all of them. So you have to read each essay and make a decision on a case-by-case basis. That's the frame of mind you need to be in in order to help your kid with his or her application.

Secret 167   **If your daughter is a shoo-in because her credentials are so outstanding, or an instant reject because she is so unqualified, chances are the essay won't help. But if she is among the majority of basically qualified applicants, the essay could be the deciding factor in admissions.**

When Should My Child Start the Essay Process?

There is no reason to wait until the Common Applications become available during the hectic fall of senior year. Essay options remain basically the same from year to year.

Secret 168   **Essays can be written in the summer before senior year—unless the applicant is spending the summer at some life-changing activity that he is sure to want to include in one of the college essays.** (In that case, have him write all of the other essays.) Students should write at least two completely different essays, both of which can be adapted to most college application requests. Although some colleges only ask for one essay, most offer students the chance to write an "optional" extra essay. Several colleges change their applications radically from year to year and a special essay may have to be written. Among them are Chicago, Northwestern, Tufts, Earlham, Notre Dame, St. John's in Maryland, Princeton, MIT, and Amherst. For most other colleges, the same two essays will generally suffice with slight tweaking.

For students eager to write their essays in advance to save time during the fall, all four of the following essays could be written during the summer:

1. Your most significant experience *or* how you overcame a risk or adversity

2. How you can potentially contribute to a university's diversity

3. "Most meaningful activity" (250 to 300 words)
4. The shell of the essay on why he or she is the "best match" for [Fill in the Blank] University, with lots of blanks to fill in course titles, professor names, appealing works by professors, names of specific organizations and clubs that the student would join, names of research projects that the student would like to participate in, and names of any special programs offered by the university (study abroad, internships, literacy projects, etc.). Keep in mind a topic for the "most influential book or person"—just in case

If the essays are completed by the end of the summer, the beginning of the senior year is much easier in terms of family dynamics. The applications are reduced to a simple process of having a parent fill in the kid's name and address and information repeatedly.

Secret 169

Among the most convincing applications are those by kids who show a passion (current buzzword) *for something that the college offers.* **Don't let anyone convince your kid that his or her passions are not interesting, if they match up to what the college offers.** A high school English teacher told a student that her essay describing her science research was "too boring." He advised the girl, who was a magnificent writer, to focus instead on something more "personal." This seemingly reasonable advice was followed by the girl, who, instead of writing about her scientific exploration on a tech-school application, described in detail her childhood hobby of baking. She was not admitted to her Early Decision school.

Is baking any more personal than science research? No. A well-written essay about the science that a student finds captivating should reveal much about a student's personal interests and concerns. Perhaps the teacher found baking more interesting than research. A college that offers a competitive engineering program is more likely to be impressed with a personal essay discussing a student's original research than a personal essay on recipes. If the student were applying to a culinary school, however, the baking essay might have been a better choice.

Childhood passions—dressing Barbie, arranging stuffed animals, running through the yard with a GI Joe, or flipping baseball cards— generally won't wow college admissions officers, no matter how literary the essay or how honest the description. The exception is when childhood passions tie in with adult ambitions. Using the examples mentioned, one can describe how Barbie led to an interest in majoring in Fashion or Interior Design; GI Joe led to an interest in Strategic Studies, and baseball cards encouraged a student to pursue a career in Sports Journalism.

Granted, life is not really about impressing or wowing colleges. But college essays should be. And when a high school student has worked so hard to acquire a passion and pursue it, denying the passion on a college essay—abandoning it for a more "popular" topic—is just plain wrong. Of course, the student should make sure that the passion coincides with a university offering. In some cases, admissions officers even may reject a student justifiably when the student's passion doesn't mesh. The rationale is, "The student wouldn't be happy here. We can't accommodate such interests, so rejecting the student is in his or her own best interests."

A trumpet player with a passion for marching bands inquired of a small New England college to find out what activities could accommodate her interest. "A trumpet player would be very unhappy here," the head of the music program blurted. "We have no marching band. We have no symphonic band either."

Making the Essay Writing Palatable

 **Parents can play a much more proactive role in college application essay writing than simply bugging the kid to write essays.** But note that if your kid is afraid to show you his or her essay, it's probably too personal for

the application. Just a reminder: Application time is not the right time to air the family's or the kid's dirty laundry.

Conscientious parents complain bitterly about how difficult it is to get their high school kids to work on their college applications. The nearer the deadline, the greater the tension level in the household, but at the same time, the harder it seems to motivate the kid. And although high school seniors often say they're eager to finally get away to college, they put off the task for as long as possible, childishly hoping that the chore will go away. The biggest stumbling block is the insecurity of not knowing what to write—worrying that nothing will measure up, believing that they have nothing interesting to say—that would impress admissions officers who've probably seen and read everything. Parents who become involved in the process are much more likely to help their kids achieve immediate success.

Secret 171 **Before approaching your son to write his essays, make a written list of some of the events in his life that you think might merit a particularly interesting story.** After all, you've been the "activities director" for seventeen years. You must have exposed your child to many interesting experiences with which you are familiar. Your son may have other ideas about what's interesting, so don't regard your list as fixed in stone. It's his essay, after all. But since you're not as emotionally invested in what to write, you can objectively highlight some topics that will spur good essay ideas. View your list instead as a jumping-off point for family discussion. Tell your daughter that you did some brainstorming to make the application process easier, and these were the best ideas you could conjure up. Don't expect affirmation, and don't expect her to instantly respond with her own list of brilliant topics. Let her absorb your suggestions. Or, more typically, let her disparage your suggestions or downplay your topics. It's okay. You don't win a prize if your child accepts all of your ideas. And many kids respond to suggestions by putting them down initially. At least there are ideas being considered, and the process has formally begun.

In presenting ideas, remind your son how exciting his life really is. Talk about some of your fondest memories—the more recent, the better. Laugh about some of the funnier moments. Tell your daughter how impressed you are with some of her achievements. Enjoy and celebrate your child in the conversation. Then leave it—and him—alone.

The next day, you might inquire of your child, "Any thoughts on those ideas for the college essay? I'll bet you can come up with much better ideas. What do you say we brainstorm together?" Kids need hand-holding in the application process. Many parents do, too. Work together. Order in food. Pizza? Chinese food? It's your kid's choice tonight. This way, nobody focuses on food preparation, and you're free to brainstorm.

Appoint your kid head of the Application Committee. You're the secretary. Take scrupulous notes on his ideas. Don't let there be an excuse for procrastinating. Discuss the ideas you've suggested, and let your kid find flaws with your ideas. It's better for her to come up with her own topic—the point of contributing your ideas is to help jump-start the process. When your kid suggests a topic, brainstorm what related events and anecdotes might be included in such an essay. Prepare to have your ideas rejected. Ask your son how he might conclude such an essay. That conclusion would probably make a great topic sentence to start the essay. Write it down as he dictates it to you. Before you know it, you've got an outline.

Now it's time for your son to write the first draft. Let him stay with you while writing if that's what he prefers. Tell him that there is a prize at the end of the process. Make the prize a surprise—a dinner out, a night at the movies, etc.

Do You Need to Hire a Consultant?

 Many families secretly work with private college consultants. Often they don't want word to get out, because they don't want their kids' peers to

hire the same adviser and gain the same strategic advantage.
In some affluent areas, kids boast about which consultant their parents
have hired, as if it's a status symbol. What do these consultants do? Typically, at the first meeting, the consultant or counselor will probably require your child to prepare a résumé and will interview your child in
person for about two hours to get a sense of her experiences, accomplishments, and interests. From there, a good consultant should be able
to recommend a short list of colleges (including reaches, 50-50s, and
safeties) and topics for two essays that provide two completely different
perspectives of your child.

After the consultant leaves, the student writes the essays and, in con-
sultation with the parents, decides on a preliminary list of colleges to
apply to, preferably including one Early Decision college (since the
odds of admission are much better if a student applies early). The first
drafts are then sent to the consultant by e-mail or fax by the student or
parent for editing suggestions.

A good consultant should be a good editor with a strong understanding of strategy. (The latter is vital yet usually underplayed, since
colleges and high schools are often still uncomfortable with the idea
that getting into the most-competitive colleges requires strategy.) When
the admissions committee is reading thousands of essays, they will not
have patience for poorly structured essays. At the same time, if the essays
are well written but not well targeted, the well-qualified applicant is
often rejected. In addition, a good consultant should be willing to devote time to the high school student's application. I have heard of private consultants who charge from $8,000 to $12,000, who state up front
that they are not willing to devote extensive time to any one applicant.
Their fee covers only one in-person meeting, one phone call, and one
revision. If you're seeking help from a consultant, find out in advance
what is included. I have found that most applications need far more attention than that.

If the consultant is good, the student should be able to rework the
essay multiple times and send the consultant each new draft, until the
student, parents, and consultant are pleased with the result. Does this

make the essay too sanitized? Does the student's "genuine voice" get lost? If the consultant is good, the student's voice should ring through more clearly after the essay has been edited.

Although consultants are expensive (some have been known to charge from $1,200 to $35,000), this option is becoming increasingly popular as parents contemplate spending $160,000 or so in tuition. Their rationale? At least their kids are gaining access to their choice colleges. Parents who feel uncomfortable supervising their sixteen- or seventeen-year-old in the application process, or who feel that the college essay process is too mysterious and esoteric to interpret, may prefer relegating the responsibility to an outsider.

Secret 173 | **Note that the most expensive consultants are not necessarily the best consultants.**

When hiring a consultant, try to get a sense of the person's track record. While no public records are available, word of mouth through friends whose youngest kid is already in college is probably most effective and reliable. No private consultant can guarantee that your child will gain admission to a particular college, but the very best consultants should at least offer creative strategies, a talent for editing, an ability to work with teenagers, and a knowledge of educational opportunities available to help make your kid a more appealing candidate. Consultants should have a good awareness of internships and jobs and other challenging experiences that improve the credentials of high school students.

Most consultants meet with their students for the first time at the end of junior year or the beginning of senior year. The best ones then are in constant touch with the parents and the student to answer questions throughout the college application process.

For students unable to hire a good consultant, I would recommend taking advantage of other available resources. Students should show their drafts of essays to teachers or guidance counselors who are willing to give feedback. But beware: Teachers who don't believe that strategy is necessary for college applications probably won't be expert at giving strategic advice. For that, the student may prefer a savvy guidance counselor or family members.

Parental Paranoia:
What If the College Asks Who Helped with
the Application?

A taboo just a few years ago, it's now okay for a kid to admit he or she received help on the application. A few years ago, the question of who helped the applicant in the application process appeared on a few college applications and occasionally came up at interviews, making parents squirm. What should you tell your kid to say? "Is it okay to reveal the fact that I helped fix a spelling error?" "Is it okay to tell them I hired a consultant?" "Is there a wrong answer?"

If asked, it's now okay for students to admit they were assisted. Students should emphasize, however, that they wrote their own essays, and that the essay represents the student's "genuine voice." And this statement should be truthful—even the best advisers should make sure that the student write his or her own essays.

Duke University, one of the colleges historically known for posing the question on its application, no longer includes it, according to Admissions Officer Randy Hackley. The college eliminated the question in 2005. "We want people to be part of the process," Hackley said. "We advise students to get help to fix grammatical errors." He says it's okay for an applicant to ask someone else "Does it sound like me?" to ensure that the student's "genuine voice" is coming through.

While colleges expect students to write their own application essays, they respect students who are resourceful enough to seek help with editing, spelling, and overall content.

Secret 174 Contrary to what many high school English teachers, guidance counselors, and writers of books on college admissions will argue, what's most important about the application essay is *not* how well you write, but, rather, *what* you write. At the most-competitive institutions, it's assumed that the vast majority of applicants write well, and writing well is a bare minimum. The student's writing ability is already measured in the ACT or SAT, which test writing skills, so admissions officers, reading college applications, are freed to focus on content.

Students' writing is also measured by grades in four years of high school English.

What's little known and more important is *what* the student writes, and what is revealed about him- or herself in the essay. Sometimes students are mistakenly advised to submit "an essay sample"—an essay they've written for an English class, based on a book they've read for school. They naively think that that will fulfill the application's essay requirement. Such essays tend to be formal, stiff, and anything but personal, as is appropriate for that assignment, but not for an essay that should paint an individual and evocative portrait of an applicant. Students have argued, "But my English teacher said this is one of the best essays she has ever read." The English teacher may be correct, but that does not make the essay appropriate for an application—unless the application specifically asks for "a writing sample" (beyond the suggested application essays).

An exception is for Hampshire College's application, which, in place of SATs, specifically asks for a copy of an "analytical essay"—the type written for school—to make sure that the student can express him- or herself in essay form.

Stock Answers

 **When trying to determine a great essay topic, first imagine the "stock answers" the college will receive from other students.** Stay away from those ideas. Procedures differ markedly at different institutions. At one prestigious university, for example, admissions committee members are told to read about one hundred applications independently over a three-hour period. Everyone on the committee reads the same essays, so each essay does indeed get multiple readings. At the end of reading session, the members come together to discuss "What do you remember of the one hundred applicants?" Perfectly qualified applicants who sound too similar to others are regularly denied admission—not that anything is *wrong* with them and not that they are even *less qualified*. It's just that

nobody can recall them when it's time to discuss which candidates are most memorable. In many cases, less qualified applicants, who make bigger impressions (because they were funnier, more intimidating, more shocking, or sadder), are offered admission. At such institutions, the applicant wants to avoid the "stock" answer to the essay questions.

A dental school admissions officers tell how applicants most frequently write about how they love to see "a happy smile." And medical school admissions officers complain that essays from their applicant pool generally focus on how some relative suffered some severe condition or died—everyone has relatives who died of something or other—and how that motivated the student to go to medical school to find a cure. As noble as this cause may sound to novice applicants (which most are), such essays sound repetitious and even phony after an admissions officer reads essay after essay in this genre. Law school admissions officers talk about *Inherit the Wind*, *L.A. Law*, *To Kill a Mockingbird*, and other popular law novels and TV shows being included in essays. Avoid these hackneyed topics. Some colleges report that every student writes about the same famous person who attended their school. "I am applying to Prestige U because so-and-so, who once was the President of the United States, attended, and I want to follow in his footsteps." Such essays become forgettable in a pool of similarity.

Many of my students applying to Wellesley have suggested that they write their essays on alumnae Madame Chiang Kai-shek, Hillary Clinton, or Madeleine Albright. I recommend, instead, that the applicants focus on their own stories, although Wellesley claims not to be deluged with essays on these three women. In contrast, at Whittier College, described in *U.S. News & World Report* as a "third tier" college in California, a member of the admissions office staff says she sees only two or three essays per year mentioning Richard Nixon—none wanting to emulate the former president. And while the College of William and Mary gets relatively few essays about Thomas Jefferson, who was among the college's most famous students, it's not uncommon to see allusions to Jefferson on applications for the University of Virginia, which he founded. Once you anticipate the stock essays, it's easier to know what *not* to write.

Make the Essay Memorable

Secret 176

In attempting to write something memorable, your child should not write anything "outlandish." Although you may presume, for example, that sex topics attract attention, essays on sex and sexuality should be avoided. While it's possible that a sex essay might titillate one admissions officer, the risk of offending the others is quite high. Other examples of outlandish topics: A student wrote about how he hears voices that direct him on his "good days." Another wrote about how she wanted to torture her cat. And yet another boasted about how he bullied another boy. Surely your kid can create a memorable impression in other ways.

Secret 177

While an essay should be bold, it should also be tasteful. The best-remembered essays are those that move us emotionally or strike a familiar chord.

For fun, imagine yourself on an admissions committee. You're asked to review essays by the following twenty students. Read the list to see if anyone stands out. Do this with your stressed-out senior, if you like.

1. John starred in the school play and enjoys Broadway shows.
2. Jessica volunteers at a local nursing home.
3. Jennifer plays cello in the high school orchestra, having taken lessons since kindergarten.
4. Samantha was vice president of the student government.
5. Justin designs Web pages for local business and likes skateboarding.
6. Jeremy published a poem in the high school literary magazine.
7. Jason entered research into a local science fair and won fifth place.
8. Eva created a school dance club, after studying ballet for three years.

9. Greg led the school's annual canned food drive for the home-less.
10. Laura modeled jeans for a local mall and enjoys shopping.
11. Jeff was captain of the bowling team and enjoys video games.
12. Amanda went to Europe to see the Olympics, and she babysits.
13. Allison went on a family vacation to Cancún and Ixtapa, Mexico.
14. Max played varsity baseball two years—two different positions.
15. Stephanie knits sweaters that she sells to help pay her expenses.
16. Jan won an accounting prize from the school Business Department.
17. Nicole was born in Qatar and moved to the United States in sixth grade.
18. Michael likes hiking and camping and is an Eagle Scout.
19. Danny leads a religious youth group's recreation hour.
20. Craig is active in Students Against Drunk Driving.

Without looking back at the list, recommend three that you remember, and explain how those three candidates will enhance the university environment. That would represent 15 percent of the twenty applicants. If you want to make a slightly more responsible choice, you may look back at the list after you've selected your three students—just to edit your choices. Upon looking back, which student did you leave out that you would prefer to admit?

Is there a right answer? No. The point is that most applicants, regardless of their excellent activities, are still not memorable. To make a decision, you would probably have to read through the list a few times and still not feel confident that you had made the *right* decision. If I were to pick my top three, I'd first choose Stephanie, who sounds both creative and responsible; Eva for her initiative in creating a new club in school; and either Justin, for being entrepreneurial, or Max, if the coach thinks we could use him on our baseball team. I'm sure you would have your own choices.

You get the picture. After reading one hundred applications and essays, nothing at all may stand out when you're asked what you remember. So you've eliminated half or more—just by purely forgetting.

Perhaps after reading one hundred full applications, four prospective college students come to mind immediately. Their applications were clean, demonstrated the student's strong familiarity with the college and strong desire to attend, and their essays were extremely memorable. One, by a shy kid who was terrified by public speaking had you in tears laughing, as she described how in the middle of her presentation at a televised fundraiser, the teleprompter died. Take that kid. One about an overseas family vacation that turned out to be the epicenter of a major earthquake frightened you so much that you worried you wouldn't sleep that night. Take that kid. One, about a student's personal hurricane-relief campaign, almost made you cry. Take that kid. And one moved you because you felt that the writer was an exemplary human being (a young Mother Teresa)—who was loved and helpful to everyone in a horrible crisis. Every campus needs more of those. Take that kid. Now the committee is left with seven other spaces to fill. The campus orchestra can use a kid that plays the bass well enough to have performed with the state's high school orchestra—take that musician. The girl who created a new local soup kitchen would be a positive addition. Take the EMT kid who described how he saved five lives. The Latin scholar who led a tour of Italy could really benefit from our undersubscribed Classics Department—take her. We have to admit the boy who worked full-time outside of school because of financial need and still managed to get high A's in every subject including AP Physics—very impressive work ethic.

Note that college admissions committees operate very differently. It's impossible to recreate discussions, which vary within every university from day to day.

Secret 178	The important picture to keep in mind is that admissions officers read hundreds of

applications, and sameness is detrimental.

No doubt some English teacher or guidance officer will tell your child that no two people write alike, and not to worry if other kids write about the identical topic—because surely your kid's personality will come shining through. But when you sit on an admissions committee and see many essays about the same topic, no matter how creative the writer, the topic gets stale quickly and the essay has minimal chance of becoming favorably memorable.

An admissions committee member of a prominent journalism program reported reading essay after essay with the same response to a question about where the applicants get their news. Applicant after applicant listed the *New York Times*, the *Washington Post*, the *Wall Street Journal*, all-news radio, public radio, *Nightline*, CNN, and public TV. Although this would seem right at first for journalism applicants, what was odd was that most of the applicants claimed to absorb all of this news on a daily basis—while they were still full-time students. In addition, most claimed to read thoroughly what they perceived to be the most prestigious magazines, including *Scientific American*, *Forbes*, the *New Yorker*, and the *Atlantic Monthly*. Such reading would have taken up their day every day, and they would not have had time to attend school. In a pool of one hundred applicants, the first student admitted was one who discussed his love of cartoons and how he gained a lot of his news information from political cartoons and other less obvious sources.

This doesn't have to mean that a student must go to extremes to find an original topic. A parent sent her daughter to skydiving school so that the girl, who had an otherwise commendable but conventional upbringing, could write about something different. There was nothing wrong with skydiving. But the girl was not particularly interested in joining the circus or air force or pursuing skydiving beyond high school. The colleges to which she was applying did not have any skydiving teams or related extracurricular activities. Unfortunately, the essay got lost in the shuffle with kids who wrote about rock climbing, tightrope walking, and magic lessons. Apparently, few schools needed skydivers to round out their rosters, and the girl, who had a stellar academic record and standardized test scores to match, was rejected from her top choices.

The message here is that if you're looking to make your kid appear more interesting, go with skills or adventures that are useful to colleges—not just exotic. She probably could have turned the essay around by discussing some of the lessons that skydiving taught her about academics or engineering. Or she could have discussed being female in a male-dominated sport, or what skydiving taught her about geology or meteorology, if those were her interests. Before spending money to make your kid exotic, be aware that costly pursuits are not inherently appealing to colleges.

Explaining Relevancy and Context

Secret 179   **Make sure your child is obvious about how his or her talents relate to the college in the essay. Tell your kid to *show* the college how his or her "passion" can somehow benefit the college.** Never assume that a college understands how a student's interests in activities relate to the college. Colleges often look at their admissions process selfishly. They try to determine who among the applicants would enhance their particular college environment. Does the fencing team need a sabre champion? Does the college have an opera company in need of a contralto? If your child is taking lessons in Indian vegetarian cooking and this is part of an essay, have your kid add a sentence to explain how this benefits the college. If your child has no clue as to how this would benefit the college, brainstorm with him or her and study the information that the college provides on the Internet. When researching the college online, check out the college "Activities" listing. Does the college have a Vegetarian Club? Does the college have any ethnic social organizations that are likely to require vegetarian cooking? Does the college offer a Culinary Arts major? Does the student plan to get a job working in the campus kitchen? If your child tutors neighborhood kids, adopts stray animals, or teaches religious school, explain how these community-service activities could potentially benefit the college.

The Kind of Essays Admissions Officers Hate

There's no right essay that works for every student, but there are plenty of wrong essays. Here are some of the types of essays to avoid.

Luxury Tour Essay

Secret 180

Avoid writing an essay about a luxury tour. A college admissions officer from a most-competitive college, speaking in an affluent community to an audience of prospective applicants, warned rather flippantly, "Don't tell me about your fancy vacations, because I can't afford to take one." He laughed and said he gets jealous and rejects anyone with a "fancy vacation essay." Although he spoke tongue-in-cheek, a lot can be learned from his statement.

Vacations can provide good grist for well-written essays, but instead of writing about a "lap of luxury" glamorous vacation, the student's essay should wreak of good values and captivating experiences (none of which should be preplanned by tour guides or itinerary designers). The essay should prove that the student is gaining something from the experience besides R&R and an album worth of photos. College admissions officers do not give you points for each sight that you "tag." If you must write about a planned tour, consider some of the following that could potentially lend themselves to essays that may impress some college admissions officers:

- Studying impressionists on an art history tour of France, or studying art or architecture in another country—particularly studies that result in the traveler being inspired to successfully complete new art
- Studying Roman history and classics on a tour of Italy
- Participating in a dig as part of an archeological tour of Israel

- Helping to build a day care center on an Indian reservation
- Immersing oneself in language where that language is spoken
- Studying Shakespeare in England
- Traveling abroad with an athletic or academic Olympic team
- Traveling as part of a natural-disaster relief effort
- Taking part in actual research or a research conference abroad (presenting your own work or assisting in some other way)
- Taking part in a scientific expedition

Tell your child in writing up travels, to specify what his role was on the trip or expedition. What did he contribute? What did she learn and how did the experience change her life and the quality of life for others? Provide anecdotes of personal interactions and unexpected experiences. Do not let your son just restate the itinerary as if he were not on the trip but just reading from a brochure. What did she see that wasn't expected? How was he treated?

Itinerary Essays

Secret 181   **Never let your kid write the "itinerary essay," which can be roughly defined as a descriptive listing of sights the student visited.** Regardless of how exotic the trip was or how much money the parents spent to send their kid there, such an essay reveals nothing compelling or even interesting about a student.

Sample sentence from an itinerary essay: "First we went to the Great Wall, a boundary rich in Chinese history, and then we flew from China to Japan to see Mount Fuji, one of the world's most breathtaking geological wonders."

And don't get fooled into thinking that such an essay can be remedied by inserting one-liners explaining what he or she learned from the experience. (For example: "I never knew that the Great Wall was so vast and imposing and that Mount Fuji was so cloudy.") Such one-liners tend to make the student look shallow and unable to contribute insight.

A much stronger essay would detail an unusual personal ascent of Mount Fuji or the problems entailed in maintaining the condition of the Great Wall and how that affected a student's visit to the historic sight.

Luxury Resort Essays

Secret 182 **Avoid writing about luxury resorts, unless your kid takes a job there or something extraordinary occurs.** A student applying to a series of Ivy League schools wrote about her family visit to a Club Med during which, she said, she became interested in French culture and French cuisine. The topic had potential—despite the fact that the trip was a luxury vacation—but in order to make it work, the story had to have a powerful, redeeming punch line—like as a result of the vacation she became fluent in French (with SAT II scores or AP French to prove it), or she attended a French culinary institute and earned a certificate to work as a pastry chef. Instead, she talked about how luxurious the vacation was and how that inspired her in the fall to take French lessons at school, for which she never demonstrated outstanding proficiency. (In fact, her SAT II scores revealed that her French-language skills were relatively weak.) College admissions officers hate this kind of essay, which only says, "I'm privileged" and shows no insight, character, energy, or inspiration. It shows no resolve to pursue studies seriously or help the community.

The Travel Wish List Essay

Secret 183 **If your kid writes about an around-the-world dream vacation, double-check the sampling of countries listed. Make sure all continents are represented, and that no offensive biases are included.** Sometimes the essay asks, "If you could spend a year pursuing any activity without worry of finances or imposing on your academic career, what would you do?" There is nothing inherently wrong with describing a round-the-world trip, but the student must be very careful about what he or she includes and excludes.

A Chinese American student who claimed to be very interested in her heritage, for example, excluded China from her round-the-world itinerary in her wish-list essay. It became obvious to the reader that she wasn't really as interested in her heritage as she claimed to be. One student's round-the-world itinerary included countries on every continent except Africa. She kept emphasizing that she wanted to see "the entire world," yet she did not mention a single African nation that piqued her curiosity. It shouldn't take an African American admissions officer to notice the applicant's exclusion of an entire continent. Is it prejudice? Perhaps not. Does one have to be interested in every culture? No. But Africa embraces hundreds of cultures, and one should not refer to the world generally and leave out Africa.

A boy wrote about his desire to visit China—where his family was from. He said he wanted to visit the Great Wall—"which is big and impressive." He wanted to see the Terra-cotta Warriors—"which must be very interesting." He planned to shop in Beijing—where he intended to "spend a lot of money," and Shanghai, where his family came from. He didn't tell the reader much about China, nor did he reveal much about himself.

Don't let the wish list sound like a laundry list. Your kid should be able to describe something intriguing about any country she mentions. She should say *why* she wants to visit the place. The explanation should be realistic and grounded in research, not based on popular uninformed bias.

Sample bad reasons

- I want to see how unsophisticated people live and witness their primitive ways.
- The culture is far more sophisticated than ours, and I want to experience it firsthand.

- I want to see sight A, sight B, and sight C, which I've always heard about.
- Everyone else I know has been to that country and has seen that sight.

Sample good reasons

- I've read about a particular archeological site/museum/attraction that I want to visit because I have a theory that [Fill in the Blank].
- I've been studying the language and want to practice through language immersion.
- I've read about some aspect of the culture (or it's my own ethnic culture), and I'm curious to explore it firsthand.
- The geological or biological landscape is unusual, and I'm curious to see it. I've read about these formations in my geology class.
- I have always enjoyed the literature/food/products of this country and would like to experience additional attributes of it.

Some of the rules are common sense. When two or more countries are involved in a current major political or military conflict—particularly with the United States—it is not wise for your kid to take sides in a round-the-world leisure-travel essay. She should not say she's eager to visit Libya or North Korea. Avoid countries where Americans have been known to be kidnapped or terrorized—no matter how intriguing or exotic the culture. Your child should not appear to be foolish, impetuous, or looking for trouble.

The Adversity Essay

 **The secret to writing an answer to the Common Application question about how your kid has dealt with obstacles or risks is not to have your**

child write about obstacles that have not been overcome—or obstacles that have not been fully overcome. Such an essay merely sells the admissions officers on why they should *not* take your kid.

A student from Florida who was applying to tech schools wrote an essay about how his adversity was a summer job that he hated as a bathroom cleaner at a luxury resort. When he accepted the position originally, he had thought that the job would allow him lots of time to use the resort's recreational facilities. Instead, he found that the cleaning process took hours longer than he had expected each day. He was slower than the other cleaning staff, probably due to daydreaming, which he used to escape the unpleasant task. He also was not permitted to use many of the resort's facilities as a member of the staff—a rule that had been concealed from him when he agreed to the job. And among the workers—cooks, chefs, waiters, dishwashers, chambermaids, concierges, bellhops, and the kitchen staff—he was paid the least and had the lowest status in the pecking order. He was very unhappy and chose to write his college essay about this situation.

The essay was badly received. Because he was applying to tech schools, he should have written about how he invented (or fantasized about inventing) some new device that would minimize the time humans spend cleaning bathrooms, or maybe how he negotiated better work conditions for his fellow employees. Instead his essay focused on how once he made a commitment for the entire summer, he felt obligated to honor it. His parents felt the essay demonstrated strong character. They, in fact, were the ones who had encouraged him to stay on the job. He was certain that this essay would appeal to the tech school, since, he said, anyone else would have quit. But it didn't. Instead it showed that he was overly passive in his adverse environment. He was rejected.

A boy who spoke only English focused on his family's sudden move from the United States back to China, and then his family's ultimate decision to relocate back to the States. Within the essay, he described his experience attending school without any communication ability in Chinese, ultimate success and mastery of his Chinese coursework, and his struggle to succeed in an American public high school having missed American middle school. The essay was very moving. It discussed the hardship of showing up in a Chinese classroom, unable to understand what the teacher was saying, being scrutinized by peers who seemed stand-offish, and not understanding the Chinese customs or procedures. But more important, the essay discussed how the boy figured out what was expected of him and how hard he worked to make friends, surpass the other students in his studies, and benefit from his experience in a very rigid, regimented, crowded Chinese school. The "adversity" essay worked well with his application. He was accepted into a few of his top-choice schools.

One girl from Ohio who hated her father's Polish accent wrote about her supposed ethnic adversity. She detailed some of the family's customs that annoyed her, and a reader got the impression that she could have bad-mouthed the family for pages. At the end of the essay, she told the reader that because a friend found her father's accent to be "cute," she came to grips with her foreign heritage and now even enjoys some Polish food. The turnaround did not sound convincing.

What's wrong with this essay? The girl never shows that she has really *overcome* the supposed adversity, nor does the so-called adversity seem adverse in the first place. Every applicant has an ethnic heritage. In other words, everyone comes from somewhere. If the admissions officer who reads the essay has Polish ancestors, he or she might be offended.

Writing about one's heritage can be very successful in a college essay if the topic is handled properly. The essays should be success stories. Enjoying some Polish food is not overcoming a prejudice against Polish culture.

| Secret 185 | **When an essay asks an applicant to describe any "setbacks, risks, or obstacles overcome," unless your kid has suffered some major personal or family illness, trauma, or natural disaster, tell your kid to focus on intellectual risks.** |

Here are more tips for the adversity essay:

- **Most important—this can't be emphasized enough— do not discuss obstacles that have not been overcome. No college wants a loser.**

- Describe how the obstacle was overcome. That should be the focus of the essay. Such discussion is more important than the hardship endured.

- The essay should not discuss stories about which the applicant feels no connection or no passion. (Parents commonly try to convince their kids to write about the parents' hardships or even compelling stories about grandparents' hardships. Usually, the kids are unfamiliar with these stories—they've been sheltered from them, up until college application time—so the parents start by sharing these stories with the kid for the first time while the kid is filling out the college application. This makes for a weak essay, since the kids are not writing about their own experience and do not feel passionately about the story.)

- The essay should not to be used to whine about the family's dirty laundry or grievances. It's okay to mention family problems, as long as the emphasis is on how the applicant resolved the problems or improved the situation.

- Any essay that deals with obstacles should have a positive outcome—something the child learned from the experience, a moral, or a redeeming factor. By the end of the essay, the applicant should have grown in some way (wiser, emotionally stronger, physically stronger, more sympathetic toward others, better at handling emergencies, etc.). The admissions officer should feel good after reading it.

- The adversity essay should reveal only positive values.

- If the applicant discusses a relative's adverse situation, that relative's situation must be directly tied in to the applicant's situation. How did the relative's adversity directly impact or pose an obstacle to the applicant? Don't let your child retell some relative's story—even the most captivating story—if it had no impact on or immediate relevance to the child.

- The essay should not "bad-mouth" people or be hateful or negative about anyone. This may be the hardest part for some applicants. Instruct your child to try to be fair in portraying all people, even those who seem to cause the adversity described in the essay. Your child should not belittle siblings, parents, elders, the school's "most popular kid," teachers, the principal, or anyone.

- Your child should not come across as a complainer or whiner.

- Make sure that your child's adversity is *really* an adversity. Not having parents who can buy a new car upon your son's sixteenth birthday is not an adversity. Being the only girl on the block who doesn't own a designer handbag is not an adversity. Having a sibling that your daughter doesn't get along with is not an acceptable adversity. Hating one's eye color is not an adversity. Not being allowed to go clubbing or drinking is not an adversity. Not being permitted to get a tattoo or body piercing is not an adversity. Being asked to help with family chores or work part-time is not an adversity. To keep things in perspective, remember that there are people starving in the world, people fighting life-threatening diseases, families struggling to make ends meet, families escaping political tyranny, people with physical disabilities, etc.—those are adversities.

- Make sure that the adversity doesn't suggest a future problem or high-risk candidate. In other words, avoid essays like "What I Learned in Prison," "Who Says My Disease Is Contagious?" "One of These Days I'll Get Even," "Surviving My Criminal Gang Upbringing," "Why I Stopped Pushing Drugs."

- Have your child avoid religious adversity essays.

- Political adversity essays—specifically essays dealing with national politics or views on real world politics—should be avoided. The student doesn't know who is reading the essay and what the reader's views are.

- The essay should not put down ethnic groups or religions in essays—even your own.

What Are Good Risks or Obstacles?

Not all risks and obstacles must be major adversities. Your child can write about auditions, performances, swim tests, team tryouts, a job interview, starting a new internship, speaking at a school assembly or meeting, settling an argument among strangers, enrolling in a difficult college-level course, asking directions in a foreign language, debating for the first time with the Debate Team, getting lost, camping out for the first time, making a new friend, training a new puppy.

The Best College Essays

The "Why Do You Want to Come Here?" Essay

The "Why Do You Want to Come Here?" essay is the student's best chance to give the sales pitch for why the college should take him.

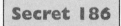 **To best answer the question of why your kid is a good match for the university, have him carefully study the literature about the college and cite specific *academic* programs, courses, professors, activities, opportunities, and/or the philosophy of the university as primary reasons to seek admission.** In addition, an aggressive (very serious) candidate will have visited the campus, sat in on courses, perhaps even met with professors or administrators, and (in extremely rare

cases) worked with a professor or professors as part of an internship. Most serious students will cite sound academic reasons for being drawn to the college.

Remember: The college seeks to admit students who specifically need what only this particular college has to offer. The college would rather that students who don't *need* this college go elsewhere, where their needs can be addressed equally or possibly even better.

A naive or unprepared applicant will cite obvious features of the college or campus: the location, climate, reputation, history. Nobody needs to even leaf through the view book to cite these features. This applicant will not have done any extensive research on the specific opportunities offered by the college—the course requirements, activities, unique facilities, internships available—and that, in turn, is viewed as an indicator of how unmotivated the student may be throughout college. This student will not present a solid case on why she *needs* this particular college. (You can't say, "I need this college because I require a warm climate." College admissions officers will think to themselves, "Apply to any of the other hundreds of colleges in California, Florida, Georgia, Texas, etc., or put on a sweater.")

In this essay, the applicant should not try to *flatter* the college or admissions staff. College admissions people don't need hear that their college is prestigious or that their name would really impress the other kids. They don't need to hear that their campus is pretty. They get hundreds if not thousands of applications reminding them of this, and they're not impressed with shallow applicants who only seek prestige, good weather, aesthetics, or to "fit in."

When mentioning a course of interest, the applicant should cite the course by name, and get the name right. He should not be vague about the department or the course. It's better to cite a bunch of classes that interest him, so it's clear that he won't lose interest after just one class. When mentioning a particular professor or professors with whom your daughter wants to study, mention them by name. Again, it's better to mention more than one professor in case the one professor who most interests your daughter suddenly moves to a different college or announces a sabbatical. Also, she should explain why she wants to work with the professor or professors. Did she read this person's work? If so, she should demonstrate that in the essay and be specific, citing aspects of the professor's work that excited her. Did she attend one of the professor's classes when visiting the campus? She should prove it in the essay by discussing what impressed her most in the class on the day that she attended.

When mentioning facilities of particular interest, your son can cite specific building names or even pieces of equipment—a specific microscope in the nanotechnology lab, a telescope in the campus observatory, a cutting-edge exercise machine in the Sports Management Department, state-of-the-art computers in the Computer Animation Department— with which he was impressed. He could cite conferences that are held on campus or that are run by the college—academic conferences that he aspires to take part in or volunteer for. Does the campus hold an annual Classics Conference, for example? Does your daughter envision herself judging the annual toga competition or establishing Latin poetry readings? Does the university sponsor a Model UN or Model Congress that your son would like to help orchestrate as a continuation of his high school activities? (Your child should not claim to want to *continue* these activities in college if he or she hasn't participated in related activities in high school. Also, this is not the time to express an interest in starting an activity that has been offered at your kid's high school but that your kid hasn't shown an interest in during high school. That looks phony. Your child may, however, express an interest in joining an organization or conference to which he or she has had no access at high school.)

When mentioning an activity or club of interest, have your child cite the name of the club or program specifically. Don't have him just write, "I'd like to sing in the chorus." Instead he should write that he aspires to sing with the Prestige U Concert Choir, the Prestige U Traveling Glee Club, or the Prestige U A Cappella Singers, and this should include an explanation of what is so appealing about the particular group—check out their repertoire on the Internet, for example, their travel schedule, or whom they tend to perform for or with. Did your son attend one of their performances? Did your daughter sing successfully in a similar group in high school? Is there something that differentiates the group from similar choruses at comparable colleges? All of that should be discussed in the essay. The more specific the citation, the more the applicant demonstrates interest in the particular college and the more compelling the candidate becomes.

In addition, your kid should imagine his or her role within a specific activity. The essay should not just state, "I'd like to work for the Prestige U newspaper." More effectively it could state, "I envision myself as one of the film critics for the *Prestige U Weekly News* and would like to someday introduce a column devoted to sci-fi films." Or "I would like to become a sports writer for the *Prestige U Gazette* and feel that Prestige U, which participates in more archery and fencing competitions than any other college in the region, would give me an opportunity to gain experience covering these underrepresented sports, which I participated in in high school as a varsity archer and fencer."

Helping your child to find a niche or angle can be very helpful. In doing your research, find out what the college *does not* already have and *might like to add*. For example, if you're able to make conversation with a total stranger, you might phone a college band director to ask if the band is badly in need of a French horn player this year (if that's what your kid plays). Or you might call the Classics Department to ask if there's any particular type of student that they're seeking (a student who can speak Ancient Greek and is interested in conducting research in that department, for example, or a student who has written a play in Latin). When making such a phone query, introduce yourself first as a parent who is seeking to find the right match for your child. Start by asking general questions about the department or program. Gradually work your way into a discussion of the department's needs and what your child could contribute. Before making the call, make sure you know your kid's average, SAT scores, and all other vital credentials—to be prepared in case you're asked. I have known of situations where parents were able to talk their kid's way into the school on the spot, based on a phone conversation.

On the application, discourage your kid from writing about some niche that another student already fills. Also have your kid avoid sounding too drastic: "If accepted, I would like to introduce an Engineering Department, since the college only offers art." Obviously, that kind of radical proposal merely demonstrates that the kid is not suited to the college.

Below are sample sentences that show good reasons and bad reasons in response to the question about why your child wants to attend the particular college. Before your son or daughter begins this essay, review some of the reasons that he or she might want to attend the university. You might help make a list of reasons and review the essay after it's written, but make sure your child writes the essay.

Sample Good Reasons

- I have read all of Professor John Green's works on the role of the color orange in curing psychological disorders and want to study Psychology with him.

- I have worked with Professor Susan Gray in Computer Engineering and would like the opportunity to continue this research with her while I pursue my undergraduate courses in Military Science in your outstanding department.

- I want to pursue studies in Nordic Mythology and Vacuum Engineering and your college is the only school in the Midwest that offers that combined major.

- The university's unique philosophy on grading is identical to my own educational philosophy, and, having studied Russian in high school, I know I would have enormous academic success as a Russian Literature major.

- I want to participate in the Baltic International Trade Co-Op Program that only your college offers.

- I spent a summer taking intensive college courses on Veterinary Medicine at your college and realized that studying to be a vet there, along with courses in Biology at your island research facility, for four years would represent a dream come true.

- I am very impressed with your college's hands-on approach to teaching Physics and want the opportunity to study String Theory with Professor Steven Marks.

- I prefer your college's encouragement of student-faculty collaboration on food-business ventures, proximity to the city's business center, and the array of management internships offered with major food-related companies.
- I know that the opportunities will be far greater for me to pursue leadership at a women's college, and your college offers more opportunities in Archaeology and Anthropology, the two fields that interest me most.
- I am impressed with the oceanfront-research facilities that will allow me to pursue work in Ocean Engineering, and at the same time you offer enough Music Theory classes to help me further my talent for composition.
- I want to study cutting-edge Astronomy at a school with an observatory in a location where I can actually see the sky at night. But at the same time, I want a college that is affiliated with a conservatory that gives celesta lessons.
- I want to study Art History in proximity to some of the nation's top museums, but at the same time, I want small, intimate Studio Art classes.
- During my two-day stay, I found myself actively engaged in a series of eye-opening discussions with students in the cafeteria. After sitting in on a philosophy class with Professor Brown and after listening to a lecture on political theory by Professor Johnson, I crave the opportunity to continue learning in such a stimulating environment.

Sample Bad Reasons

- You have a good reputation and the university is very prestigious.
- I like the campus; it's pretty and located just where I want to live.
- I fit in well with the other kids at your college.
- I can handle the work.
- Two of my friends attend your college, and we're hoping to get an apartment together.
- Your school has lots of school spirit, and I enjoy spectator sports.

- This is the most prestigious university I could get into. I would love to put a decal on my car.
- My parents want me to go to this college. They say it's right for me.
- I'm most familiar with the campus, since I live just down the road.
- I like your junior year abroad options. I want to visit other countries.
- Nobody from my high school goes to your college, and I want to get away from everyone from my high school.
- Your business program has an excellent reputation, and even though I've never done business so far, my parents say I'd be very good at business.
- Your drama program has an excellent reputation, and I want to be a star.
- I want famous teachers. Your professors have good reputations.
- I like the climate and want to attend school in this region.
- The kids who come here are very smart, and I think it would be good for me to surround myself with smart people. That would bring my level up.
- I was bored in high school, but learning here looks like fun.
- Your school is located in Boston, which has good architecture and a lot of other college students. So I think it would be fun.
- My parents always talk about the great parties from when they went there.

Unpublicized Honors

Students have complained about arriving on campus and finding out that their roommates are some special kind of scholar—not just an ordinary student—and as such are getting special invitations to exclusive lectures and meetings, dinner with the university president, etc. **When your child writes the why-this-college essay, look for special programs online and make sure she refers to any that interest her** in the essay. For example, University of Pennsylvania has Benjamin Franklin Scholars and Joseph Wharton Scholars. Columbia has John Jay Scholars; Yale has a Directed Study Program. (*There are no other applications to these programs.* Most are not prominently featured, so it will take some hunting.) The student is notified of being accepted into these not-so-publicized programs at the same time he is accepted into the college. (For Penn, students who are not chosen may *apply* during the second semester of freshman year.)

The Make-Your-Mark Essay

Secret 187 **Students should show hard-to-reach aspirations, but at the same time, be able to demonstrate a deliberate track record to prove that these goals are not just pipe dreams.** What are your child's aspirations? That's the crux of the question in the make-your-mark essay. The challenge appears in many forms: "How do you want to be remembered a few years after you graduate?" "What would you like to be doing fifteen years after graduating?" "If you were to write your autobiography, what would page 250 contain?"

Encourage your child to brainstorm on career options and plans to save the world. It is okay to wish for an ambitious, even grandiose, career. If one doesn't show major aspirations, chances are he or she will not achieve lofty goals. This essay should be upbeat, ambitious, optimistic, and energetic, projecting a strong self-image and good values.

Avoid the humble, pessimistic, defeatist, failure essay—the one that says, "I'll never amount to anything." Candidates who write humble essays may think they're being perceived as polite or modest—the "right" kind of person—but when an admissions counselor has to sort through hundreds of essays, modest students tend to look like dead wood at a time in life when a young person should be bursting with energy, enthusiasm, and aspiration. Understandably, colleges want to admit students who are eager to achieve, pioneer, innovate, and improve the world.

Example of a Bad Essay

A student, thinking he was entertaining the admissions staff and hoping to make his essay memorable, wrote about how he would like to be remembered as the kid who was thoroughly tattooed. He said that years after his graduation, people would refer to him as "the tattooed kid." An admissions officer easily could have interpreted the tongue-in-cheek essay as flippant, immature, or insulting. Another officer could have viewed the essay as a case of rebellion. Was the essay memorable? Probably. But not in a positive sense.

The Right Approach

Where *should* your kid want to be in fifteen years? There is no single right answer, of course. Yes, it's okay for your kid to say that fifteen years after graduation, your kid would like to be accepting a Nobel Prize, Fields Medal, Pulitzer Prize, or an Oscar. Tell your kid to aspire. But at the same time, the student should try to demonstrate in the essay that he or she has already taken preliminary steps to pursue that lofty career. The seeker of the Fields Medal, for example, should be starting to show a track record in mathematics. The Pulitzer Prize winner should be an editor or photographer for the high school newspaper or should be writing plays.

The "Most Meaningful Activity" Essay

| Secret 188 | Consistency is what is most essential in the "Most Meaningful Activity" Essay. |

Make sure your kid's essay supports other statements made on the application. Elsewhere on the application, the student will be asked to list the most important activities in priority order. So this essay, theoretically, should be about item number one from that list.

If your daughter wants to write about something else, she needs to explain: "While competitive diving is the most important activity in my repertoire, I've described that activity amply in another essay, and would rather focus this one on another vital activity that I devote hours to—volunteering at the local hospital." Or "While competitive diving is the most important activity to me, I also spend considerable time entertaining children at the nearby hospital." In other words, she should acknowledge that she is aware of the list of prioritized activities on a previous page of the application and explain why the essay is about something else.

Secret 189	**Make sure that your kid's "most important activity" is something that he is suc-**

cessful at. So many kids foolishly write about an activity that they think will look good and that they are not particularly adept at. It looks bad when a student says that a particular activity is important, but the student has not taken the time to master it. How will the student do in college if he doesn't even excel at his "most important activity"? Also, make sure that the "most important activity" is something that's offered at the college to which he's applying.

A student applying to a small tech college, for example, initially said that his "most important activity" was playing his violin in an orchestra, thinking that that would impress the admissions office. I said to him, "But the college you're applying to doesn't have an orchestra or even a string ensemble. If that's your most important activity, surely you should apply to a place that will not only accommodate your violin playing, but that will appreciate it." Although many other tech schools have orchestras, he really wanted this one. He changed his essay.

Often students are oblivious as to what subjects truly interest them or what subjects the particular college even offers until it's time to write such an essay. Should you suddenly find that your child has a strong interest in something not offered by the college to which he or she is applying, suggest other colleges. The student should not stifle his or her top interest to attend a prestigious college that doesn't accommodate that interest.

A girl who claimed in her application to have the deepest interest in a medical career focused her essay on her love of her high school's Asian Culture Club. She described the club's events with a degree of enthusiasm and detail that dramatically outshadowed any discussion of medicine. The contrast was so significant that the reader was left to think that she had only claimed an interest in medicine to please her parents—or maybe to impress the college.

A boy who worked every day after school at a local drug store used the essay to describe his job, the interactions between customers and sales clerks, and how the job taught him a lot about resolving disputes. He became interested in labor relations through his daily job experience and applied to a labor relations program. The essay strongly supported the information contained in the rest of his application, and he was admitted.

A boy who did an internship in genetics one summer and wanted to package himself as a science student listed his activities in order of importance: trivia team, tennis, piano lessons, debate clubs, and National Honor Society. Finally, at the bottom of his list of activities, he got to a science-related club that entailed minimal time commitment. Any admissions officer reading the essay could see that he had relatively little interest in science—even if the boy, himself, hadn't realized it.

The "Describe a Person, Book, or Event That Influenced You Most" Essay

Secret 190 The secret in the influential person/ book/event essay is for the applicant to focus on *how* he or she was influenced. Don't make this a book report, biography, or schedule list. A well-written essay should provide a sense of your child's values, sophistication, and world awareness. Many students choose to write about their parents, their grandparents, or a relative who lives with them. This should be done with enormous caution. The applicant should make sure that the relative has a genuinely compelling story, but more important, the student must feel that this story is an important part of his or her life. Don't regurgitate an old family story third-hand. Also, although parents might appreciate seeing their kids' gratitude in written form, parents have the tendency to oversupervise (and write) the "parents as most influential" essay.

Two students whose parents immigrated to the United States (one from Europe and one from Korea) wrote essays about how their parents arrived with less than ten dollars (six in one case, eight in the other) in their pockets and a dream to start a new life. In both cases, the parents worked very hard and became successful. Both kids wrote about how their parents' work ethics inspired them, and how they intended to follow their parents' examples. But more important, both described their own experience with poverty—before their parents began making money.

If your child chooses to write about someone famous as "most influential," make sure your child is familiar with that person's story. Often such an essay requires research. And you, as a parent, may want to do some legwork as well to make sure your kid's essay doesn't misrepresent the person. Remember that the admissions officer may be familiar with the famous person's story and could catch any inaccuracies—particularly if the famous person is a graduate of the university to which your child is applying.

Have your kid avoid the "major catastrophe essay" (9/11, Hurricane Katrina, the 2005 tsunami, or a major earthquake), unless your child had a *firsthand* experience with it.

If your child decides to focus on an influential book, you may want to read the book too, to make sure the student truly understands it and is explaining it fairly and accurately with a reasonable interpretation. Book essays can be risky, as readers on the admissions committee might have their own preferred interpretation. Obviously, the essay is safer if the child is writing about a book that was read and discussed in school, but some application essays suggestions specify that books read in school may not be included in the essay. Also, be careful to avoid a traditional book-report style. The essay should detail how the book influenced your child and what changes in thinking or practices your kid has experienced as a result of the book. The essay should not be a summary of the book or a compilation of other people's reviews, interpretations, or thoughts.

Example of a Weak Essay

A student wrote about his grandmother and how she was the most important person in his life. He described fond memories of sitting in her lap as she told him stories. He never revealed the content of those stories, or how he was affected, or how his own behavior changed as a result. Instead, he kept mentioning that she was nice, a good role model, and that she treated his grandfather royally.

Example of a Strong Essay

A student wrote about her grandmother, a woman in her nineties who lives in India and has more than fifty grandchildren, who visited the United States specifically to see the girl receive a national award. Although the girl identified many major U.S. political figures at the awards ceremony, the girl said that the most important member of the audience was her grandmother, who had traveled all the way from India for this occasion, and who, for once, was focused solely on her.

The Humorous Essay

Secret 191 | **If your kid chooses to write a supposedly humorous essay, have an outsider (non–family member, non–guidance counselor) proofread the essay to tell you if it's funny.** What may seem funny to a high school kid during a late-night essay-writing session may not in fact be funny at all—not even to the kid the next day. But parents should also be aware of their own lapses in judgment. What may seem charming to a doting parent may not be at all amusing to an admissions officer who is outside the family loop and who may not understand the family's offbeat sense of humor or inside jokes.

If your son insists on going with humor, make sure it doesn't offend any group—defined by gender, ethnicity, race, religion, sexual orientation, nationality, disability, or economic standing—even if he is applying to a college with a religious or ethnic affiliation, or a single-sex college.

The "Describe Your Ideal Roommate" Essay

 **Secret 192** The "Describe-Your-Ideal-Roommate" Essay is really asking that the applicant describe *him- or herself.* A variation is, "If you could be a character in one of your favorite novels, who would you be and why?" Although pop psychology says "opposites attract," few applicants will seek their supposed opposite as a roommate. Instead, they seek roommates with similar late-night habits, study hours, musical taste, and social schedule. In this essay, the applicant should reveal all his or her better qualities.

Without having to state straightforwardly "I don't do drugs," this essay permits the applicant to describe the ideal roommate as a non-drinker, non-smoker, or non–drug user. Think carefully about what qualities you want to reveal to the admissions officers and note that anything that's conspicuously missing could be suspect. Of course, you can add "lighter" qualities, like wanting a roommate who shares your passion for sushi, or who likes movie posters (so you can coordinate room decor), or who prefers to keep the windows open at night. Is it more impressive to seek a "neat" roommate? No. Is it more impressive to seek a roommate who likes to go to sleep early? No. Is it more impressive to seek a roommate who prefers classical music to current music? No—unless the kid is applying to a conservatory.

Make sure your child does not advocate for or against a roommate of a particular background—racial, ethnic, nationality, etc. Remind your child not to view this essay as an opportunity to share all of his weaknesses. He should not say things like, "I need a very tolerant roommate, because I have a short temper," or "I need a very cheerful roommate, because I tend to get depressed easily."

The Optional Essay

Secret 193 There is nothing optional about the optional essay (except the title). When a

**college application invites a student to submit an optional es-
say, always have your kid write it.** Submitting extra suggests that the
student really wants admission. It's one last opportunity for the applicant to sell him- or herself to the college. Not writing the extra essay
may be interpreted as lack of enthusiasm. One essay is rarely enough to
give a college a full perspective. Two may not provide enough, but it's
twice as much.

Empty Essays

Secret 194

**None of the application essay paragraphs
should be empty. Each should include in-
formation that will help to promote your child.** When outlining
an essay, the student should consider what elements he or she wants to
reveal in each paragraph—not necessarily new credentials in each paragraph, but also qualities that define his or her character or curiosity.

In an essay explaining a kid's achievements, beware of the laundry-
list essay that just consists of a list of achievements; the admissions officers will not feel that they are getting a real sense of who the applicant
is. Only key achievements (three or four, maximum) should be
smoothly woven into the flow of the essay. Before beginning the essay,
prioritize which most-important achievements *must* be present and
warrant further elaboration.

Secret 195

**In writing about achievements, your
child should clearly spell out the significance of each achievement mentioned, so the admissions officer can make no mistake about how impressive each
credential is.** If your child's greatest achievement, for example, is
winning first place in a national art competition, assume that the admissions officer has never heard of that competition—even if it's the
biggest national competition, even if everyone you know has a kid who
has submitted work to it, and even if Rembrandt himself once won
that contest. The people who read your child's application may be far

from the world of art, science, math, humanities, or whatever your child specializes in. In specifying the significance, make sure that the following questions are answered:

- What is the exact name of the achievement?
- How many other competitors participated? Did these competitors have special qualifications? (Had they been preselected from a previous round of winners?)
- Were there multiple rounds? If so, how many participated in the starting round?
- Was your child ranked in any way? Was there a first place? Second place? Gold Medal? Grand Prize?
- If your child was ranked, how many other students earned an equal or better rank? Was your child the only first-place winner out of 100,000 students who applied? Was your child one of only twenty second-place winners out of thousands?
- Did your child win by doing something pioneering, unique, or risky?

Admissions officers claim that parents whose kids are rejected are often clueless as to the strength of the competition pool. But sometimes admissions officers are clueless as to how deserving a particular child is because they have no idea about the significance of the child's achievements, and the student's application doesn't adequately spell out the context.

Take the following math students:

Jerry won third place in the county in the Mandelbrot Competition.
Jessica was one of twelve third-place winners in the one-day County Math Competition.
Jonathan won third place at ARML, at Penn State.
Jenn won third place in the five-round County Math Competition.
Jackie won third place at the County Math (research) Fair.
Justin won third place in the U.S. Math Olympiad.
Jason won third place in his county on the AMC-12 exam.

Jared was named captain of the High School Math Team.

Jill was named captain of the All-County Math Team.

Jacob got a perfect score on the Canadian Math Exam.

If you're not an expert in math education—let's say you're a member of the admissions committee who just graduated last year with a major in Slavic Languages and Culture—you might not know which student has won the most prestigious award. If you could choose only two from the group, you might be clueless—even though these contests are considered "common knowledge" for any math teacher. That's why it's important for your child to explain every award listed—even if it's a Nobel Prize, Pulitzer Prize, Academy Award, or Olympic medal. Do not assume that any awards are common knowledge.

"But don't all admissions officers have to know the most prestigious awards in every field?" you ask. No. They don't. And many student awards change from year to year—new ones pop up that can quickly become very prestigious but that nobody has heard of because the awards are so new.

"Fun Questions"

Secret 196 **There is nothing fun about "fun questions." And fun questions do not reduce stress.** That's the secret I am hearing from stressed-out parents as they struggle to help their kids answer these. Some high-pressured colleges have introduced "fun questions" to make the application process less stressful. If an application asks the applicant what he or she does for fun, don't be fooled into letting your kid let down his or her guard to write something that makes your kid sound lazy, passive, a wannabe, a follower, a partier. Make sure your kid emphasizes *constructive* activities that can be accommodated by the university to which he or she is applying.

I frequently get calls from frantic parents trying to find the "right" answer. In previous applications, Penn has asked, "Tell us what you like to do for fun." MIT asked, "Tell us about something you do simply for the pleasure of it." Harvey Mudd asked, "What fun, cool, or interesting things about you won't fit into the categories on the application? Feel welcome to be clever or funny." Right.

While any parent of an applicant would welcome stress reduction, parents report to me that adding a "fun question" does not do the trick. If anything, these Band-Aid questions bring greater stress to the applicants with whom I have spoken, as they struggle to figure out what fun they should speak of. After all, they observe that everyone they know who has been admitted to these colleges had no time for "fun" in high school, having pulled many all-nighters and faced weekends and vacations filled with homework. In order to be seriously considered for these colleges, one must ace many time-consuming AP or IB courses—some students take five or six per year—which eats up all time for fun.

What's the right answer? I recommend competitive sports "purely for fun"; discretionary reading (science fiction, Russian literature, British humor, etc.); any art form; a non-school-assigned academic pursuit (reading history for fun, conducting science experiments in your basement, writing poetry, keeping a journal as opposed to a diary); practicing a musical instrument; or exploring new musical repertoire. Lean toward *constructive* activities that might be appreciated (and accommodated) by the colleges to which your child is applying. For example, fencing is preferred over trapeze. (Lots of colleges have fencing teams; few have trapeze.) Snow skiing is preferred by a northern college over waterskiing. Waterskiing is preferred by a southern college.

Regardless of what anyone else may tell you and your image of what students at these universities actually *do* for fun, don't let your kid write any of the following: violent computer games, card games, fantasy sports, shuffleboard, low-brow board games, gambling, hanging out, summer camp, teen tours, surfing, skateboarding, face wraps, spa treatments, clubbing, spectator sports, partying, collecting things, watching music TV, shopping, listening to CDs, makeovers, laser tag, darts, scrapbook making, camp crafts, surfing the Web, talking on the phone, eating, dieting, drinking, reading junky romance novels, reading comics.

Why can't your kid, who wants to become a published writer or game designer, for example, admit that she reads romance novels or plays violent computer games for fun, if she already has top SAT scores and top grades? While these may be activities that already-admitted students *actually do* once they get into top colleges—and your daughter might have spent a weekend on campus and saw that all the students play violent computer games all weekend—these still aren't fodder for an application. Every space should be viewed as a potential marketing opportunity. After all, think about how you would select students if you were on a committee reading thousands of responses to the "fun" question. Would you prefer the kid who *wrote* a romance novel and *designed* a bestselling computer game, or the one who entertained him- or herself by reading and playing these?

Once the essays are written (or possibly during the same time period), the next step is for your child to pursue teacher and guidance counselor recommendations. Many teachers and advisers are kind about sharing what they write with the student, but some insist on keeping their recommendations confidential. Parents can be very helpful in making sure that their kids get solid, enthusiastic support from high school faculty members even if teachers are unwilling to let the kids see.

CHAPTER 9

Guaranteeing Excellent Recommendations

A student who was liked very much by her teachers happened to get a glimpse at three recommendations written for her when she was applying to a competitive summer research program. One, by a science teacher, was hand-scribbled, almost illegibly, with positive raves balanced by spelling and grammatical errors throughout. One, by a health teacher, was neat and seemingly well intended, but it didn't present a compelling enough case for the student to get into this summer program that was only accepting one student per state. And the third, by her math teacher, attempted humor with phrases like, "She's not bad for a kid who grew up on the wrong side of the tracks."

The occurrence was obviously an eye-opener for her family. Her parents wondered if well-intending teachers ever inadvertently block a student from gaining admission to a most-competitive college. Is there anything that parents can do to guarantee that the recommendations will be strong enough and helpful?

Secret 197 | **It's possible to prescreen a kid's teacher recommendations, even if the kid has to sign a waiver for college applications.** There are several ways to do this. Just because your daughter signs a waiver saying that she agreed to forfeit the right to see her recommendation does not mean that the teacher *is not allowed* to show her the recommendation. Instead, it means the teacher *doesn't have to* show her the recommendation. But a teacher may elect to show a student a recommendation. The teacher never has to sign a waiver promising that the applicant won't see the recommendation.

Secret 198

Nice teachers who are proud of the recommendations they write make a point of showing the applicant the recommendation before it is submitted—without being asked. Some very nice teachers will even photocopy the recommendation so that the kid (and the family) can keep a record of the recommendation. And some will ask the student if he or she has any corrections or suggestions about anything to add to the recommendations. "Was there anything that you wanted me to focus on particularly for *this* college? Were there any credentials or anecdotes that I neglected to mention?"

Teachers are people who have applied for jobs and college before. They know what it means to be able to see a recommendation. And, of course, you'll get plenty of whiners who will say to you, "Nobody ever let me see *my* recommendations—so I'm not letting you see what I write about you." Or they'll say, "When you trust me to write a recommendation, you have to trust what I write without seeing it. That's what trust is about." They can choose to be nice and open about the process. Or they can choose to be secretive. Secretive often means halfhearted. Don't listen to teachers who say that they're *not allowed* to show the kid the recommendation—*not required* is different from *not allowed*.

If the teacher does not offer to show the recommendation to either the kid or the parents, you should not assume that the letter is necessarily *bad*. But screened letters do tend to come out stronger, since more parties (parents and applicant) get to offer input.

That said, it is not correct etiquette for a student to ask a teacher if he may see the recommendation. The teacher should offer it voluntarily. If not, the student should not ask unless he has a particularly close rapport with the teacher. Once the student has signed the waiver, the teacher is under no obligation to show the student the recommendation. And the student should not risk annoying the teacher—who is supposedly only saying kind words about the student and might have written the recommendation only as a result of the confidentiality agreement. Some teachers actually believe that it's bad for kids to hear good things said about themselves. The argument is, "I don't want this to get to the students' heads." Such teachers argue that if the student sees the recommendation, the teacher won't feel at liberty to really boast about the student—"lest the student see." Some teachers say they want to insert a lot of their "personal" feelings and feel that it would be inappropriate for a student to see these feelings in writing. But, if the teacher is writing a truthful and appropriate recommendation, there should be no harm in letting the student see it.

Other Ways to Prescreen

Secret 199

Long before your kid hits senior year, he or she should apply for internships and programs that require teacher recommendations. Most of these *other* applications will not include a waiver and will therefore let a student (and parent) screen them. Many of these will even require that the applicant submit the recommendation along with his application, so you'll have easy access to the recommendation. Once a teacher has written a recommendation, let's say for an internship sophomore year, in all likelihood, the teacher will at least rely on the "shell" of that letter when composing all future recommendations. Some teachers will continue to use the reference verbatim. Chances are, the initial recommendation will be saved onto the teacher's computer. So the sophomore "preview" letter will be pretty indicative of later letters, unless something in the student's behavior, achievements, or relationship with the teacher changes significantly. Keep a copy of that letter. Keep a file of copies of all recommendations. When college application time comes, you'll be able to compare the recommendations and have a good sense of which teachers would be most supportive.

Secret 200

If your child has no reason for recommendations in sophomore year and arrives at junior year without any references, start finding programs and internships to which she can apply to necessitate some. By senior year, it's late to start "shopping" for recommenders, so junior year is the best time. There are three primary advantages to seeking recommendations as early as possible. First, regardless of recommendations, scouting opportunities and having your kid apply to wonderful programs and internships is a task that you should be doing anyhow. But second, having your kid apply for different opportunities will give you a chance to prescreen the recommenders. Seek lots of recommendations from teachers, so you get a wider selection in senior year. And the third reason is that when you ask a teacher to recommend a child, it forces the teacher to *think* about the kid. This often is a very successful way to create some rapport with teachers early in high school, particularly if your kid is relatively quiet or shy.

Who Should Write the Recommendation?

Secret 201

If your child arrives at senior year without having accumulated a file of teacher recommendations, you or your child might ask a school guidance counselor who writes the best recommendations. They often know. Many guidance counselors get to see the teacher recommendations on an ongoing basis and would be able—if they're willing—to offer some advice on which teachers to select.

Aim for teachers of varied subjects. Preferably, your child will find a math or science teacher for one recommendation, a social studies or English teacher for another, and a third from any other academic department or a course that pertains to your kid's college plans. The recommenders should all be teachers of classes in which your child did well—preferably an A—and teachers who, you feel, appreciated your child. Note that teachers are less likely to "glow" about B students—

even in high schools that claim to have no grade inflation and where a "B is considered a good grade."

In choosing a recommending teacher, start your search in September at the latest. (Granted, you won't be able to ask a current teacher that your senior has for the first time in September, because the teacher should know the kid for a longer time. But it's wise to make up your mind early.)

Is a recommendation from a Physics teacher stronger than a recommendation from an English teacher? No. But if you've stated on the application that the kid wants to pursue Physics as a major in college, it might make more sense to have a recommendation from the Physics teacher. Likewise, if the kid wants to pursue American Literature and has stated so on the application, a recommendation from the English teacher might be stronger. Is a Physics teacher recommendation stronger than a Music teacher recommendation? Possibly. Regardless of your philosophy, we live in a society that simplistically believes that scientists are smarter than musicians. But note that if the student is planning to major in Music and has stated so on the application, a Music teacher's recommendation is a must.

More important, make sure the teacher *knows* the kid and can write personal anecdotes—rather than listing kind, bland adjectives. A personal, impassioned recommendation from a Music teacher is much more convincing than an uninspired recommendation from a Physics teacher. Also, make sure the teacher *likes* the kid. Just because the kid gets an A in the class, doesn't mean that the teacher likes him. Ask your kid—most kids know. Some kids will tell you that "every teacher hates me" (many teenagers say that out of low self-esteem). But if your daughter genuinely feels that nobody likes her, September is as good a time as any to try to turn that situation around.

Parents' Role in Recommendations

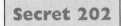 **No matter what other parents or school officials tell you about the importance of**

your kid's independence and parents not meddling in their kids' school careers, wise parents know to create a nice dialogue with their kid's teachers. Make a point of meeting some of your kid's favorites—even if the only time you have access is Open House or Open School Night. Develop rapport. Send a note to school when the teacher does something that impresses you or that is particularly helpful to your kid. Let each teacher know that you are very supportive of his or her curriculum and program. You want the teacher to feel like part of the "team" that is educating your kid, and you want the teacher to know that you, unlike many other parents, are also a team player. Teachers never complain about meddling parents when the meddling is in their favor.

| Secret 203 | **Do not restrict your child's choice of rec-ommenders to teachers from junior** |

year—particularly if your kid was savvy enough to maintain contact with teachers from freshman or sophomore year. Instruct your child to maintain contact with teachers from previous years. This can often be accomplished by participating in after-school activities that are organized, coached, or supervised by these teachers. Make sure your kid does not become a stranger to good teachers at the end of each school year—maintain those contacts. Parents can assist in this process by occasionally sending helpful notes to school: an article that you think that the history teacher might enjoy, or a new opportunity for students that you think the teacher might like to know about.

Sometimes a recommendation is stronger if the teacher is able to say something like, "I have known Amanda for three years now and have seen her mature into one of the most hardworking students in our school." Or "To really appreciate Amanda, one would have to note her development over three years from a very quiet, seemingly shy foreign student who spoke little English into a confident and eloquent leader at our school." Often the school's junior-year teachers are overtapped for recommendations, whereas teachers who typically focus on the younger high school grades are eager to write recommendations for the "right" kids.

How Many Recommendations Per Teacher?

Secret 204	**Don't feel guilty about having your kid request teacher recommendations.** Nowa-

days, most teachers write their recommendations on the computer—which means that most teachers have the basic prose stored on their hard drive. This should make it significantly easier to write each new recommendation as it is requested. At a minimum, the busiest teacher only needs to adapt the name of the college on the stored recommendation. So instead of saying, "I enthusiastically recommend Tara Jones for admission to Duke University," the teacher changes the "Duke University," to "University of Chicago" on the second letter, and the address to where the recommendation is being mailed (indicated in the header) changes as well. The rest of the letter might remain the same. Or if the college asks for slightly different information, a sentence or two could be added. This should not be cause for guilt. Students should feel comfortable (yet appreciative) asking teachers to write multiple recommendations.

Some high schools restrict the number of colleges that students may apply to, partly to save teachers from having to write too many recommendations. If that's the case, the limit is clear. In other cases, do what you have to do.

Secret 205	**It's best to tell the teacher up front—when seeking the first recommendation—how**

many colleges the student is intending to apply to overall and how many recommendations will be needed. Your son might say, "I am applying to Northwestern Early Decision, but if I don't get in Early, I will be asking you for recommendations for six additional colleges." That way, the teacher knows not to delete any files, and when he needs more recommendations, it won't be as difficult to approach the teacher each time. You won't get a response like, "Again? Another recommendation? How many do you expect me to write? Do you think you're my only student?" Teachers generally prefer to receive all the paperwork at once, so they can structure their own time.

Americans Versus Foreigners

| Secret 206 | **American-educated teachers write much more positive recommendations than** |

foreign-educated teachers. Americans' social code is *not* to bad-mouth people in recommendations. American recommendations are not expected to be balanced, but instead polite and supportive. Some Americans would even consider it *deceitful* to write a recommendation that mentions an applicant's negative qualities—they view the job of recommending as the chance to state the positives and advocate for the applicant.

At the same time, college admissions officers mention that references by foreigners tend to seek balance. To an American, a foreign reference can sound extremely negative and downright rude. In other countries, recommenders often go out of their way to try to cite negative qualities in order to sound credible, combining an equal amount of positive and negative. They view this as a more honest approach, since nobody is perfect, and the assumption is that the admissions officers want to hear about the severity of the imperfections as well as the glories of the achievements. Americans argue that if one has something negative to say, the recommender should not agree to write the recommendation at all. College officials say they are accustomed to the disparity. Nevertheless, savvy parents need to know to turn to an American-educated recommender if the student wants a recommendation that oozes with enthusiasm.

This is not a bias against any particular ethnic, national, or religious group. Americans view the purpose of recommendations differently than the rest of the world—and this applies to American-educated people of all different ethnic and religious backgrounds. We expect to see only the positives. We compare one candidate's attributes to another candidate's attributes.

That said, is there any assurance that each teacher or guidance counselor recommendation will be positive? Once one waives the right to read one's recommendations, there is no assurance, but writing positive recommendations is considered the norm in America, and most educators are instructed by school administrators to abide by that custom.

Weak Recommendations

Secret 207

In America, weak or bland recommendations are far more common than negative recommendations, and can be just as harmful. Parents are often fooled by weak recommendations that sound pleasant enough. Very few teachers go out of their way to destroy a kid. But bland, noncommittal recommendations can prevent a student from standing out in an admissions officer's mind and keep the applicant from gaining admission to prestigious programs and colleges. A weak recommendation is one that focuses on qualities about which the college doesn't care or is done sloppily. Nowadays, for example, colleges generally expect teachers to submit typed (on the computer) recommendations. A handwritten recommendation with cross-outs, misspellings, or serious grammatical errors sends a message and can weaken the recommendation.

For the most part, teachers do not intentionally write weak recommendations. Many teachers don't have a good sense of what colleges are seeking and therefore don't know how to be strong advocates for their students. But sometimes, knowledgeable teachers will knowingly write weak recommendations because they are caught in a bind.

Imagine that you are a teacher and a kind, well-meaning, not-so-strong student asks for a recommendation. You feel that the student is reasonably bright, but you haven't seen this student working to potential. You are hesitant to recommend the student because you can't think of anything helpful to write. You might even politely suggest to the student, "There must be a teacher who knows your work better than I do." But then the student seems desperate and insists that you are the teacher best equipped to write the recommendation. The student even tells you that he or she feels particularly close to you or that you're his or her role model. You feel both flattered and obligated. You want to be truthful, but you don't want to compromise your integrity.

You need to write the most positive, truthful description you can in good conscience. You might ask the student to bring you a copy of his or her résumé for backup information. You might even ask the student to ghostwrite a draft of the recommendation for you to edit or rewrite. Or you might conjure up a series of polite statements that you hope the colleges will understand and interpret in good faith and won't offend the student.

Sample Bland Descriptions

- Monika seems to get along nicely with her peers.
- Jason shares well with others in the class.
- Allison always appears well put together. Her peers admire her fashion sense, and she clearly devotes time to proper appearance and hygiene.
- Robert has been a pleasure to have in class.
- Emily is certainly one of the students who fit in best with the others.
- Mitchell's sense of humor will take him far in life.
- Caitlin is always well prepared for class.
- Adam has the best attendance record in the class. He shows up on time and his assignments are never late.
- Megan seems to charm everyone around her. Though she's quiet during class discussions, everyone seems to respect her, and she's never controversial.
- Brett is one of the most athletic students in the class. Whenever I've needed someone to carry heavy books, I know I can count on Brett to respond with a smile. I will miss him next year.

While none of these statements will destroy an application, they lack the necessary *umph* needed to support a borderline application. Ethical teachers will inform the student in advance if they are unable to write anything at all that's positive about the student.

Foreboding Hints of a Weak Recommendation

| Secret 208 | **Teachers often won't feel comfortable warning students that they intend to** |

write a bland recommendation. Teachers who are afraid to say no to a request for a recommendation might make a polite excuse. Take the hint. Tell your kid to get a recommendation from someone else.

Sample "Polite" Excuses to Watch For

- You (the student) should seek a recommendation instead from someone "more familiar with your work."
- I would love to write your recommendation, but I'm too busy to write it now. If it could wait two months, until my workload has lightened. . . .
- I would love to write your recommendation. You'll have to meet with me and tell me a bit more about yourself.
- I would love to write your recommendation, but it's too bad you didn't come to me sooner. I have to write thirty recommendations within the next two weeks, and am not sure that I can fit yours in . . . and I don't want to do a rush job.
- Although I think very highly of you, as a policy, I only write recommendations for students who have earned at least a high A in my class.

Sometimes a teacher will ask the student to ghostwrite the recommendation—and then the teacher agrees in advance to sign it or to alter it and then sign it. This is not necessarily a bad sign. Parents should view this as an opportunity to take over the task or at least offer good input.

How Many Recommendations Are Too Much?

Secret 209

The vast majority of colleges are willing to read an extra recommendation or two, in addition to the number of recommendations they request. But don't "overstuff" the application with recommendations.

Colleges generally specify how many recommendations they require. Some colleges advise against additional recommendations, complaining that "stuffing the file" makes the application more time-consuming to wade through and can even give the impression that the student is trying to compensate for weak recommendations by offering quantity rather than quality. A spokesman from Denison University, Senior Associate Director of Admission Michael Hills, warned that applications that have five or six similar-sounding recommendations and other unrequested documents may also raise suspicion that the applicant is trying to "pad" an otherwise weak application. If you're going to add recommendations, limit the extras to one or two extra recommendations.

Secret 210

When submitting additional recommendations, note that each letter should add a different perspective to the picture. Otherwise, don't include it. Recommendations that just reinforce or repeat already provided information may be greeted with annoyance.

Guidance counselors are often fast to advise students to stick to the number of recommendations required by each college—not to request more recommendations from teachers. Sometimes this is a matter of trying to protect their colleagues from work overload. After all, if every student doubled the number of recommendations he or she enclosed with the application, the letter-writing workload for teachers would also double.

If you want your kid to supplement the recommendations, suggest other people besides classroom teachers who know your child well and could write from a different perspective. Have your kid ask employers, a sports coach, faculty members of after-school or summer courses, internship mentors, or community organizers with whom your child has worked. A key here is that the recommender should *know* your child. Seeking out a prominent person or celebrity to write the recommendation is *not* suggested. Colleges prefer to hear from people who can really offer insight into your child, instead of polite endorsement, regardless of the celebrity's name recognition.

How Do You Know a Great Recommendation When You See One?

Secret 211 A great recommendation should gush with superlatives, telling the college in what context and for how long the recommender has known your child, going on to positively describe how your child compares to every other child this teacher has ever had. A great recommendation is written by a teacher who has taught many children for many years and can do a worthy comparison. Surely your child's teacher can point to some outstanding characteristics of your child that differentiate him or her from every other kid this teacher has ever taught.

Sample Statements

- In the fifty years that I have been teaching, I have never had a student who could enliven a class discussion the way Grace does. While she clearly devotes herself to her work, she adds new perspectives and occasional humor to classroom discussions, and I envy any university class that will be privileged to have her presence.
- Of all the students I have had in my AP class in recent years, I have never had one as able as Jacob to master the most esoteric mathematical principles so quickly and explain them so succinctly to other students.

- Sometimes I think that Beatrix could do a better job teaching this class than I can. I have never before met a student who understands the material so thoroughly, as if she were born knowing it. She politely corrects students when they err or seem confused, yet she is loved and well respected by her peers.

- As faculty advisor for the Environmental Club, I have noticed that Brian, who is the club's president, has been an outstanding role model for the younger students. He is soft-spoken, encouraging, and extremely charismatic. He rules by example. As a result, he has built the organization from a ten-student club two years ago, to a group with more than sixty active members.

- With Victoria, when the class bell rings, the lesson is never over. She pursues each topic aggressively, with a thirst for knowledge that goes well beyond the call of duty. She isn't satisfied until she is an expert on each topic we cover in class, and brings new material to discussions based on research she does outside the classroom, out of sheer interest.

Code Words on Recommendations

Secret 212 Contrary to common parental paranoia, college admissions officers say there are no code words or buzzwords routinely written into recommendations that secretly bad-mouth students. So parents don't have to be too suspicious of each word in a recommendation.

If a teacher recommendation says, for example, "I would recommend this student without hesitation," the parents don't need to worry that the teacher inserted the conditional "would" instead of saying, "I recommend this student without hesitation." Also, admissions officers say they don't comb through every word to seek multiple interpretations. They tend to read recommendations the same way other people do.

But teachers may write generally unenthusiastic recommendations that sound positive on first read, but then sound very mediocre from the perspective of one who is reading hundreds of applications. The giveaway is the topic or topics covered in the recommendation.

Weak topics include: behavior, appearance, popularity, apparent affluence, receptivity to learning, handwriting, attention span, and regurgitation of grades that are already apparent on the transcript (without further explanation or discussion).

Strong topics include anecdotes about insights the student has shared, knowledge or expertise the student brings to the class, the energy of the student to further explore topics covered in the classroom, the willingness of the student to take academic risks, leadership skills, innovative thinking, overcoming obstacles.

The Celebrity Recommendation

| Secret 213 | Celebrity recommendations are useless unless the recommender knows your kid |

well. A pleasant recommendation from a famous person (unless the person is a *major* donor at the college to which the kid is applying, depending on the "development policy" of the university) adds no weight to the application and makes the parent feel indebted to the celebrity. In cases where the celebrity doesn't even know the applicant at all, such a recommendation could backfire and hurt the child's chances. As a general rule, parents need not go running to their client who happens to be the CEO of a major corporation, or the politician for whom you campaigned, or the distant relative who is a famous author or who starred in a movie or concert just because they are famous. However, if the recommender is able to tell a good anecdote or two about working with your kid in some capacity, the famous person's recommendation could be very helpful. Did your kid help the famous person win the Nobel Peace Prize? Did your kid help the candidate become elected in some way that the politician can cite specifically? Did your kid appear in the same movie with the famous actor writing the recommendation? Did your kid help make the breakthrough for the prize-winning scientist? If the famous person just describes a "nice deserving kid," the recommendation probably won't help.

In order for such a recommendation to be helpful, the celebrity must be a *real* advocate for the kid. The recommender must be able to provide a "missing piece," highlight some other aspect of the kid that the rest of the application doesn't do justice to. And the recommender must show evidence of really *knowing* the kid.

The Alumni Recommendations

 **Alumni and alumnae recommendations have the most power when the writer is a major donor to the university or is very active and currently known within the college community.** Again, the recommender must *know* the student and the student's work, or else the recommendation is useless.

If your child seeks such a recommendation, make sure the recommender cites personal anecdotes and specific examples of your kid's work and explain how he or she was able to see the kid's work. Because the recommender is familiar with the campus and the college, he or she should refer specifically to how the particular student could enhance the campus or contribute to the college community—and how the kid could benefit from the particular college. If your neighbor is the recommender, you might want to ghostwrite the letter to save him or her time, and to maintain control of the wording.

Peer Recommendations

Secret 215 **The best bet for a peer recommender is another teenager who is willing to collaborate with a parent.** Some colleges, including Dartmouth, request peer recommendations. Others, like Princeton, offer it as an option. Savvy parents have a heavy hand in overseeing this process.

Before having your kid request a recommendation from a peer, discuss the choice of friends. Your kid's best friend may be a sweetheart who can't put a sentence together. Or the kid may be the "busy" or "overburdened" type that *never gets to it*. Your best bet is probably a kid who likes your kid and has very supportive, savvy parents who will guide the kid through the process in the same way you would if it were your kid writing the recommendation for their kid. (But don't make an exchange agreement with another peer applying to the same college: "I'll write your letter if you write mine." I have heard stories of Dartmouth applicants who got into disputes over whose letter had more positive adjectives, whose letter sounded more literate, and whose letter was better supervised. The last person a student should want a recommendation from is a kid who is competing possibly for the same opportunity.) In seeking a peer recommendation, speak to the other kid's parents in advance to make sure that they'll show you the recommendation.

If a peer writes a recommendation for your child, make sure you screen it carefully first. The good thing about a peer recommendation is that any peer who writes one will usually be willing to show it to you before it goes out. There are no sealed and signed secret envelopes. More likely, they'll expect *you* to mail it out for them, lest they be bothered with going to the post office.

Teenagers often have no sense of what works in a college recommendation. Most have never seen recommendations until their senior year of high school. This can provide helpful and candid information to a college, since the information is probably less polished and less rehearsed. But you as a parent should be cautious in overseeing what goes out to the college. Your kid's best friend could be mad at your kid the day the recommendation is written, and the hostility could slide into the recommendation—or that could be the opportunity to "get even" before the two kids make up again a few days later. Or, lacking judgment, the kid could write an overwhelmingly positive review of your kid and just mention one turnoff point, not realizing that it's a turnoff. "Annabelle has been my best friend since we both lost the elections in ninth grade." "Even though Annabelle was failing chemistry, she still managed to be a role model for me and my peers in the chemistry class." "Although she never speaks up in class, I know Annabelle is a very smart girl, and, being her best friend, I can vouch for the fact that she's not at all depressed."

Parental Recommendations

Secret 216

Recommending your own kid is a treat not to be missed. What college would want to hear parents boast about their kids? Princeton and Washington University in St. Louis, among others, have been known to invite parents to recommend their own kids. If you're asked to write your kid a recommendation, go for it. Have fun with it. No, this is not license to talk about your kid's dirty room, lack of grooming habits, or negative sibling relationships. This is only your chance to boast. Tell the college all the things that your neighbors, friends, and especially your kid's siblings don't want to hear: how brilliant and talented your child is.

Don't feel the need to be objective about your kid. Be supportive instead. Your role is to advocate. Remember while you are writing about what an exemplary human being your kid is, other parents are also writing about their saintly children. If you detail your child's worst points, how will that compare with the other children's all-positive recommendations? Some parents think it's necessary to point out their children's blemishes in order to sound credible. Not the case on a parent recommendation. If you truly want your child to be admitted, provide good, positive reasons why your child and the college are a perfect fit.

If your child has a disability or situation that you feel the school should know about, this could be an opportunity to share this information with the admissions officers. But be very wary about pointing out deficiencies. If the disability could sound like it might prevent your child from keeping up with the students at the college, you might be smart not to mention it. Colleges are impressed with disabilities that are *overcome*. Colleges are also impressed when they hear about hardships that the student has *successfully* faced (students who hold full-time jobs while maintaining a high average), as long as the hardships are behind them and don't act as predictors of additional hardships yet to come.

Never use the parental recommendation to confess family short-comings; this only undermines your own recommendation. It's okay to boast. Boasting is expected. But note that the elements you choose to boast about reveal much about your family values. Don't boast, for example, about your kid attending the "most prestigious sleepaway camp," or winning the local bar's "darts championship," or being the designated driver when his or her friends are all drunk, or being "a good loser," or acting kind to children from "lesser" or "more primitive" backgrounds.

Ghostwritten Recommendations

Secret 217 When a teacher asks a kid to ghostwrite the recommendation, the parents should step to the plate and do the writing, unless the kid really wants to do it. No kids do. Sometimes a teacher who is overburdened and really knows and likes the kid, asks the kid to ghostwrite his or her own recommendation. And the teacher says he or she will sign it. This is one of the most difficult tasks. Parents are much more able to "boast" about their kid. Teenage kids suddenly get extremely modest when they have to write their own recommendations—for fear of being labeled conceited or showing off. Parents tend to be much more in tune with the qualities that a college might be seeking. Is it dishonest to ghostwrite your kid's recommendation? No. As long as the teacher signs the letter.

Most teachers will receive the ghostwritten recommendation and will then want to embellish, delete, alter the style, or elaborate on what is written. By editing the ghostwritten letter, the teachers are making the recommendation their own—while saving themselves a lot of time. The recommendation is only signed once the teacher *likes* or feels comfortable with the recommendation.

Parents who are ghostwriting a recommendation should note that only positives should be included. Do *not* try to balance your kid's recommendation with negatives. Think of the recommendation as an advertisement to try to sell your kid to the college. Your job is to promote your kid to the best of your ability. The parent-written ghostwritten recommendation should include the following information:

- How long has the teacher known the student and in what capacity?
- Which class or classes has the student taken with the teacher?
- Has the student joined any clubs or teams that the teacher supervises?
- Do you (parents) recall any positive anecdote your kid has told you over the years in relation to that teacher? Does your kid recall any that the teacher might be aware of that you should add? Ask your kid.
- Did the teacher ever tell you any positive anecdotes about your kid?

Be generous with adjectives—but try to back them up with anecdotes or stories.

Sample Good Adjectives

bold	independent
brilliant	innovative
charming	intellectual
committed	leader
compassionate	logical
concerned	mature
courageous	methodical
creative	multidimensional
critical thinker	multifaceted
curious	one-of-a-kind
determined	original
devoted	outspoken
demanding	outstanding
driven	passionate about a subject
effervescent	perfectionist
empathetic	resourceful
energetic	respectful
enthusiastic	role model
exacting	self-disciplined
exemplary	self-respecting
expert	serious
generous	talented
gifted	thoughtful
honest	unifying
inclusive	

Sample Weak or Bad Adjectives

above average

adorable

aggressive

argumentative

attractive

authority-fearing

bashful

bubbly

competitive

conceited

cute

follower

friendly

future Einstein

genius

good

good sense of humor

"in"

insubordinate

interesting

introverted

kind

laid-back

loner

loud

marches to his own drummer

materialistic

modest

mysterious

neat

nice

obedient

obsessed

outsider

partyer

patient

placid

playful

polite

popular

private

quiet

rambunctious

religious

respectful of authority

self-centered

selfish

serene

sets her own pace

shy

sloppy

slow paced

social

sowing his oats

subordinate

talkative

tolerant

traditional

trendy

type A

undisciplined

well dressed

well groomed

well liked

well mannered

well meaning

wild

youthful

At the end of the letter, you need to write two more sentences declaring under what circumstances, if any, you recommend this candidate for admission. Write something like: "I recommend Peter Johnson enthusiastically and without reservation. Prestige U would be lucky to get him." Or "Prestige U should grab Peter Johnson. He is a mover and a shaker, and Prestige will someday want the credit for educating this talented young leader." Or "If Prestige U could take only one student from our entire state this year, Peter Johnson is that student. He is outstanding and would make a significant contribution to your college." Do not write wimpy endings: "So, in conclusion, I would recommend that you accept Peter Johnson at Prestige University. I know he would be very happy there." Or "Please accept Peter Johnson for admission. We shall miss him very much." Or "While we'll miss Peter Johnson at Central High School, we know that he'll have many new opportunities at Prestige University." Or "As I've shown, Peter Johnson is a very capable student and would be able to keep up with the work and the other students—even at Prestige University, one of the nation's most-competitive colleges. I highly recommend him."

When to Request a Recommendation

Secret 218

Reserve your teachers. Have your kid ask teachers for recommendations as far in advance as possible—even before the student gets hold of the proper recommendation forms. Recommendation season is often a hectic time for teachers. Imagine having twenty students or more ask you for a recommendation, when each of the twenty students is applying to an average of six colleges apiece. That's 120 recommendations that you're asked to produce. Students are generally expected to give two- to three weeks' notice—usually right before Christmas vacation—the same time that you are grading exams, reports, and papers so you can get as much work as possible out of the way before the holiday. You want to do a good job with the students' recommendations. You don't want to send off the wrong letter to the wrong school.

You might even announce to your students that three weeks' notice will not be enough—that you need to know who needs recommendations in October or November.

Each student needs at least two teachers—preferably from different subjects—to show off the kid's multiple facets. Many teachers will limit the number of students they are willing to recommend. Usually the teachers with the best rapport (the "most liked teachers") are the first to become oversubscribed.

Have your kid ask in September if you're sure about whom he or she wants to ask. This is usually hard for kids, but it's necessary. Rest assured that most kids are afraid of rejection at this point—but, as I tell my students—most teachers who want to say no will do so in a very polite palatable way. Most students leave the recommendations until the last possible second because they're afraid to ask. But let's face it, if your kid is a senior who is applying to college, you know in September that your kid will be needing recommendations. So there is no real valid argument for waiting.

(Note that this advice only applies to students at high schools that permit students to ask individual teachers for recommendations. In a minority of high schools, students fill out a "brag sheet" form and a teacher in the school is randomly assigned to write the student's recommendation—without necessarily ever meeting the kid. That way, the large public school guarantees that all students get recommended and all teachers are "burdened with" an equal number of recommendations. If your child attends such a school, regardless of the limits that the high school and colleges suggest on numbers of recommendations, you might suggest that your child add an outside recommendation from at least one adult who knows the child's work well and can write something personal.)

How to Request a Recommendation

 **Appreciating how busy teachers are during recommendation season, savvy parents help to organize the teacher who is writing the recommendation by assembling a neat packet for the teacher.**

Before giving the recommending teacher any materials, your kid should ask the teacher politely for a recommendation. Once the teacher has agreed to write a recommendation, assemble the necessary materials in a pocket folder/portfolio with your kid's name on it. In fact, each page of the folder should contain your kid's name.

The folder should contain the following items:

- A cover letter from the student (signed by the student) thanking the teacher in advance for agreeing to write the recommendation and specifying any information or details that must go into the recommendation. This is a great opportunity for the student to remind the teacher of some of the student's qualities that are particularly pertinent. ("Prestige U has asked that you comment on my interaction with other students. You might want to mention the fact that I lead the class study sessions before all exams." Or "Prestige U wants to get a sense of my mathematics abilities. As you recall, I was the only student from the high school this year who was chosen to represent the county at the State Math Competition." Or "Prestige U wants to know about my interaction with adults. You probably already know that I was just elected student rep to the Board of Education, where I was successful in negotiating a new pass-fail option.")

- A copy of the blank recommendation form (a photocopied version is okay) with the student's name and personal information already filled out on top (preferably typed). If no recommendation form is provided by the college, mention this in the cover letter and ask the teacher to create his or her own letter of recommendation.

- A new stamped, addressed (to the college) envelope—so the teacher does not have to pay postage or go hunting for envelopes. (No, official high school stationery is not necessary.)

- A self-addressed (to the student), stamped postcard that you insert into the envelope that you have provided for the teacher. The postcard says, "Dear [Student's Name], [Name of College] has received your recommendation from [Name of Teacher]." The college will know to send you this postcard as soon as the recommendation arrives.

- A copy of the student's résumé—for the teacher only. This will help the teacher write the recommendation. Make sure to write in the cover letter to the teacher that a copy of the résumé is inserted for the teacher's reference only—not to be mailed out to the college. (See the appendix.)

Secret 220 **If you want each recommendation to be separately tailored to a specific college (preferred), then for each recommendation that you are requesting from the teacher, use a *different* pocket folder and a *different* cover letter.** (Don't expect to get the folders back.) Each cover letter should detail what is expected of the recommending teacher for *that particular* college. This will save the teacher lots of time and prevent confusion. The letter to the teacher should specify what information the colleges are seeking. Make sure to provide the teacher with enough background information (in the cover letter and packet) to answer the questions. One recommendation form may ask the teacher to comment on the student's "inventiveness." Another may ask the teacher to comment on the student's "ability to grasp new material." The first cover letter should then say, "Please make sure to emphasize my inventiveness. You might recall the time that I designed a new grammar video game for the French class." The same student's cover letter for another college might say, "Please comment on my ability to grasp new material. You might recall the time I was out for a month with mono and had to teach myself the entire pluperfect tense in French to catch up with the class." You get the point.

Parental Paranoia: Do Recommenders Ever Sabotage Applicants?

Although adding secret messages is not a common practice, admissions officers say they have seen secret Post-Its or received confidential phone calls from recommenders reversing what is written.

In one case, parents who were very angry that their daughter was deferred by her first-choice college stormed the high school principal's office, demanding that the principal write a recommendation. The principal, who seemed to like the girl, wrote a glowing recommendation and showed it to the parents before submitting the letter to the college. The girl was ultimately rejected anyway.

Is there any chance that the principal submitted the recommendation with a Post-It that said something like, "Written under coercion" or "Submitted under protest" or "This application was censored by the girl's parents"? Although it may sound crazy, yes. In general, if you ask someone to recommend you, you are at the recommender's mercy. You need to have some element of trust in that person, what he or she might write, and how the person knows your kid! Chances are, if the recommender is willingly showing you the recommendation and if you didn't coerce the recommender to recommend, there are no secrets.

Make sure that your kid asks only teachers and administrators who you are confident like your kid. Don't coerce you kid's principal or headmaster to write a recommendation. You'll never see the Post-Its, only the rejections.

Guidance Counselor Recommendations

Secret 221

Guidance counselors and high school college advisers *do* wield power, and colleges require recommendations from them. A savvy parent should make sure that his or her kid develops a positive relationship with the counselor. A suburban family sold their home and moved to a different suburban public school district claiming that the school guidance counselor had, in effect, shortchanged their daughter when the counselor was asked by a college admissions officer to compare the top competitors at her highly competitive high school. The parents believed that the guidance counselor gave their daughter the lowest ranking of the applicant pool—despite her high grades and test scores—and, as a result, the girl was rejected from her top-choice university.

College admissions officers deny that such scenarios occur. The most-competitive universities claim that they don't survey guidance counselors as a general policy to ask who should be accepted. Instead, admissions officers claim to take pride in making their own evaluations. As part of every college application evaluation form, guidance counselors are asked to *rate* each applicant according to specific qualities listed on a chart. Qualities usually include ability to get along with teachers and peers, academic achievement, personality, character, and extracurricular accomplishments. On Yale's form, "Creativity" is also rated. The rating levels on typical applications are below average, average, good (above average), excellent (top 10 percent), outstanding (top 5 percent), and "one of the top few encountered in my career." For the top ten students who are applying to the same college, the guidance counselor obviously can't rank all ten applicants as "one of the top few encountered in my career." So some are rated outstanding, and some are rated excellent, etc.

While "excellent" sounds, well, excellent, if your kid is applying to Harvard, Yale, Princeton, Stanford, Duke, MIT, or Caltech, do you want your kid to have all "excellents" if the other nine have "outstandings"? Your kid's guidance counselor can give your kid all "excellents" and still write lovely essays to show you. So even seeing the guidance counselor's written recommendation, you have no guarantee that your kid is getting the highest support.

Secret 222 **Savvy parents who develop good rapport with the adviser have been known to ask to see the entire reference form.** The worst a counselor can say is no.

| **Secret 223** | **Have your kid seek out his or her guidance counselor as early as possible in high** |

school. And have her remind the counselor regularly that she still exists. Have your kid bring in her résumé updates as conversation starters. Don't have a polished résumé ready? Bake cookies and have your kid bring them in to share as an icebreaker with the counselor. No, cookies will not be perceived as bribes nor will they violate public school antigift policies, because guidance counselors understand how difficult it is for teenagers to walk in cold and start up a conversation. And home-baked cookies have minimal monetary value, but major value in breaking down barriers. The idea is to create an excuse for interaction.

Once your child has finished making arrangements for recommendations, you should check into the college interview process. At some colleges, your child may get a phone call from an interviewer as soon as the initial materials are received. At other colleges, it is your child's responsibility to phone the college to arrange an interview. Check the college website or phone the particular admissions office to find out what is expected.

CHAPTER 10

Preparing Your Child for Memorable and Effective Interviews

Regardless of films your kid saw in AP Psychology, admissions officers do not sit behind mirrored windows observing twitching, shuffling, panicking kids in the waiting room. The mirror on the wall is not a two-way mirror, and there is no camera behind it. And the two magazines placed near him on the coffee table—one serious science journal, one pop culture—do not represent a test.

Your kid will not become part of some secret psychological study when he or she makes an appointment for an interview. Interviewers sometimes do fall behind schedule, and nobody cares what you read in the waiting room. Instead of focusing on these fears, parents can play a very active role in helping their children prepare to give memorable, effective college interviews.

Nevertheless, the following habits and good body language are always advisable, particularly if your kid is scheduled for a "formal" (admissions office–based) interview. Have your child rehearse some in your presence.

| Secret 224 | **Rehearse good eye contact and a solid handshake.** (These are age-old secrets, but the |

current generation, accustomed to e-mail contact only, is often oblivious.) Observe your own kid's speech habits. If your son tends to talk to the ceiling, floor, or the "distance," rather than making eye contact, have him rehearse eye contact for days in advance. Some kids will make perfect eye contact when they speak to family members or peers, but when they talk to authority figures (school principal, a dean, or a college interviewer), their eyes suddenly divert—usually down. If possible, check out your son in such a situation to see if eye contact is made. Tell him about his eye-contact patterns—not to make him nervous, but aware. Then practice good eye contact.

Practice the handshake choreography, too, or it will never happen at the interview. For most kids, initiating a handshake represents a risk. Practice coordinating the handshake with eye contact. Your daughter should be looking at the person with whom she is shaking hands. Most kids don't know this and look away as they shake hands. No, the admissions counselor does not have a checklist of items that says, "Did the girl look at you when she shook your hand?" But the subconscious message is that the kid is shy and may wilt in college if a professor so much as looks in her direction. She wants to come across as a "mover and shaker" at a very competitive college, not an academic wimp.

How hard must the grip be? Conventional wisdom used to dictate that the firmer the grip, the better—that people judge a person by the firmness of their handshake. This is true to some extent. But direct your football-player kid not to pump the person's arm off or shatter the greeter's hand bones. If the recipient of the handshake is wearing a ring, an extra-firm handshake could hurt, so tell your kid to be cautious. The aim isn't to hurt the other person. This will not impress the interviewer. If the person's right hand is in his or her pocket, or if the hand is bandaged, tell your kid to proceed cautiously—and take a cue as to whether the person is able to shake hands before offering it. This may sound ridiculously obvious to some parents. But it's not always obvious to nervous kids who are unaccustomed to meeting new authority figures, particularly those they are trying to impress. Remember, they've spent years of their lives speaking almost exclusively to peers and family members. Practice introducing your kid to new people.

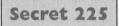 **Secret 225**   **Remind your kid to act polite with the office staff, not just the admissions officer.**

You want your child to make a good impression on everyone he comes into contact with. If he is rude to an office staff member, that message is sure to be relayed to the admissions officer.

Secret 226 | **Teach your kid some of the conventions of American introduction and what is expected of him.** When the interviewer says, "Hi. My name is Jane Doe, and I'll be interviewing you," tell your kid not to just say, "Hi," or even "Hi, nice to meet you," in return. Instead, this is your kid's cue to tell Jane Doe his or her own name. Even if your kid's name is written in Jane Doe's appointment book, Jane Doe might not have looked back at her schedule recently, and might not remember the name of her next interview subject. Even if your kid's name is written in bold letters on a visitor's badge in sight of the interviewer, your kid should still clearly pronounce his name for the interviewer. In fact, your kid should probably say, "Hi. I'm Joe Johnson from South Mills, Idaho," to give the interviewer a little more context. This could even spark a positive discussion with Jane Doe about South Mills, or about Idaho. Perhaps Jane Doe has admitted other kids from South Mills. Once again, practice with your kid. Many kids mumble their names, and the interviewer suddenly goes running off to check the appointment book, rather than humiliate the poor kid by having to ask the kid her name again and risk another mumble. Of course, some clever interviewers will ask, "How do you spell that name?" But if the answer turns out to be "R-O-S-E" or "J-O-E," both parties will be embarrassed.

Arranging the Interview

Secret 227 | **Parents can indeed make the arrangements for a college visit including the interview. Gone are the days when it had to look like the visit was being arranged entirely by the student.** Some admissions offices may have a snooty secretary who says, "Why isn't your son or daughter making the arrangements if he or she is so interested in the college?"

Luckily, that approach is vanishing, and admissions offices are getting more used to parents making arrangements. But if you're greeted by such a quip, say politely, "My daughter asked me to make the arrangements, since she won't be home till eight tonight, when your office is closed." Or "My son is working full-time this summer and is not permitted to make calls during the workday." Or "I'm orchestrating a whole trip to the college for the family, including hotels and sibling activities, so I really need to be the one coordinating the interviews."

Do Interviews Count?

| Secret 228 | **At some colleges, interviews don't really count at all. At others, interviews are very** |

important. Don't guess. Advise your kid to treat each interview as if his or her career hangs on it. Whether or not an interview counts for admission depends a lot upon the college and how the interview goes. If, for example, a kid acts very rude, dishonest, or unkind, or appears dirty or drugged out, word of this behavior would get back to any college and could destroy a student's chances, regardless of how little the interview was supposed to count originally. If a kid seems outstandingly bright, and the discussion is engaging to the interviewer, a very positive recommendation could emerge in support of the student's application. This applies even when a college student is the interviewer—the practice at many top small colleges.

Articles that have appeared in popular publications indicate that some colleges offer alumni interviews just to humor alumni—that such interviews really aren't valued heavily by the universities. At other colleges, however, the alumni interview is one of the most important factors of the application. The college gets a sense of which students would fit in best by hearing what alumni have to say about future generations of students at their alma mater. Never assume that a local interview is powerless.

At most colleges, an alumni interview adds one more piece to the puzzle. Most of the time, the interview is consistent with other parts of the application, and just confirms the application. But occasionally, some new aspect arises at the interview. Sometimes it is a positive aspect—some new credential that the applicant neglected to include on the application because "there was no room," it didn't seem to fit anywhere, or the new credential was earned after the application was submitted. Sometimes there is a negative element that emerges—a student confides in the interviewer that he really isn't interested in the particular college and that the parents are forcing him to apply. (Sounds crazy, but it happens.) Regardless of the usual weight allotted to alumni interviews, such a statement could heavily impact a child's chances of getting in, once word gets back to the college that the kid really doesn't want to attend.

A senior student interviewer at Dartmouth claimed that student interviews probably bear a little more weight than alumni interviews in that the students are closer to the campus and have a better sense of how the applicant would fit into the culture. Also, applicants are often more willing to confide in a peer. The Dartmouth student said that usually the interview helps to complete any missing information. He said the student interviewer doesn't have the power, however, to give a definite yes or no.

How to Handle a Nervous Kid

| Secret 229 | **Every kid, nervous or not, should bring conversation starters to an interview to** |

help get a good discussion going. The best one is probably a résumé. Start with the premise that *everyone* is nervous. The interviewer understands that the student is nervous, and often the interviewer is just as nervous. Many alumni interview students because they enjoy the endeavor, but are relatively inexperienced.

Make sure your kid is ready to start a conversation. If your kid doesn't have a résumé by senior year, create one before the first interview. You want to avoid a bland, weak interview—one that typically starts with "Tell me something about yourself." Kiss of death. Then the kid usually mutters something like, "I have always wanted to go to Prestige University." And the interviewer asks something awful, like "What is it about Prestige U that interests you?" half quizzing the nervous child and half filibustering while searching for a more captivating question.

 **Secret 230** **Your kid doesn't have a résumé? Have her bring props that demonstrate some of her interests.** Recommended props include photocopies of art work, science papers that have been entered into competitions, creative writing that has been published in school or professional publications, photos of athletic achievements, newspaper clippings mentioning her name, a musical instrument that she has mastered, origami masterpieces, and rare photos from her travels. Make sure the items can easily be carried and don't make a mess. Also, tell her not to bring too much and overwhelm the interviewer. The idea is to spark a memorable conversation.

Your child should not bring certificates, personal photos, a family album, or scrapbook. He may bring photos—if they're not photos of him—if he's a photographer eager to show off his art. The props should easily fit into a flat portfolio or backpack, in case his interview includes an unannounced walking tour or a visit to a campus lab, for example. He should not bring original art or anything breakable. Nor should he expect the interviewer to read all of his materials on the spot—or any of the materials at all, aside from a résumé—reading may be too time-consuming in the limited time of the interview. But bringing along some articles or journals will be helpful just to spark a discussion of the child's interests.

Come with Questions

Secret 231 **Students should prepare to ask at least five questions that don't make the kid appear negative, angry, depressed, or coerced—or like the kid**

hadn't read up on the college or prepared for the interview.
The interviewer will *always* ask, "Do you have any questions?" The student should make sure to listen to the interviewer and not ask any questions about information that has already been covered. Warn your kid about this. Some kids get so nervous, they don't listen to a thing the interviewer says. They only worry about their next question. The student should be able to demonstrate that she has good listening skills and knows if the questions have already been answered during the dialogue.

The questions the student asks can be very revealing. Rehearse questions with your child. Obviously, some questions may arise spontaneously during the interview, and you want to encourage this. This shows that the student is really experiencing a dialogue and is listening to what the interviewer is saying.

Tell your kid to avoid posing questions that are overly controversial—not that anyone should deliberately censor questions or stifle them, just that during an interview it's better to focus on what both parties have in common rather than differences. When your daughter is trying to pitch herself to the college, she should avoid discussing current campus issues: labor relations on campus, drugs and alcohol on campus, driving policy, sexuality, religious practice on a secular campus, and political affiliations. Aim instead for questions that bring a smile to the interviewer's face and tap the interviewer for his or her knowledge or expertise: "What is the best part about attending Prestige University?" "What is your fondest memory from Prestige University?" "If I attended Prestige, would I be able to explore multiple fields?" "Which departments would you personally consider to be the strongest departments at Prestige University?" "Could you recommend the best course or best professor at Prestige University?" "If you were to do your education all over again at Prestige, what would you do differently that I might learn from?" The following is a sample list of good interview questions:

- Does the university offer many research opportunities and internships for undergraduates? What is the commitment of the professors to undergraduates who want to pursue research? If

I had my own idea for a research project, would I get support at the university—or is research here limited to staffing other people's work?

- I'm considering majoring in _____, _____, or _____. Which of these do you feel is the strongest department?

- Do you feel that students really bond and network at this university or in this department? Do people keep up with each other years after they graduate? Or do they have little contact later on? (To an alumni interviewer: Do you keep up with anyone from college still—aside from the admissions office staff?)

- On the weekends, do most students stay on campus? If so, what activities are offered? Do multiple activities take place at once?

- Do the academic departments sponsor guest speakers? Faculty speakers? Lunches? Relevant movies? Other social activities?

- If you were in my situation now, choosing between this college and, let's say, Yale, for a potential major in _____, which would you choose? (Use comparable schools that you are truly considering.)

- In the large lecture classes, are there smaller "breakout sessions," tutorials, or recitations? Where do students ask their questions? Do students have any direct contact with professors to ask questions and pose ideas during or outside of class?

- Does the university achieve real cultural diversity? Do people of different cultures mix on campus? Or do students self-segregate?

- Are freshmen shut out of programs on campus? Can a freshman, for example, audition for shows? Write for the campus newspaper?

- Do you permit students to double- or triple-major? Are there any special programs that I might not have noticed that might be of interest to me—like a four-year BA/MA degree, or seven-year BA/MD degree, or five-year BA/MBA or BA/MEng.?

The following is a list of bad interview questions. What makes them bad is that they sound suspicious and portray the kid negatively. They imply that the inquirer only cares about socializing and partying, rather than savoring academics and studying—which the most-competitive colleges view as the primary purpose of college:

- How many hours would I have to devote to studying per night? Is there any time for social life during the week?

- Is the drinking age really enforced on campus?

- Where do most students hang out during free time?

- Are there dorms for smokers? Is drug use tolerated?

- Does class attendance matter?

- What happens if you don't like a roommate?

- Is there a wakeup call in the dorms?

- Is there a service to clean the kids' rooms?

- How do you prevent kids from bringing other kids in to sleep in their rooms?

- How do you guard against kids bringing strangers into the dorms?

- How much school spirit does this place have?

Your First Choice College

Secret 232

Before each interview, psych your kid up! Convince yourself and your child (genuinely) that this particular university is indeed the best possible choice for your child—or at least that this university could potentially be the best placement for your child. Review the benefits of the college with fervor and enthusiasm. Comb through the view books and websites, and find the particular characteristics of the college that make it stand out as the best for your kid. When an interviewer asks your son if this college is his first choice, he should be able to honestly answer yes. This is tricky if your kid secretly has aspirations to go elsewhere. You want to tell your child to be honest. But for the day of the interview, make sure your kid feels like this place *is* the best. If your kid says that he would prefer to attend another school, the interview is over, and your child is not likely to be offered admission. The college would rather offer a coveted place to a student who genuinely wants to be there.

It is perfectly acceptable for the student to say that this college is *potentially* his or her first choice, although the student has not yet made a decision. It's perfectly acceptable for the student to say that he or she is hoping that the interviewer will help the student finalize his or her first choice by answering some questions.

What If the Interviewer Doesn't Seem Interested?

Secret 233

Tell your kid not to push her work on the interviewer. Some interviewers prefer not to examine works of art or writings during the interview, but would rather hear the kid speak about the works brought to the interview. She should not tell the interviewer, "You must read my poem," or "You must watch my video," or "You must listen to my CD," or "You must read my science paper." Instead she should be willing to leave these work samples with the interviewer for inclusion in the application file—to be read or enjoyed by the committee at a later date. Don't bring papers that are not file size or are physically unwieldy—since they cannot be easily filed and therefore are likely to be discarded by a well-intending file clerk, or, if you're lucky, sent back to you. Now that most of the applications have been computerized, many colleges are hesitant to accept extra papers of any size.

Conversation Starters

| Secret 234 |

Instruct your kid to be observant and willing to start a conversation based on the interviewer's displays. One alumnus interviewer, for example, had an office filled with baseball memorabilia and a car parked outside with baseball-related bumper stickers. If the student has any interest in any aspect of baseball, this could spark a good discussion. Beware, though. If your kid is meeting with a die-hard fan, he may want to avoid a discussion of particular teams, since the interviewer could be a dedicated fan of an opposing team and that could alienate the student or vice versa. Also, tell your child not to get into an in-depth discussion of something that he or she knows nothing about. Your kid should not try to impress the baseball aficionado with his interest in the sport, if he really has no knowledge of the game whatsoever. If your child does slip into a discussion that seems over his head, tell him not to be afraid to end the particular discussion with a polite comment like, "I'm so impressed with your knowledge of the sport. I'm not as familiar with it, but you've inspired me to learn more about it." Then move on to the next topic.

Another interviewer—one who was interviewing kids all day, in back-to-back interviews—had an office filled with *Star Trek* and *Star Wars* memorabilia. The entire interview focused on the TV shows and film series. The student left feeling that he had had an enjoyable time, swapping sci-fi insights with another aficionado, and the interviewer also apparently enjoyed the talk with a young person who shared his passion. The student was eventually admitted.

Taboo Topics

Secret 235

Of course, your kid should be instructed to maintain a positive tone at all times during the interview. An interview is not an appropriate time to "air one's dirty laundry," confess, change world politics, convert everyone to his or her religion, or "get something off his (or her) chest." The kid should not speak about his or her annoying sibling, micromanaging parents, unsympathetic teachers, disagreeable politics, argument with religion, peculiar eating habits or disorders, sexual quandaries, character flaws, qualities that other people don't appreciate, bad or questionable taste, bodily inadequacies, feelings of anger or depression, incidents of misbehavior, or moments of feeling misunderstood.

Horrible, Sticky, Trick Questions

Secret 236

One of the toughest questions that students tell me they are asked by one particular university's interviewers is "Give me a reason that this university should accept you over the tens of thousands that apply nationally." Not such a terrible question, but when you're not expecting it, it could sound arrogant and throw a teenager off guard. This question goes back to the original questions posed in this book, basically, "Why should we take you?"

One student, a top grade–achiever in her high school with top-level SATs to match, was stumped. "I'm the only captain of my high school's table tennis team this year," she replied. And she knew at once that she had blown the interview. She felt that the interviewer was seeking national "stars," and she had limited her answer to a local achievement.

How should your kid handle such a question? Be prepared in

advance. This isn't necessarily an aberrational question for certain extremely competitive colleges. And even if the question isn't directly asked during the interview, the question is often implied at colleges that like to perceive themselves as collectors of the very top kids in America.

| **Secret 237** | **The best approach is a composite approach.** |

Refer to your child's résumé to help pick out a few unique or relatively unique achievements, and have your child practice combining them into a single sentence. "Of all your applicants, I am sure that I am the only local table tennis champion who also managed to publish a poem in a national publication and who also was able to raise twenty thousand dollars for a new day care center for children of working single mothers in our city." "Of all your applicants, I'm the only one who founded a madrigal quartet company that performs at fund-raisers, studied flying trapeze for three years, and taught myself to speak fluent Arabic."

Another applicant to the same university says he was seated in a room with a bunch of students from his high school who were applying Early Decision to the university. According to his story, the students all knew one another, having been in classes together for years. All of the students had previously discussed their college applications—but none of them had admitted to each other that they were applying to this university. Imagine their surprise at seeing each other in the Early Decision interview site together. Nevertheless, all were too nervous to really speak with each other. When the boy's turn finally came, he said the interviewer's first question was, "While you were in the waiting room, did you recognize any of the other kids—all of whom should know you? If so, why should we take you over those other kids?"

The boy was stuck. A student government leader, he knew to be circumspect, but he didn't want to sound evasive. He worried, of course, that some of his competitors might have bad-mouthed him, but he was determined not to sound bitter or insulting toward them. Correct thinking.

| Secret 238 | **Tell your child to focus on his or her own accomplishments and answer the question much the same way you would answer the question about what makes you more worthy than all the other applicants in** |

America. "Of all the kids in the waiting room, I'm the one whom the students chose to lead the student government. In addition, I founded an Astronomy Club, conducted independent science research that resulted in a paper, have EMT certification, and am working almost full-time after school to help support my family," he said.

Questions of Religion or Politics

| Secret 239 | **Tell your kids not to let anyone goad them into making a political or religious** |

statement at their interviews. The college interview is not a good time to take a firm stand on political or religious issues that are emotional for many people. On the rare occasion that she is asked about politics or religion, the student could easily get caught in a sticky bind, because she has to second-guess the politics or religion of the interviewer. The student should come to an interview prepared with some upbeat answers. In response to political affiliations, probably the most intelligent way to answer is to say, "I view myself as a thinking person and don't believe in putting myself in a box and classifying myself as an across-the-board conservative or liberal. I respond to each issue independently. I am conservative on issues of drunk driving, for example, or public health and public safety. I am radical on issues of foster care reform and education." The student might even ask the interviewer if he or she has a particular issue that he or she meant to discuss. Chances are the question will be dropped—no points gained and, more important, none lost.

Religion is even harder. But very few interviewers will ask about it—unless your kid is applying to a religion-affiliated college. At all other colleges, asking about one's personal beliefs is generally not considered professional. In any case, it's better for a student not to "put himself in a box with a label," because even if the interviewer is of the same religion, the interviewer may favor or oppose certain practices within the religion. You *don't* want to go there. A student can be politely evasive by saying something like, "The religious texts obviously took years and years to assemble. Outlining my own religious insights for you could take equally as long. I don't think that's what you're after. Is there anything specific you're looking for?" Most religious discussions should stop there.

If your child is asked for opinions on specific religious or political issues (abortion, same-sex marriage, contraception, prayer in schools, "God" in the Pledge of Allegiance, Alaska pipeline, etc.), he can say that he's continually refining his views and is not ready yet to offer a dissertation on the topic, and then ask the interviewer for his or her opinions. If the interviewer seems to be pressing for a short cliché "radio spot" response, the student may ask, "Is this what we're supposed to be discussing?"

Dress Like You Want to Get In

Secret 240

While there is no "dress code" as such for most college interviews, parents should note that attire is often interpreted as an indicator of enthusiasm for a particular college. A boy from Oregon was interviewing for Columbia University. He showed up for an alumni interview in Oregon in a swimsuit that was somewhat damp and sandy. He apologized, saying he had just interrupted his day at the beach for this interview and hadn't had time to change. The interviewer was not particularly formal or conservative, but he was surprised to see an applicant show up so casually—as if the boy had no concern about what kind of impression he made. In fact, the boy's body language seemed to indicate that he felt that this interview was a major intrusion on his day, and he was eager to get back to surfing as soon as possible. The interviewer took the hint and asked the boy directly, "How interested are you really in Columbia?" The boy said, "Not very." "Why are you here?" the interviewer asked, somewhat daunted. "My parents made me come for this interview. I have no interest in Columbia." Needless to say, the boy was not recommended for admission.

It's not the old-fashioned notion that a jacket and tie for men and a skirt suit for women is right for interviews, but rather a psychological notion that when one wants to be offered a particular opportunity badly, one will do everything to achieve this goal. This includes dressing convincingly, bringing appropriate materials to the interview, and speaking politely.

High school seniors often tell one another how to dress for interviews. They advise each other not to bother with a skirt suit or tie and jacket. And the majority of kids nowadays do not show up at most of the most-competitive college interviews with a tie and jacket or skirt suit. Do not let the other kids influence your kid. Tell your kid to "dress for success." Dressing conservatively (unless the kid is specifically applying for an art school) sends the message that your kid definitely wants to be admitted—more than your kid wants to "fit in" with peers. For girls, a formal pants suit is as good as a skirt suit. Chances are likely that your kid will meet with an admissions officer who is not dressed as formally. A male interviewer may wear a jacket without a tie, or a female interviewer may wear a coordinated blazer and slacks that is not an actual suit. Let your child be more formally dressed. A boy or girl could remove a jacket if necessary during the interview. But make a grander entrance in formal business attire to make a first impression that says, "I don't normally dress this way, but I want to get into this college really badly, so I'm dressing for the part."

An exception is the alumni interviewer who specifies in advance that the interview is going to be casual. Students have said that interviewers have invited them to meet at their homes, a local coffee shop, a golf club, or park. The applicant should still err on the formal side. To an interview that the interviewer specifically states is casual, both boys and girls should probably wear nice slacks with a blazer (jacket) and clean, relatively casual shoes (loafers)—no tie, no athletic shoes. A golf shirt for boys may be okay; a shirt with sleeves for girls is mandatory.

If the interview is in the alumnus's home, dress formally, unless the interviewer specifies otherwise. The interviewer probably will not be dressed formally. This doesn't matter. And although many of the kid's classmates may show up in less formal attire, your child's attire will demonstrate how badly your child wants to be admitted. Ignore the other kids' attire for a day.

Will your kid be penalized or denied entry for not dressing formally enough? Probably not. Many kids have gotten admitted to the most-competitive schools after showing up at interviews in T-shirts and jeans or other casual clothing. And most interviewers do not measure the student based on his or her fashion statement—unless it's extremely inappropriate. More important, the way your child dresses for the interview is just one more indicator of his or her drive in getting admitted. If the kid really wants to get in, why neglect any opportunity to demonstrate this?

Also note that while the university might not care about how your child dresses for an interview, the individual alumnus interviewer might. Perhaps your kid's interviewer is an investment executive or a fashion designer or the CEO of a corporation. You don't want your kid's interview to focus on the difficulty of speaking with a pierced tongue, the rear-end tattoo that becomes visible every time your kid bends to retrieve a résumé from a bag, or the tattoo with the name of your daughter's ex-boyfriend on her shoulder. While you don't want your child to be too self-conscious during the interview, you might have your kid wear a shirt she can tuck in so that the bellybutton isn't the primary focus of the interview.

Practice Interviews

 **Don't let the college interview be your child's first interview experience if possi-ble. Your son or daughter should have many interviews (for summer jobs, for after-school internships, for school-year vol-**

unteer positions, etc.) before senior year. If your kid still has not experienced a formal interview by the time he or she is a senior, arrange some "practice" interviews at colleges that are *not* your kid's first choice but that he or she is considering seriously. Do not set up "fake" interviews at colleges that don't make it on your kid's radar screen. Doing so is unfairly time-consuming for the interviewer and rude, and does not really simulate an actual interview, since your child will not be appropriately nervous or eager to impress.

Obviously, it's nearly impossible to have a practice interview with your own kid. The tension and the adrenaline rush are never there in a practice session. Nevertheless, it's important to have some discussion about the interviews in advance, and it's also smart to practice.

If you can arrange for a friend to come to interview your kid just for practice, that sometimes works better than a family member trying to be serious. Have your kid assemble all of his or her interview "props" (résumés, photocopies of art work or news clippings, etc.).

Talk to your kid about trying to control the direction of the interview. Props help in this endeavor. Have your kid throw out the first question. "May I assume that you are a graduate of Prestige University?" When the alumnus interviewer says, "Yes," the kid can say, "Tell me, what is it you liked most about it? How, in your mind, does it stand above all the other options you had?" This gets the discussion going on a positive note. Then the student should whip out the résumé.

| Secret 242 | Prepare in advance four résumé-based topics that your kid can address on a mo- |

ment's notice. Typically, for a kid who wants to appear well-rounded, this should include one academic passion, one art form that the student is proficient or talented in, one sport or athletic endeavor, and one community-service cause to which your kid is dedicated. In addition, the kid should have one pop culture topic to discuss, ranging from sci-fi books to new films, pop music stars, fashion, computer games, or high-tech gadgets.

How'd It Go? Debriefing Your Kid

Secret 243   **Always make sure you are well out of range of the interviewer (and that doesn't mean standing outside his or her window) before you debrief your kid after the interview.** Do not *loom* during the interview—do not locate yourself in a place where the interviewer or your kid can see you.

Contrary to what most people think, kids usually do have a reasonable sense of how the interview went, and what the likely outcome is, immediately following the interview. Although few interviewers are given license to tell the kid right on the spot that they're in or out, most will give a strong hint one way or the other—if they know or if they think they might have a strong influence.

Many kids report that interviewers will say to them right on the spot, "I'd be shocked if you don't get accepted. But it's not entirely up to me." That's obviously a good sign. Some say, "I'll do everything I can to support your admission, but I have no power in the process." This is usually a good sign. Some say, "You'll be admitted unless something really quirky happens." This is also good.

Some say nothing after an interview in which there seems to be no connection. The interviewer just thanks the kid on the way out and wishes the kid luck with the future. This is often a rejection if the interviewer has any say.

Students should note that interviewers will all start with a disclaimer saying something like, "I don't make the ultimate decision," or "I'm only here to answer questions, but I have little power in admissions," or "This interview is only one element of the application." But most have more power than they admit, particularly if they're enthusiastic about a candidate, or if they feel very negatively about a candidate. When your kid emerges from an interview, find out what the exact final words were. Comments vary, and some interviewers just automatically say things without attaching meanings. Don't focus on this—it's not productive. Based on my years of experience packaging students, here are my interpretations of some of the most commonly made end statements:

- I'd be shocked if they don't take you. (very positive)
- I expect to see you here in the fall. (very positive)
- Expect good news in the mail soon. (extremely positive)
- If it were up to me, I would take you. But we'll see what the others say. (50–50, noncommittal)
- You're obviously well qualified, but sometimes the college is unpredictable. (50-50 positive, but noncommittal)
- Now you can relax. The interview is over. (negative, but friendly)
- It was great to meet you. Have a safe ride back. (negative and attempting to distract)
- Your projects sound interesting. I hope to hear great things someday. (negative)
- Good luck in your college search. (negative)
- I encourage you to continue your college search. (very negative)
- Thanks for considering this college. We'll see what happens. (very negative)
- I enjoyed speaking with you. And enjoy that vacation you spoke about. (negative)
- It was lovely to meet you. And what a great _____ (fill-in-the-blank: outfit, notepad, hat, story you shared, etc.) (negative)
- I have no power in the process, and I have no idea what they'll decide. (very negative)
- I should warn you: The competition is extremely stiff this year, so even the most qualified students may not get in. (very negative)
- We have a larger applicant pool than ever, but we'll keep your application on file. (extremely negative)

Sometimes parents ask a kid how the interview went and the kid mumbles "Okay." It's not that the kid is inarticulate, but rather that the

kid has been through a stressful experience and may not recall a thing
that happened during the interview. Parents who are eating their in-
sides out, waiting to hear the results of the interview, should persist and
ask a few more questions, such as:

- Do you recall any of the questions you were asked?
- Did you feel that you connected with the interviewer? Did you
  like the interviewer?
- Did you especially like any of the questions?
- Was it handy to have your résumé (or props) with you? Did you
  use any of the information?
- Were you asked any questions that you couldn't answer or didn't
  like?
- Did you enjoy the experience? Was your adrenaline going?
- Did you find you had anything in common with the inter-
  viewer?

Time allotted can give you some sense of how the interview went,
but it's not a perfect indicator. The student is usually told to expect the
interview to last for twenty minutes to a half hour. An excellent interview can last an hour and a half at some universities, depending upon
the time of year and the interviewer's schedule of appointments. A
shorter interview may not be an indicator of a poor interview, however, but rather a limited time slot. At some schools, the interviewers are
on a very tight interviewing schedule.

But often, if the interviewer finds the discussion entertaining or intriguing, the interview will run overtime.

Secret 244   **Tell your kid not to worry about the interviewer's time and tell your kid not to be
the one to cut the interview short.** Parents, be sensitive and sensible. Don't rush your kid or imply as your kid goes into the interview
that you're in a rush or that you'll worry if your kid doesn't come out
soon. You want your kid to feel relaxed, and you want the interview to
last for as long as it should. At the same time, your kid should attempt to

make sure that the important information is communicated during the first few minutes of the interview. Some kids like "punch endings" or "surprise endings," and they think that their interview is leading up to some climax so they "save the best for last." Bad practice. Tell your kid to get the important information out early, to make a good first impression, in case the interview is cut short. Your kid should not feel selfish if his interview is running into overtime. Assure your son that if his interview runs long, the next kid's interview will just start later, and the kid will still be allotted the set amount of time. Sometimes the interviews are scheduled with ten-minute cushions (for the interviewer to grab a cup of coffee or take a stretch between interviews), and the interviewer may opt to use that time on your kid, forgoing a break between interviews.

Should You Escort Your Kid to the Interview?

Ten years ago, it was considered universally wrong for parents to visibly escort their teenager to a college interview. If kids relied on parental transportation, the parents knew to make themselves invisible. College applicants were expected to present an image of being independent.

| Secret 245 | The etiquette has changed, and many more parents are no longer hiding in the |

bushes outside the admissions office. Whether or not college admissions offices like this increased parental presence, kids seem to be getting accepted anyway. When interviewers see parents escorting their kids, the parents are often politely offered a seat in the waiting area while the kid is being interviewed. It's usually better not to accept the offer. Tell your kid you'll meet him or her at the campus bookstore or at a nearby eatery. That way, your kid will not feel like he or she must rush through the interview so as not to keep you waiting. Hanging out in the admissions office waiting area will put pressure on both your kid and the interviewer not to use up extra time.

| Secret 246 | If you accompany your child to the admissions office or to an alumnus interviewer's house, *do not* attempt to attend the interview itself with your child. And do not grill the interviewer after the meeting to find out what he or she thought of your kid. |

Don't even ask.

If you drop your kid off for an alumnus interview, instead of lurking in front of the interview location, it's better to send your kid in with a cell phone, drive elsewhere for about twenty minutes, direct your kid to phone you when it's time to be picked up. In an urban or suburban setting, drop off the kid away from the home, a few houses away, perhaps, so the interviewer doesn't feel obligated to invite the parents in (which can work against your child's interview). Drive by first to point out the actual house or building, and then drive away a few houses or buildings and let your child walk back.

In an urban center, instead of having your kid phone for pickup after the interview, you might arrange in advance to meet your kid after the interview at a nearby location—a coffee shop perhaps, or a public library, or at a bench in a nearby park area. Tell your kid not to rush—you (obviously) won't leave without him.

What If You Know the Interviewer Personally ?

| Secret 247 | If you know the local interviewer personally and worry that the person might be prejudiced against your kid, have your kid phone the university to request another interviewer based on potential "conflict of interest." |

Obviously, the situation is sticky, particularly if the person is a neighbor or someone that you see regularly. More often, the interviewer will back out of the interview first—citing "professional reasons"—when he or she recognizes your kid's name on the list. Many universities require alumnus interviewers to take a sabbatical from interviewing when their own children are high school seniors—so the interviewer doesn't try to sandbag everyone else's kids—or if they know the kid personally. From the interviewer's perspective, if your kid does not get accepted, the situation could be awkward, and he or she might worry that you'll hold a grudge forever.

But if the interviewer doesn't back out first, you should politely explain the situation to the university. Or if you live in a remote area where there are no other interviewers and you're really daring, your kid might ask the interviewer directly if he believes that despite familiarity with the family, he would be able to give a fair shake. If the answer is yes, you have to trust the person, but at least you're on the record for having expressed your concern. If the answer is no, you're at liberty to phone the university to discount the interview.

If you're stuck with a questionable neighbor or someone you're not sure of, you might contact the person in advance to tell the person that you're "so happy" that he or she was chosen to interview your kid. Affirm the person, and make sure that he or she is 100 percent comfortable with the situation. Sometimes you might know the interviewer and feel confident that the person would give your child a very supportive recommendation. Warn your kid in advance that if the interviewer asks if your kid knows his or her kid, to say only positive things.

The Optional Interview

Secret 248

There's no such thing as the "optional interview," although lots of applications specify that a personal interview is optional. Some schools do not offer interviews. At all others, parents should note that if the student is serious about the college, no interview is optional—it's mandatory. Instruct your child to always go for the "optional" interview, just as you should instruct your child to always include the "optional" essay and to always do any "extra credit" assignments at school. Both essay and interview demonstrate serious interest.

Should the Kid Eat?

| Secret 249 | Advise your kid not to order anything sloppy—this isn't the time for a leafy

salad, for example—or expensive. It's impossible to talk while you're struggling to cut a tough piece of lettuce or meat, trying to capture the right number of strands of spaghetti onto your fork, or while you're chewing heavily.** If you're asked to meet the interviewer at a restaurant or coffee shop, the interviewer usually pays, using money provided by the university for such interview situations. Nevertheless, the student should thank the interviewer for the meal and probably write a thank-you note for the meal and the interview in the days following the interview. The student should also bring along enough cash, just in case the interviewer does not plan to pay—a rare situation—and the student should be prepared to offer to pay (as a courtesy). The kid should not *insist* on paying, however, since protocol dictates that the interviewer (the college) should pay.

The savvy parent will definitely want to visit the restaurant in advance to preview the menu and to give advice on what to order to make the event run smoothly. You don't want your kid to order the most expensive thing on the menu. That looks tacky. Advise your kid in advance. Nor do you want your kid to order "from each category," if the interviewer is only having a cup of coffee.

And it's humiliating to sit through an interview once you've dripped tomato sauce or other wet and colorful sauces onto one's clothes. Advise your kid, instead, to order a simple sandwich. Even if there's something else she craves on the menu—save that for the next time she's in that restaurant. For some kids, it's better to eat a light bite before the interview, so they don't find themselves shoveling food into their mouths when the interviewer is expecting them to be talkative. Sometimes, it's also advisable to promise the kid to "celebrate" immediately after the interview by going out to another restaurant, so she feels free not to order much or feel obligated to eat a whole lot during the interview meal. Successfully experiencing an interview could be a good cause to celebrate. Remember: After senior year, the kid is off to college, and you won't have quite as many bonding opportunities. Regardless of how the interview went, it's nice for family members to celebrate this milestone with the kid.

Before the interview, instruct your child not to behave like this is the first time she has ever been to a restaurant. Try to avoid focusing on food issues. Discussing one's vegetarianism might not be a good topic if the interviewer happens to be a hunter, for example. Ordering a simple cheese sandwich is a better way to handle the situation. Your daughter can binge at home after the interview. Or if the interviewer is very overweight, and your daughter is on a carb-restricted diet, tell her not to make a big point about calories or fat content. Order an omelet.

What if you're kosher or have other dietary restrictions that forbid your son from eating in a particular restaurant? He should mention this up front, when making arrangements to meet. You should have a comparable restaurant in mind that meets the dietary criteria. Or be able to suggest another venue. If you wait until your child gets to the restaurant to inform the interviewer, the interviewer is bound to feel embarrassed, and the interview will be off to a wrong start.

What Some Interviewers Are Looking At

Secret 250   **If your kid claims to be a member of an underrepresented minority group, be ready to provide documentation if appearance doesn't immediately vouch for his or her ethnicity.** Claims of lost records don't cut it, admissions officials say. A biracial Native American student with fair skin was told by her interviewer, "You don't look like an Indian." However rude and inappropriate, apparently, the interviewer had a stereotyped image of what Native Americans looked like. The application stated that the girl had one grandmother who was Native American, but that the grandmother had died, and no written proof was available of the grandmother's ethnicity. Weeks later, the college sent the family a form to fill out, seeking further evidence of the girl's minority status and "blood percentage." If this sounds like something out of World War II Germany, apparently, this is accepted practice among many universities.

Should You Send a Thank-You Note?

Secret 251 Thank-you notes are not required, but if your kid really wants to attend the college, sending a thank-you note provides one last opportunity to inform the college of your interest. Many students don't send notes, and that's usually okay. But if the interviewer gives your kid his or her card, take that as a strong hint. Also, if the interviewer specifically requests that your kid keep him or her updated on his decision or on his activities, have the kid write a note. The note can be an e-mail, if that's more comfortable and if the interviewer provides an e-mail address. The note also provides an opportunity to mention something that your child may have forgotten to say during the interview—one last chance to add credentials. Or think of the note as a way for your child to stay connected with someone locally from the college.

If your kid gets good news and decides to attend that university, you might encourage your kid to thank the interviewer once again for his or her part in the process. Interviewers like to know how *their* kids fare, and thanking the interviewer acknowledges his or her role in a favorable decision.

Once the interviews have taken place and the applications and recommendations have been submitted, you should encourage your child to continue working hard. While you hope to hear good news from your child's first-choice college, you don't want your son or daughter to be complacent in case he or she is wait-listed. Your child should accumulate new and appealing credentials throughout the second half of senior year, and the next chapter will focus on the steps you can take in the event that he or she does end up on the waiting list.

CHAPTER 11

Getting Your Kid off the Waiting List and into the School of His or Her Dreams

When the letter finally arrives in April, it's not unusual for a child to feel hurt or disappointed if he's told that he's wait-listed. The majority of students will either be accepted or rejected, and the waiting list may seem terribly anticlimactic after waiting all winter to hear positive news. Kids and maybe teachers will ask in school the next day, "Well, did you get in?" And your kid is still without an answer, seemingly hanging by a thread.

Don't despair. It's time to be very proactive if you want positive results.

Is Being Wait-listed an Insult?

Secret 252 **If your child is wait-listed, don't encourage him or her to boycott the college. It's not unusual for kids to feel insulted when they're wait-listed, but if the college is still the "dream school," encourage your child to get over it and become more aggressive about the application.** Let your daughter mourn for a day or two as you aggressively help plan her next strategy. Don't let the mourning period last too long. Affirm your son: "Obviously, they made a bad choice." Or blame demographics: "They probably were afraid to admit too many kids from your school or from the county." Meanwhile, check your child's application to see what can be improved.

Some students who have gotten accepted into their first-choice college off the waiting list have been known to be so hurt initially that they reject the college once they're admitted and stubbornly insist on going to their second-choice school. This punishes the student, not the college, which then recruits another lucky student off the waiting list. A year later, nobody from the college remembers. But your child will remember, and may resent his or her choice. If your child specifically wants a school that wait-lists him or her, pursue admission aggressively. If he or she ultimately receives a rejection, at least you can feel better about trying.

The overall message is that waiting lists are not for waiting. Many exciting opportunities exist for imaginative teenagers and their supportive parents who want to be proactive and go the extra distance to help their kids become innovators and leaders and get into first-choice colleges.

Don't Wait Patiently

Secret 253

Patience and passivity are not virtues when it comes to the waiting list of a college. The waiting list should be viewed as a special opportunity for kids to market and repackage themselves. Parents always ask if the waiting list is really just a polite rejection, or if it is equal in status to a deferral. But the waiting list *is* better than a deferral. "This is a great opportunity," a Caltech admissions officer says. "This is a chance to improve your credentials and update your résumé"—but only if spaces remain. (Note that Caltech did not take any students from its waiting list in 2005—because it was "overenrolled.") A waiting list letter may be flattering or matter-of-fact. It could state, "We are pleased to inform you that you have been placed on the waiting list of our college." Or it could state, "We are sorry to inform you that since so many qualified applicants applied this year, we are putting you on our waiting list." The letter may state that the college really wants your kid, but they've just run out of room. That's probably true.

What do most kids do in response? They wait. And wait. And wait. After all, they figure, it's a *wait*ing list. Wrong response. In the end, these kids ultimately receive a rejection letter.

Without sounding like Pollyanna, you should explain to your kid that the waiting list means that the college really *did* want your kid (should space become available), but not quite as much as they wanted the other kids whom they admitted. In other words, your kid is right on the borderline—a tightrope of sorts. If the wind blows in the right direction, your kid is in.

What does it take, then, to get your kid admitted? Phoning the college to yell and scream doesn't help. Your kid is so close to getting in, you don't want to alienate those who make the decision. You know that the college will likely take *some* kids from the list. But how do you make sure that your kid is one of them?

When your child makes the waiting list, it is time to step back just for a moment and think about a quick but very aggressive résumé and application overhaul. Remember: It's been months since your child's application was submitted. Is there something you would elaborate more on this time? Is there some credential that your kid buried into the application originally that now merits more mention? For example, maybe your kid mentioned that he was planning to try out for the high school's varsity baseball team come spring—but you didn't know at the time that he would be named captain. Or your daughter mentioned casually that she sang with the high school chorus, but had no idea back in December that she'd have the big solo in the Spring Music Festival.

Once you've looked over the application, it's time to update the résumé: Surely your kid did something worthwhile in the interim period before hearing about the waiting list. Compile a list of every award, honor, achievement, new skill, athletic victory, school production, published work (the school newspaper will do), new club, contest, competition, internship, and after-school job that your child has engaged in or won in the aftermath of submitting the application. Granted, if your child is a senior, he or she might have been out to lunch—or at the beach or local park "hanging out"—for the past few months, waiting to hear from colleges and unable to focus on academics and constructive activity. But assuming you've been able to motivate your kid enough to continue to remain a productive student or citizen, it might not be unrealistic to assume that your child has accomplished *something* in the remaining few months of high school. If your list of your child's accomplishments amounts to at least one item—maintaining his or her A average, for example, when other seniors slumped—you might be able to have your child send a letter, fax, or e-mail to the college to update his or her application.

The First Update Fax

Address the fax "To the Admissions Officers" or to "Dear Admissions Officers." (You should also find out who the local recruiter is in your area and, if possible, address a copy of the fax to that recruiter. To find out who that recruiter is, just phone the college's admissions office and ask.) Then write "I have been wait-listed at _____ College, which remains my first choice school. I *promise* to attend if admitted. (Say this and mean it.) I am eager to update you on new credentials I have earned since submitting my application to you months ago, and I hope this will help convince you to admit me."

The second paragraph should focus on the kid's most impressive new credential. Devote the entire paragraph (since there might not be additional credentials at this point) to elaborating on the credential. How many other students from your kid's school were involved? How important is this credential to your kid? More important (from the admissions office point of view), how might achieving this new credential contribute to the college, enhance your kid's college experience, or influence your kid's decision to attend this college?

Devote separate paragraphs to each additional *new* credential (only credentials achieved in the aftermath of submitting the application count), describing each in detail and being as specific as possible as to how each credential might benefit the college. Did your kid take up bassoon lessons, for example? Might she be able to play in the college orchestra by September? Did your kid publish in a local paper to gain experience in college journalism?

Sit with your child. Do some soul-searching. Tell your son or daughter to think about why and if he or she still wants to attend the specific college. Have him write a final paragraph about how he envisions life there. Name specific clubs she would join and courses she would take. The fax should be summed up with the following reminder: "Please include this update in my admissions application folder. I am hoping to hear good news from you soon." The P.S. should indicate: "I am sending a copy of this letter to you by regular mail as well, to make sure you receive my update." At this stage, faxing is better than e-mail because it creates a guaranteed paper trail.

If the parent is writing the "shell" of the letter (which often happens when the wait-listed student is too distraught or too busy with schoolwork), be sure to include your child's full name, address, phone number, and Social Security number (or application number, if the college has assigned your child such a number), so the college is able to easily find the application and add the new material to the file.

Your child may not get a response. It is okay for your child to phone to see if the fax arrived. Some admissions officers may say that they're too busy to check, but that's usually not the case if your child phones minutes after sending the fax. On rare occasions, students have been known to get immediate acceptances (by phone) within minutes of the initial fax. Don't count on it, however. As soon as the first fax is sent, start thinking about the next fax.

Successful parents help plan a barrage of faxes and letters to help secure a spot for their kids. (The reason faxes are preferred over e-mails is that faxes result in paper copies that no secretary or clerk can claim not to have accessed. Faxes generally still come through on paper automatically, without having to be printed out by a third party. E-mails can be left unopened or not printed out. As long as colleges still use paper printouts when reviewing applications, faxes are a surer guarantee that your child's added information will make it into his or her file.) To do this, you and your child will have to creatively think of new ways to add new last-minute credentials to the application. Some obvious additions: Did your kid get a new summer job? Can your kid help tutor other students or set up tutoring for final exams? Is your kid speaking at graduation?

Some people will argue that this last-minute "Band-Aid approach" is not only wrong, but it doesn't work. ("Don't colleges see through it? Don't the newfound commitments seem insincere?") No. If your kid is very borderline, colleges may expect to see which candidate will now go out of her way to demonstrate that she should be admitted. I have told students (with success) that if only one space opens up at your first-choice Ivy League college, make sure that you're the one. By strengthening credentials and aggressively writing updates to the college, my students have gotten in off some of the shortest waitlists.

| Secret 254 | **Attempting to remedy a weak application or résumé when your kid is wait-listed** |

can be viewed as smart, proactive, resourceful, and responsible. It teaches the student that it's never too late to improve oneself or to enhance one's experience. Even last-minute improvements matter. The improvements should not be superficial: Have your daughter inform the college of her enriching summer plans, a weekend language-immersion program she enrolled in, her organization of a food drive, or her aid to storm victims. Have your child demonstrate to the college that he isn't satisfied to passively await news, but that he wants to be aggressive and proactive about his future, and this is a good quality in a potential student. This is also an excellent indicator for how motivated the student will be in college. Sometimes waiting list notification can be just the ticket for a less-motivated high school student to turn his or her life around and become more academically assertive. Many colleges report that such last-minute faxes and credential enhancements significantly increase a student's chances of getting in—as long as the added credentials are honest and the achievements significant.

Although sending an update letter sounds good in theory, motivating a just-wait-listed kid to write a note to the admissions office may be a daunting task. After all, the kid feels like he has just been rejected (half true) and writing another note represents yet another risk and "waste of time" (his words). Be very sensitive. A little hand-holding can be helpful. Help your kid to formulate the letter. Write the "shell." Brainstorm about your child's accomplishments in the aftermath of the application. Suggest worthy achievements. Sit with your child as he or she writes the letter (or let the kid dictate to you). Offer a prize, if necessary, to make the process fun. Proofread the letter before it's faxed.

The Second Fax

Again, the second fax should be addressed "To the Admissions Officers" (with a copy sent to the local recruiter). This time, your child will want to indicate up front that this is the second fax being sent—partly as a reminder and assurance that the college received the first fax and filed it properly, partly so the admissions office doesn't confuse the two faxes, and partly to demonstrate to the college that your child is still aggressively pursuing admission. When phoning to make sure that the fax was received, it is okay for your child to ask for reassurance that the first fax was also received and was correctly filed. (Before your daughter picks up the phone, make sure that she knows the exact date that the previous fax was sent, so that she can refer to "my letter of May 25," for example.) You, the parent, should be in charge of bookkeeping and keeping track of old correspondence. The answering officer or secretary may agree to check or may not. Advise your son to be polite, cheerful, and upbeat in any case, and thank the staffer for his or her time. Your child's telephone voice should say "Winner." If you have the mumbling or grunting type of kid, practice the phone conversation in advance. Or let your kid make the phone call from a private room—so that he or she doesn't feel obligated to coolly mumble or grunt in front of his or her family during the phone conversation.

The second fax should contain all new material. It should be positive and enthusiastic. The gist should be, "You may recall that when I heard about my waiting-list status, I sent you an update of my credentials. Now I am sending you a second update. Note that I am adding new credentials that were not contained in the application or the first fax. But first, I want to stress that Academia College remains my first choice, and I intend to enroll immediately if accepted."

The second paragraph should describe in detail your child's most impressive new credential. Again, devote an entire paragraph to each additional credential.

When should the second fax be sent? As soon as you can muster up more credentials to merit a second fax. A week later is ideal, since the waiting-list process is relatively short. Many colleges have the waiting list summed up by the end of June. (Some colleges admit kids as spaces become available, others take all their wait-listed kids at once.) A single, major credential will do, but obviously, it's better to have as many new credentials as possible. Sum up the letter once again by reminding the admissions office to include this second fax along with the first fax update in your kid's admissions folder. Also, your kid should remind the admissions officer of his or her enthusiasm and eagerness to hear good news. Once again, be sure to include the kid's full name, address, phone number, and Social Security number (or application number, if the college has assigned such a number), so the college can locate the file and add the new material to the application.

A Third Fax?

How many faxes should you send? That depends upon how long it takes the college to admit your kid. Plan to keep going until the college either accepts or rejects the student. Plan to send a fax a week. That means you need to keep adding credentials. Add them if your kid really wants to attend the college. Tell your kid to go out and do good things that he or she can write about.

Nothing to write about? Visit the college again. By the time your kid is wait-listed, classes will probably be out for the summer. Arrange meetings with professors in the departments that interest your kid. Try to set this up—quickly—so your kid can refer to these meetings in his or her third fax. "I am eager to report some of my latest activities to you. This is my third fax, and I want you to know that I am still very much hoping to be admitted off the waiting list. I visited the campus again this weekend and was thrilled to be able to meet with Professor _____ in the _____ Department. She showed me her lab and invited me to ask questions about her research. I was intrigued by the setting since I strongly want to major in _____, and I learned from this experience that _____." Your kid should sound like he or she has already moved into the university and would be at home there.

Last-Minute Rescue

Secret 255 **Parents can be enormously helpful in scouting out wonderful new opportunities and credentials to enhance the "pedigree" of a wait-listed child. Be constructive. Be dazzling. Think big.** Kids who play an instrument, for example, might consider staging a concert or concert tour at local day care centers, hospitals, or senior centers. An art student or photographer might seek out exhibition space at a local town hall, library, park nature center, or bank. A student whose friends have eclectic talents could stage a "vaudeville" fund-raiser, bringing in other students with talents for magic, juggling, and gymnastics to raise money for cancer research. A socially oriented kid might organize a fund-raising costume ball, or a fund-raising golf tournament, or a community clean-up day.

Think from the college admissions decision-maker's perspective. What kind of kid would you want to admit at the last moment? If the college still has needs, you would want the kid who fills a need (the French horn player, the political cartoonist, the track star, etc.). If all needs are met, you want the most motivated kid who desperately wants to come to your college and promises to attend if admitted. You want the kid who demonstrates energy and promises to contribute to the life of the college. You want the kid whom you should have taken the first time around. You want the kid who *doesn't wait.*

The Orderless List

Secret 256 **Contrary to what most people assume, many most-competitive colleges *do not* rank kids on the waiting list. That's right—no ranking, no priority, no preference for this kid over that kid—just a pile of names in no particular order.** Parents like to imagine their kid is on top—the next one in line, urgently desired by each college, but wait-listed for some technical reasons or demographics. Forget this myth. Few of the most-competitive colleges *rank* the waiting list. Yet if you phone the admissions office and ask where exactly your kid is on the list, many staffers feel uncomfortable admitting that there's no order. Instead, you may get a very evasive answer or typical: "I don't have time to check," or "I don't have access to that information," or "I'm not permitted to divulge that information," or "Be patient," or "We'll be sending out the letters next week."

Likewise, if you phone to ask how many kids are on the waiting list or how many kids the college typically admits from the list, the answer again could be vague, although some colleges will tell you.

Some colleges do have an actual ranking system for their waiting lists. Of these, few will divulge your child's ranking. Instead, they may give you a noncommittal answer or suggest that you proceed with another college, not counting on the waiting list to deliver good news. Does it hurt to inquire? No. Inquiring is a wise response. At best, it may give you a handle on how to proceed and may answer the question of whether or not you should put down a deposit at another school. Usually, you should put down that deposit—and hope to lose it, as wait-listed students are usually notified long after the deposits were due at the other universities. If you don't put a deposit down anywhere, your kid may have no college to attend in the end.

The Green Pen Approach

Secret 257

If there's no order to the waiting list, and there's no *list* to the waiting list, what does a waiting list look like? At some schools, the list consists of a series of note cards or even a pile of single sheets of paper. The candidate with the most green pen marks is the first one admitted off the list. Each card or page has a different wait-listed student's name on it. Admissions officers write notes in the margins of these sheets supposedly in green pen (hence the name, "the green pen approach") as new information on a particular applicant is added—even at the very top colleges. For example, if an admissions officer learns that a wait-listed applicant just won a Congressional Award, the officer might enter in green pen a notation (with the date of the entry) on that student's sheet that after the original application was submitted, the "Student won a Congressional Award." If a student wins a science competition or a poetry competition, another green pen notation is added in the margins. For a very aggressive applicant, the margins fill up quickly. For a passive applicant, no green pen marks appear.

How do admissions officers learn of the applicants' additional accomplishments? Naive parents note: Few admissions officers scour the newspapers looking for names of prospective candidates who are silently, patiently occupying the waiting list hoping to be discovered. So the responsibility rests on the applicants or their parents—usually their parents, in fact—to inform the admissions office of the applicant's newest achievements if they want these accomplishments added to the application. Regardless of who writes the updates, the updates should be signed by the students.

Each time the student contacts the college by fax with an updated piece of information, an entry is made on the application in green pen. An admissions director of a prominent university said that eventually, when a space opens up, the admissions officers look to see whose card or sheet has the most green marks in the margins. It's that easy. The kid who badgers the admissions office most is the one accepted, assuming that the updates are legitimate.

Staying on Top of the Pile

Secret 258 | **Other college representatives speak of a similar approach to getting in off the waiting list. They say the secret is "staying on top of the pile."** Each time your kid contacts the college, his or her card is pulled from the pile and a notation is made. The card is then put on top of the pile. The cards belonging to the most proactive applicants tend to be found at or near the top. When spaces open up, the college fills them by taking the cards at the top and offering those candidates admission.

Few colleges reveal their method—if they even have a method of admitting students from the waiting list. If either method is used, constant updates pay off.

For paranoid parents' information: No colleges say, "Oh this kid has been updating his application too much so we won't accept him." Just make sure that the updates contain *new* credentials—*worthy* events that occurred after the filing of the original application. And make sure that the fact that the information is *new* is spelled out in the update—so admissions officers don't think you're reiterating previously disclosed information. Provide the dates of the new activities.

By the time of year when waiting lists are announced (April and May), it becomes harder for applicants to acquire new credentials—and I emphasize that the credentials should be *meaningful* activities, not fraudulent, fake, or trivial. (For example, don't let your son say he's founded a bird-watching club, when he hasn't. Or don't let your daughter claim to tutor elderly people on the computer, when she doesn't.) For some of the more competitive students, spring is when they hear from some of the contests that they entered previously. This is another reason why it's important to encourage your seniors to remain active in clubs and contests. With luck, some of the results represent good news (winning a contest) that can enhance one's credentials in late spring. For students who were less active during the year and are not awaiting competition results, more aggressive behavior is required in manufacturing new credentials. Yes, *manufacturing* new credentials is okay, as long as you're being honest.

The Proper Perspective

Secret 259   **Developing new credentials is a constructive activity that may teach the child a long-term lesson in marketing and presenting oneself.** New credentials could consist of repackaging or reengineering previous accomplishments. For example, with minimal work, an art student can take a series of paintings that the student has already created and organize them into an exhibition at a local bank (tacked onto a bulletin board). A performing-arts student can organize a performance (of previously mastered works) at a local day care center, senior center, or hospital. A student who has excelled in community service can put together a fund-raising drive, a clothing drive, or pizza sale. Although the activity may be last-minute, the project should be constructive and a new learning experience for the student in order to qualify as a legitimate additional credential. To a college admissions office, such activities demonstrate willingness to take already polished skills and abilities to new levels, initiative, and determination to pursue admission aggressively. These are positive predictors of success in college, even if the initial motivation is to help secure admission.

Is Creating New Credentials Ethical?

Secret 260   **Building last-minute credentials should not be viewed as a façade meant to fool colleges. The secret is that with proper parental support, this experience can be an eye-opening experience that expands your child's horizons and encourages exploration of new subjects.**

But be warned: The very idea of *manufacturing* new credentials may at first seem corrupt. And, depending on how it's done, it could indeed be corrupt. A group of wait-listed students from one high school considered setting up a fake ethnic news magazine. According to their scheme, each staff member would be made an instant editor just for joining. The plan dictated that the publication staff would never meet and the editors would have no responsibilities. But the students, eager to get off the waiting lists at their respective colleges, thought that the creation of such a publication would impress college admissions officers and show leadership and initiative. Luckily the fraud never happened. Although some of the students might have gotten away with the scheme, the overall lesson would have been very negative—promoting dishonesty and laziness. Parents should encourage a wait-listed child to enhance his or her credentials honestly, so the student benefits from a new experience and maintains honesty and integrity.

What kind of credentials or updates are worth reporting?

- Contests, competitions, and scholarships won
- Honors and awards earned
- New publications (school newspaper articles; literary magazine works)
- New artistic achievements: performances, exhibits, displays, films
- New jobs
- Success at a community-service project: raising money for a good cause (specify how much you helped raise in total), helping to construct a day care center (specify what your role was)
- Tutoring a student (specify any tangible sign of improvement)
- Enhancing a sports team at your school (if your kid creates a team newsletter or yearbook, organizes a tournament, changes the way athletes warm up or train, solicits more spectator involvement, etc.)
- Creation of a new club, team, organization, or chapter of an established organization at school
- Visits to the college campus, meetings with professors, attendance at college classes

- New grades and test scores if they show significant improvement
- Having a gratifying new experience (flying in a blimp, taking tap dancing lessons, white-water rafting, appearing on a local TV show)
- Finishing a book or article that had major impact on your thinking

When writing an update about new credentials and achievements, make sure your child explains the achievements carefully and in context. For example, if your son wins a local science fair, he should describe the project and what effort he contributed in the long term, how many other students entered, and how many placed in the same category. Your child should let the admissions office know the significance of this honor as the student is best able to describe it (with parental support, of course). Have your kid emphasize the originality of the project.

Assuring the Admissions Office

Secret 261 State up front and in all subsequent correspondence that if your child gets off the waiting list and into the college, the child promises to attend. The family that is oblivious of this secret is likely to lose out to a more savvy family. Colleges want "sure things." There is no wiggle room. The college does not want to be rejected by a kid admitted off the waiting list (although many colleges say they don't count the waiting list statistics when calculating their yield or ratio of accepted students to the number of students who actually end up attending). Each transmission that is sent to the college should restate the child's commitment to attend the college if pulled from the list, and your child must stick to this commitment if ultimately accepted. If your child is unsure if he or she can stick to this commitment, do not have him or her pursue admission beyond the waiting list.

★   ★   ★

Although the waiting list may seem disappointing at first, the more difficult response to deal with is a deferral or rejection from a student's first-choice college. With deferrals and rejections, it may be time for parents to investigate other options more seriously. Perhaps some of the student's second-choice colleges have special programs—Honors programs, for example—that would make those colleges seem just as special and appealing as the first-choice college.

CHAPTER 12

Success After Deferral
or Rejection

In the event that your child is either deferred or rejected, you'll need to not only console your child but also quickly determine and act upon your options. Savvy parents will have encouraged their kids to prepare applications to a range of other colleges in addition to the Early Decision choice, to be ready if the kid is not accepted in December. (This preparation should take place in November and early December, after the Early Decision application is submitted, so the student who gets rejected or deferred doesn't have to spend the Christmas holiday week filling out applications in a state of depression to meet the early January deadlines.)

Focusing on polishing these additional applications is a good way to turn the student's rejection into a constructive response, although it probably won't eradicate all of the disappointment. Our society tells high school students that senior year is supposed to be one of the best years of their lives—filled with proms, leadership opportunities, high school sports stardom, and college acceptances. For students who don't get into their first-choice college in December, senior year often turns painful, as they wait all winter and early spring hoping that they will receive good news in April. Be sensitive to your kid, but don't harp on the negative.

Are Deferrals Really Conclusive Rejections?

| Secret 262 | **Deferrals are not rejections.** I have known many cases where deferred students have been |

accepted in April. The trick is not to treat a deferral as a rejection by passively sulking about it. Instead, the parents should take leadership by showing the student how to respond to the deferral as an opportunity to add credentials and repackage him- or herself. Treat the deferral the same way as being wait-listed (see chapter 11). Submit new material to the college to demonstrate that your child has added credentials and should be added to the pool of those students that the colleges will accept in April.

Dealing with a Rejection

Rejection is tough in December, since, in all likelihood, the student will have only applied to the one Early Decision college and won't have positive news to balance the negative. But a December rejection still leaves plenty of time to find a range of suitable colleges—including safety schools—to apply to Regular Decision. Make sure that the safety schools that are selected are palatable. Sometimes kids agree to safety schools never really envisioning that they may have to *go* to those schools. I have seen students who applied to top colleges at other ends of the country (as their safety schools) suddenly feel traumatized, when they realize that no nearby college had accepted them, and they will be stuck going far from home. I have seen students use small rural colleges as their safety schools when their first-choice colleges were all large urban universities and then become despondent at the thought of having to go to a remote or isolated campus. And I have seen the opposite: Kids who dream of serene college campuses free of city lures and distractions suddenly finding themselves with only urban options.

April rejections are more difficult, if the student doesn't receive at least one appealing offer of admission. Remember, you only need one.

Savvy parents make sure that their kids apply to a range of colleges to improve their odds.

Rejection Versus Deferral Versus Waiting list: A Crash Course

For students who apply Early Decision and are not accepted, two kinds of notices may be sent by the university or college (usually in December). A deferral notice means that the college has delayed the student's admission decision until spring, when the student will be compared with a larger pool of applicants seeking Regular Admission. Outright rejection letters are less common, but they are final decisions and close off the university to the recipient. Of the Ivy League colleges, Penn has the reputation for rejecting the largest percentage of Early Decision applicants. When colleges defer students, the implication is that the student was worthy, and the college needed more time to consider the student. In contrast, an immediate rejection sends the message "not even worthy of consideration." The most common reason for rejection is that the applicant's numbers (GPAs and scores) aren't in the right range. After Early Decision is over, and students apply Regular Decision, notices are sent out in the spring either accepting, rejecting, or wait-listing the remainder of the students.

After Early Rejection or Deferral, Can My Kid Apply for Early Decision 2?

Secret 263   **Many students who don't get accepted Early Decision (1) at their first-choice school turn around and apply to *another* college Early Decision 2, *when the odds are even better*, since the pool is smaller.** If your child has already heard—usually in mid-December—that he was either deferred or rejected from an Early Decision or Early Action choice, he is free to apply to a college that offers Second Early or Early Decision 2 ("ED2"). The ED2 deadline at Washington University in St. Louis, for

example, has been January 1 in recent years, and the student hears by
January 15. The turnaround is very fast, according to the Director of
Admissions Nanette Tarbouni, because the bulk of students apply either First Early Decision or Regular Decision. The Second-Early applicant pool is much smaller. Washington University has been offering
this option for fifteen years because, "Many students decide sometime
after the first round that Washington University is their first choice,"
Director Tarbouni says.

Many of the colleges still cling to the concept that students should
only apply to one college early—whether it's Early Decision or ED2.
Students applying Second Early should go out of their way to affirm
that this ED2 college is really and truly their first-choice college—even
if they previously applied to another college for Early Decision 1 and
were either deferred or rejected. Do not even mention any college that
might have been a previous Early Decision choice.

None of the Ivy League colleges offer Early Decision 2. Among the
more competitive colleges that offer an ED2 option in addition to
Washington University are (alphabetically):

Bates	Claremont McKenna
Boston U.	Connecticut College
Bowdoin	Emory
Bryn Mawr (called "Winter Early Decision")	Middlebury
Bucknell	Oberlin
Colby	Pomona
Colgate (apply any time be- tween November 15 and January 15 and you'll hear within two weeks)	Reed
	Smith
	Tufts
	Union
Carleton	Vanderbilt
Carnegie Mellon (not for its art, design, drama, or music program)	Vassar

Most have deadlines of January 1, but ED2 deadlines range from December 15 to January 15, and may change annually, depending on the college. When considering this option, check with the individual college.

Reversing a Deferral

Secret 264 **Deferrals (but not rejections) can be reversed by proactive guidance counselors sometimes at both public and private schools.** Parents can play a major role in helping their kids find new, legitimate credentials (that somehow were omitted from the original application) to support this effort. If the guidance counselor phones the college with new information to add to the application, this could be influential. One admissions officer at a most competitive college said that her institution has "never turned over a *rejection*" based on a phone call from the guidance office, school official, or parent. Nor do other colleges.

Is it wrong for a parent to ask the guidance counselor to advocate for your deferred kid? No. There is no harm in asking—if you know that the guidance counselor genuinely likes your kid. A guidance counselor who strongly supports your kid's application will agree to advocate firmly. A guidance counselor who is coerced can come across as negative. Make sure you are confident that your kid's counselor really wants your kid to gain admission before you ask the counselor to phone the college to change a deferral to an acceptance. If you don't ask the counselor, it is extremely unlikely that your counselor will take the initiative to phone the college to inquire—particularly if your kid attends a public school.

Typical negative responses: "If I advocate for your kid, shouldn't I, in all fairness, have to advocate for the other seven as well?" The proper response is, "But we're requesting this because my kid really wants this college—as demonstrated by my contacting you. The other parents are not requesting your endorsement, thus showing that their kids may be happier with other colleges. Endorsement should only be given to those who seek it."

Reversing a Rejection

Can a parent reverse a rejection decision by complaining to the admissions office or by meeting with college administrators?

 **Decisions are never reversed when _parents_ complain, but sometimes the discussion can be therapeutic. Many admissions officers view complaining parents with sympathy.** In fact, many of the admissions officers at some of the most prestigious colleges field the parents' phone calls instead of relegating the nasty job to a subordinate.

The primary reason parents feel _wronged_, admissions officials say, stems from a lack of understanding of the scope of the applicant pool—the achievements of today's graduating high school seniors. Today's applicant pool is far more accomplished and competitive than the pool of twenty, ten, or five years ago, admissions officers say. Parents whose kids are applying to the most-competitive colleges mistakenly think that a 2100 or even 2300 SAT I and an A average will get their kid in anywhere. These parents should be reminded that the handful of the nation's most-competitive colleges—Harvard, MIT, Princeton, Yale, Stanford—turn away many students with perfect SAT or ACT scores and A-plus averages.

Does it hurt your child if you phone to politely complain about or question a rejection? No. Does it help your child? No. **But sometimes you can learn something to help any younger children you may have who are planning to someday apply to college,** assuming that the discussion remains civilized and open-minded. If a kid phones—or even some kids have been known to show up at admissions offices to complain—getting a concrete explanation from an admissions officer is sometimes helpful.

(While I have never known of a high school student who was able to reverse a college rejection, one of my students talked his way into a top magnet high school the day after he was rejected, convincing the head of admissions to reverse the decision. He even wrote about this initial setback for his college application, and the essay helped to win him admission into his first-choice college.)

If you phone, you'll be in good company. "We get hundreds of them (phone calls from parents)," said one admissions administrator at one of the nation's most-competitive schools. "Usually, it's the father," she said, explaining that the admissions officers do, indeed, speak with these callers. She says her office offers some explanations. She said that most parents of the rejected kids have "no idea of the ocean of talent. They don't believe that other kids can be better qualified." The admissions officer said that the applicant pool has gradually been increasing in quality and quantity over the years, and that families that rely on admissions statistics from ten years ago, find that their context is outdated, and that admission is much more competitive. She said that some parents sound like they have been "on Pluto" for ten years.

Does it hurt the kid's chances of getting into *another* school if the parents question the rejection? No. Admissions officers are not known to compare negative phone calls with other colleges. They say they don't view questioning phone calls as incorrect responses. And they don't seek to punish the kids of callers.

Do Colleges Ever Reverse a Positive Decision?

| Secret 266 |

In response to a frequently asked question: Yes, neighbors, competitive parents, competing kids, nasty teachers, or others *can and do* phone or write to admissions offices to ask that other people's kids be disqualified from admissions. If your kid has no skeletons in the closet, nobody can blackmail or blacklist him or her. But if your kid has been suspended, or arrested, or fails a course and doesn't report it, or drops a course after applying without reporting it, or lies, or cheats, or plagiarizes, or hides other infractions, your kid is vulnerable. Make sure your kid's application is honest and forthcoming.

Admissions administrators report that they receive two kinds of tattling phone calls: one more common, and one more influential. At the most-competitive colleges, officers say they frequently get unsigned letters (with no return addresses) undermining an "unnamed student." The gist of the letter is that, "I want to inform you that you are among several universities that have incorrectly accepted a student who fraudulently wrote information in her application that just isn't true. She doesn't deserve to go to your college. You should investigate this immediately, but I will not reveal her name." Usually these letters are written by students who were rejected or disgruntled parents of students who were rejected. Most don't identify the student that they accuse. And most are not signed.

When admissions officers get these letters that do not name names they do not respond. They have nobody to respond to, and nobody to research, based on the lack of information provided. They feel that such letters are just a matter of people "blowing off steam" in response to rejection. People are hesitant to sign their names or identify the accused students when they are not sure of the facts. This kind of letter has no impact and is viewed as just plain irresponsible.

A second kind of correspondence, however, is relatively rare, but has more impact. Occasionally university admissions officials receive a letter providing the name of a supposed offender who has been offered admission. For example: "Lucy Smith, whom you admitted to your college, recently was suspended from high school for cheating—and has cheated her way through high school—and does not deserve to go to your college." Or "Sarah Anderson, whom you recently admitted, has just been arrested for shoplifting." Or "Victoria Gray, who is to be a member of your freshman class, was recently given probation on drug-selling charges." Or "Robert Williams wrote on his application that he was editor of the student newspaper, when, in fact, he never worked for the student newspaper."

These letters are also rarely signed, but they identify the person they accuse. Beware! College admissions officers say they follow up on negative, unsolicited letters, if the letters identify a specific student—even if the letters are unsigned. In the first step, the university typically phones the high school. The admissions officer wants to know if the accusation bears merit. If the school confirms the accusation and admits that it suspended Lucy Smith at one point, the admissions office wants to know why the student and the school did not report this before a whistle-blower or tattler did. This looks bad for the high school, admissions officers say, although they realize that public and private schools are often mired in politics that forbid them from reporting anything negative about their own students.

How is it bad for a high school? The school loses some credibility in recommending future students. Admissions officers feel that it's the schools' duty to be forthright with information. Many high school officials do not concur.

After the negative information is confirmed with the school, the admissions office contacts the individual candidate to seek two explanations. One explanation is for why the misdeed was done, and the second is for why the misdeed and the punishment were never reported to the university. (Some applications specifically ask if the student was ever arrested, or suspended, etc. Many do not, however. But students are still expected to voluntarily report infractions.)

At this stage, the admissions decision is not necessarily reversed. The student may still stand a chance. One head of admissions said that if the student, at this point, expresses remorse that sounds sincere, the offer of admission is likely to remain—particularly if the student discusses what was done to remedy the situation and how the student intends to prevent such a situation from ever occurring again. If, however, the student tries to rationalize or glibly dismiss or excuse the misdeed, the offer is likely to be reversed. As a general rule, make sure your kids are honest in their applications. If they manage to fool the admissions staff, they still won't fool themselves, and they'll never feel that they genuinely earned admission.

Admissions officers have found that most of the letters that name a specific kid tend to be based on some truth. So they take these letters seriously. Does this mean that you should tattle on your kid's competitor? No. My advice to parents is to focus on helping to promote your own kids' merits, rather than teaching your kids to step on others to get ahead. If you want your kids to become caring, compassionate adults, and those two qualities are included in your definition of success, the application process is probably one of the best opportunities a parent will ever have to demonstrate integrity.

Can You Back Out of an Early Decision Acceptance?

 **You can back out of Early Decision if you're accepted and find that you can't afford it. That's the one acceptable excuse for not going.** Most colleges and guidance counselors keep this a secret. They tell you that you can't back out of an Early Decision college once you're accepted—never, ever. But what if you find that you don't have the money and the college doesn't offer you enough scholarship to make the college affordable to you? Of course you can back out if you can't afford the college. But colleges don't want this information known. They prefer that their Early Decision applicants be "sure things," and don't want to worry about people backing out for financial reasons. However, some colleges may try to offer you more aid to "sweeten the pot" to keep your kid in, if they are convinced that there is a genuine financial need that has not been met.

What If My Kid Gets in Nowhere?

Secret 268 **Many of the most-competitive colleges have openings in the spring semester that are difficult to fill.** A student's odds are much better midyear. Your son can temporarily enroll last-minute in a local public or community college—saving you lots of tuition for one semester—and plan to transfer out after that single semester into the school of his choice. It helps to note that the community colleges each summer are filled with Ivy Leaguers, who routinely take their introductory Biology, Chemistry, and Pre-Med courses there and transfer in the credits to their more competitive colleges as a way of passing their Pre-Med requirements in a less stressful environment. If your kid must do a semester of community college, have him or her take Pre-Med requirements, freshman English, or any other potentially stressful course to get them out of the way in a less challenging setting and then transfer to the goal institution.

| Secret 269 | **A second option for a student who has not been offered admission anywhere is** |

to pursue a two-year associate's degree (AA) and then apply to transfer into a competitive college. Many top colleges accept a significant number of junior transfer students. Princeton is one of the few that does *not* take transfers. Often transferring is an easier way to get in than applying for freshman admission.

| Secret 270 | **Probably the most palatable option when your child has been rejected everywhere** |

is to go online and seek out colleges that did not fill their enrollment maximum for that year. Go to the website of the National Association of College Admission Counseling: http://nacacnet. org. Click on the NACAC Space Availability Survey and the state in which you're interested to find colleges with space available. College availabilities are posted starting the first week in May and lasting through the summer, with constant updates. Just to give you an idea, as of July 2005, some of the following colleges were listed as still having space available for September 2005: University of Arizona, Pittsburgh, Clark, Goucher College, New College of Florida, Illinois Institute of Technology, Rochester Institute of Technology, University of Maine, University of Oregon, Drew University, Webb Institute (free tuition),

Fordham, Alfred, Hofstra, SUNY Purchase, SUNY Oswego, SUNY Brockport, U. Mass at Lowell, U. Mass at Dartmouth. (Note that the list changes each year.)

| **Secret 271** | **If your child has not been accepted any-where, have him do something extraordi-** |

nary for a year and then reapply. What can your child accomplish in a year? Your science-bent daughter can, for example, participate in a research expedition, do an internship in a local laboratory, or volunteer for a Student Conservation Association (SCA) expense-paid, tuition-free national park internship, (http://www.thesca.org/con_int.cfm). Your social sciences–bent son can travel and participate in an exchange program or language-immersion program, or volunteer in an emergency-relief program, or for a political campaign. Habitat for Humanity's Collegiate Challenge welcomes students over age sixteen (http://www.habitat.org/ccyp/col_chal/default.aspx) year round. Your artistic kid can write a novel, or choreograph a ballet, or arrange a painting exhibit, or compose an opera. The one-year project does not have to be costly, but it should be very goal-driven, ambitious, and out of the ordinary.

| **Secret 272** | **Have your child enroll at an extension, continuing education, or general studies** |

college at a prestigious university. One of the best such programs is offered by Harvard University's Extension Division, whose administrators stress that their school is *not* a back door for Harvard. Ignore what they say for a moment. If your kid can handle attending college without all the activity hoopla and tuition expense, and without the hassles of regular college applications, your kid might be the perfect candidate. Most of the courses meet at night, and the kid would graduate after four years with, get this, a genuine "Harvard University" degree. What's the catch? There are several listed below, but for many kids, such drawbacks pale in comparison to the benefits and glory of receiving a Harvard degree.

Major Drawbacks

- Most classes meet at night.
- About half the students in the classes may be older people who hold full-time jobs (about half are college age).
- Most Harvard extracurricular activities are closed to Extension students, but Extension students may use athletic facilities and libraries.
- No dorms are provided, although the students can live in Harvard apartments.
- Although it says "Harvard University" in big letters at the top of the diploma, in the middle, where it would normally say "Harvard College," it instead says "Extension School."
- Diplomas are in English instead of Harvard's usual Latin.
- Extension students are not in the same classes as Harvard College students, but often they'll share professors and classrooms.

Major Advantages

- Tuition is shockingly low; average course cost is $550 to $825 per course, $2,200 to $3,300 per semester full time; or $4,400 to $6,600 per year.
- In the end, the student *does* get to write on his or her résumé that he or she received a Bachelor of Liberal Arts from Harvard University.
- Twenty majors are offered.
- Admission is a lot easier.
- The Extension School has its own student government and publication, and is a lot more accessible if a student wants to run for office or become an editor.
- After a specified number of courses, Extension students may take two courses per semester in Harvard College.
- A student can graduate in four years, and many go on to Harvard, Yale, and MIT for graduate, medical, law, or business school.

Northwestern has a School of Continuing Studies program that is very similar to Harvard's. Similar programs are also offered at Columbia, University of Pennsylvania, and Pittsburgh with more restrictions. At Columbia, the student must be out of high school for at least a year. At Pittsburgh, the student must be out for at least two years. At Penn, the student must be at least twenty-one. NYU's General Studies is a "back door" of sorts; the student earns a two-year AA degree and then applies to another NYU school to complete the bachelor's with two more years of study.

If your child initially does not get into his first-choice college or any college at all, the important thing to remember is that many exciting options are still available, and parents can be most helpful in sorting them out. Be flexible and don't be stuck on the idea that only one college is able to meet your child's educational needs. Focus, instead, on which opportunities would be most important for your child, and seek those out.

A FINAL NOTE

Gone are the days of parents sitting on the sidelines, oblivious or helpless as their kids apply to college. Parents today are playing a far more active role in the college application process than check-writer. And they're not apologizing for their increased involvement, nor should they. Savvy parents recognize that the world of college applications is competitive—and they need to devote energy and attention to help guide their children's pursuit of opportunities.

Packaging entails a sophisticated involvement. Today's most successful parents take responsibility for seeking out opportunities for their kids—or hiring someone to do that. Savvy parents see it as their mission to give their kids more skills, help their kids develop more talents, provide their kids with more experience, expose their kids to more adventures and different customs, teach their kids ethics, enrich their kids' lives with cultural appreciation and awareness, and make their kids more capable and ready to take advantage of the opportunities that are out there. Parents are also responsible for helping to inspire, encourage, and support their kids. These are the tasks that good packaging entails, and parents who embrace this mission will find, as a side benefit, that their children maintain good family rapport and are very marketable to the most-competitive colleges. These are the kids who won't feel stifled when it comes time to apply to college.

Now is an exciting time to be a parent if you're up for the challenge. You don't have to be a marketing executive to be successful at parenting. Packaging your kid for college is the capstone on your kid's growing-up-at-home years, the ultimate gift for your child—setting him or her up on a challenging and rewarding path.

APPENDIX:
SAMPLE STUDENT RÉSUMÉ

When helping your child put together a résumé, you don't necessarily have to list Education as the first category, particularly if your child has accumulated special credentials in a subject that he wants to emphasize. In the following résumé, for example, Jane Jones's passion is Plant Conservation, so that subject is listed first. Also, I always recommend that my students highlight their positions of leadership and awards won by using bold letters. Admissions officers have limited time, and you want to make sure to draw their attention to the most impressive credentials.

Keep in mind that this is not a business or job résumé, and therefore, you're excused from some of the rules of standard résumé writing. If your child has more credentials, for example, than can easily fit on a single page, let the résumé take up two or more pages. Explain all activities and honors so that the reader understands the significance. Most of all, make sure that the child's role in each activity and award is described. And for awards and honors, the reader needs to know how many competed for these achievements (the applicant pool) and how many others won.

JANE JONES

Phone: (212) 555-1212   200 College St. Urbanville, NY
Email: jones@address.com

Plant Conservation

The Adventurers Club International, elected member in 2003 and 2004

National Winner of Junior Adventurers' Grant for botany research, 2004

One of 56 top U.S. botany students (**only 2 high school students**) to win grant

Prestige University Summer Botany in Brazil, summer 2004

One of only 44 high school students selected nationally to conduct three weeks of research in Brazilian jungle, working with Prestige University professor

Botany World Terrarium, Urbanville, NY

Exhibit Interpreter, Lizard Touch Tanks and Snake Exhibit, 2003–04 and 2004–05

Information Volunteer for Urbanville Foundation for Wildlife Preservation

Underwent extension training program and exam

Helped design and set up new Tropical Flower Exhibit for Botany World

Student Conservation Association (2004)

Conservation Crew Member: Worked for a month at Yellowstone National Park

Tasks included researching, identifying, and removing invasive plants

Neighborhood Botanic Garden, Localtown, NY

Volunteer Performer in major fund-raiser for botany research, 2003 and 2004

Ocean Conservancy, Beach Cleanup 2004 (certificate for helping identify pollutants)

Selected as **Top Biology Student at Urbanville High School**

to represent school in 2004 contest sponsored by Urbanville Nature Museum

Urbanville High School Ocean Sciences Bowl Team, **Founder and Captain**, 2003–04

Led team to 2004 U.S. Ocean Sciences Bowl Regional Contest

Jane Jones Résumé (page 2)

Urbanville High School Botany Club, President, 2003–04 and 2004–05

Education

GPA 3.95 unweighted (out of 4)

Standardized test scores:

> SAT verbal 720; SAT math 720; SAT writing 720; SAT II Spanish 720

Urbanville High School straight-A student, at a most competitive public high school

> Courses completed:_____

> Current courses: _____

Urbanville Community College, Introduction to Botany summer 2003 (4 college credits)

Language Skills, Publications, and Achievements

English (fluent, first language):

> *Urbanology,* high school literary magazine, **Editor**, 2004–05

Spanish: **Treasurer**, Spanish Culture Club, Urbanville High School, 2003–04 Member 2004–05

Music Honors and Activities

Sang a solo in fund-raiser for local botanical gardens, 2004, 2005

Urbanville High School Choir, 2002–03, 2003–04, and 2004–05

Athletic Achievements and Awards

Urbanville Girls' Athletic Association Award, 2003, 2004

> Lettered in softball in 2003 and 2004

INDEX

From the author of *What Colleges Don't Tell You*,
300+ secrets for raising *the* kid colleges
will compete for

AVAILABLE WHEREVER BOOKS ARE SOLD.

Hudson Street Press
A member of Penguin Group (USA) Inc.
www.penguin.com